Foxhole Radio

Foxhole Radio

the ubiquitous razor blade radio of WWII

Brian Carusella

First Printing, 2019

ISBN: 978-0-578-53658-3

Canyon Wren Press
Dallas, Texas

info@canyonwrenpress.com

canyonwrenpress.com

foxholeradio.com

To all the veterans who shared their tales,
and to all of those who couldn't.

To Anna and Henry
for their encouragement and extraordinary patience.

CONTENTS

ILLUSTRATIONS

Preface

My first encounter with the foxhole radio was in *All About Radio and Television*, a children's book written in 1958 that seems to have been in every grade school library for several decades. The author Jack Gould, who was the radio and television critic for the New York Times, mentioned in the beginning of the chapter on Foxhole Radios that "American G.I.'s in Italy put several of them together".

Years later I included what I knew of the foxhole radio on my web site, which documented classic children's science projects. Before long most of the email I received regarding the website was about the foxhole radio, from people who had built sets as children or remembered that a relative had built one during WWII. By the time I received an email from a veteran who had made one during the War, I was beginning to realize that there was more to the foxhole radio story than a handful of sets built in Italy. The history of army radio, early solid-state electronics, morale, improvisation, the persistence of lore, and military grooming all came together in these improbable little receivers.

Searching for contemporaneous newspaper articles on the subject led to veteran interviews, which led to a much more complex story than anticipated, and then, years later, to this book.

One of the greatest joys of working on this project was meeting so many fascinating and encouraging people. To Mary Elizabeth Ruwell, Academy Archivist and Chief, Special Collections, McDermott Library, United States Air Force Academy, for locating and providing copies of George Owen Squier's correspondence from 1896-1898, and to Doug Johnson, IT specialist for taking on the challenging job of digitizing them; to Floyd Hertweck, U. S. Army Communications-Electronics Command (CECOM) Staff Historian, for locating pictures of George Owen Squier and the electrical lab at Fort Monroe, and for his encyclopedic knowledge of all things Squier; to Robert Kelly, Casemate Museum Historian, Fort Monroe Authority, for locating information regarding Building 27, Fort Monroe, home of Squier's electrical lab; to Malgosia Myc, Assistant Director for Reference and Academic Programs, Bentley Historical Library, University of Michigan for locating Squier's 1897 London Diary; and to Karl Fritz, for generously providing copies of Board of Ordnance and Fortification papers mentioning Squier's wireless work. Much more could be written about Squier's early research and these archives hold much of the story.

H. H. C. Dunwoody's story was especially interesting to piece together as he left little if any written record of his radio researches. Karl Messmer went above and beyond in his search for Dunwoody related documents. General Ann E. Dunwoody and her father General Harold H. Dunwoody provided some very useful information and encouragement. Radio historian Bart Lee provided insight into the working relationship between Dunwoody and deForest. Marsha Brown provided me with a copy of collected Dunwoody family papers that included some details about H.H.C. that were not available elsewhere. Maura Kenny, Processing Archivist, Rio Grande Historical Collections, Archives and Special Collections, New Mexico State University Library located some later letters in the library's collection, mostly concerning Dunwoody's mining business.

Dr. John B. Pickard helped enormously with photos and documents belonging to his father, Greenleaf Whittier Pickard. Mary Ann Hoffman, the Archival & Web Services Manager for the IEEE History Center, provided a portrait of Pickard. Hal Wallace, Associate Curator at the National Museum of American History, Electricity Collections, helped track down Pickard's notebooks and provided a very useful index. Kay Peterson, Alison Oswald and Christine S. Windheuser of the Smithsonian Institution Archives tracked down documents related to Pickard. Alan Douglas provided copies of Pickard's testimony regarding Dunwoody's carborundum detector, which went far to round out the story. The staff of the U. S. Army Heritage and Education Center, U. S. Army Military History Institute, generously located and copied documents in their collection pertaining to early army radio. Signal Corps Historian Rebecca Robbins Raines provided guidance, encouragement, and some lively discussion about early army radio activities.

Melissa Ziobro, Command Historian at the U.S. Army Communications-Electronics Command, Fort Monmouth, NJ located information about Dunwoody in their collection and steered me towards George B. Ferree's radio at the United States Army Communications Electronics Museum, Fort Monmouth. Mindy Rosewitz, curator of the U.S. Army Communications - Electronics Museum at Fort Monmouth, located Ferree's set and gave me an amazing tour of the museum followed by a delightful and informative lunch with Pat Blair, daughter-in-law of radar pioneer William R. Blair. Evelyn "Evy" Reis of the Chenoa, Illinois Historical society went above and beyond in helping find information on George B. Ferree. She was one of Ferree's students in high school and took a great interest in the project, corresponding frequently. She is very much missed. I am also grateful to Bud Vercler of the Chenoa Historical Society for providing copies of articles about Ferree, Kev Varney of the Illinois High School Glory Days web site for putting me in contact with Evy Reis, and Karen Moen, Local History Librarian of the Bloomington Public Library, for finding George Ferree's obituary and other articles. George Ferree's story could not have been told without help from his son, Eddie Ferree, who allowed me to copy his father's wartime journal and other documents. Our visit with Eddie and his wife Helen was one of the highlights of my research.

Lance Borden, WB5REX, and Maxim Olchanyi have both been very encouraging and have shared with me their knowledge of foxhole radios. Maxim Olchanyi has studied a variety of improvised radio detectors and I am grateful for his insight into their design and for his directing me towards P.O.W. built sets in museum collections.

Sergeant Major Herbert A. Friedman provided scans of WWII propaganda leaflets for reference. Edmund Goldshinsky of the Marlin Firearms Company sent some very useful information about the Marlin Razor Blade Division. Barry Fairwood and Robert K. Waits helped shed some light on the blue razor blade, and Dennis Manuel of Houston Electron Microscopy confirmed just why they were blue. Lewis L. Gould corresponded with me about his father, Jack Gould.

Jim Carstensen provided a wealth of information about his father, Vern Carstensen, and allowed me to quote from his excellent website based on his father's 5th Army Mobile Radio scrapbook. Anne Cornell

McNea graciously photographed the radio built by her father, Paul Cornell. Tom Roscoe K8CX at hamgallery.com provided information about one of Paul Cornell's QSL cards displayed on his site and put me in touch with John Kroll K8LJG, who kindly sent me a scan of the card. Ursula Bourgault has corresponded with me about her husband Ed Bourgault and has been very encouraging, as has been Goldie Phelps, who I had the pleasure of interviewing about her husband Eldon. Charlie Plumb shared his story of a radio he built while a POW in Vietnam, perhaps the only documented POW made razor blade radio. I enjoyed a very entertaining series of emails from and an interview with Dr. Ray McAllister. Maxie Rupert sent several very useful letters as well as copies of material relating to his radio and the advertising campaign based on it. I visited William Lloyd Wiley and his wife Helen for what was supposed to be an hour-long interview and ended up staying for the better part of the day. I am grateful for their many stories and for the delicious lunch prepared by Mr. Wiley.

To all the veterans who sent letters, sat for interviews, or pointed me in the right direction, including James Broughton, Charles Cleveland, Anthony D'Angelo, Derk Doombos, Russel Weiskircher, Zack Roberts, William Kocher, Eugene Ligget, John Zapitello, Kenneth Muston, Frank Stevenson, Albert Sidge, Herbert Hatley, Harold Deane, Bill Van Luven, Leroy Good, Waldon Johnson, Leo Hill, Lee Palmer, Thomas Pradetto, Carl Fish, Joseph Manni, Norris Dupre, Francis Taphorn, Barney Streeter, Warren Niceley, Phil Caccavale, Warren Garman, Victor Kubilius, Thomas Fitzgibbons, Bryan Compton, Meta Politi, Ray McAllister, Pat D'Amato, Ed Butwell, Bill Bastian, Mace Broide, Louis Kunofsky, Clark Lease, George Avery, Wesley Waggoner, Charles Myrick, Waldon Johnson, Donald Taylor, Kenneth Sliter, Doug Bailey, Hidenobu Hiyane, Don Welling, Isaac Caudle, Paul Wilson, and Howard Waugh, I am sincerely grateful. There would be no book without their generosity.

Introduction

A foxhole radio is a crystal radio receiver that uses one or more razor blades as part of its detector. They were first built by soldiers during the stalemate of the Battle of Anzio in 1944 from whatever parts could be found. The sound they produced was faint and they usually would not hold a station for very long. But the servicemen who built them found them worth the effort, and they spread across the beachhead and into radio lore.

The crystal radio takes its name from its detector, a crystalline piece of semiconducting mineral, often galena, used with a fine wire cat whisker to separate audio from a modulated radio wave. Because they require only a few simple parts, are powered by radio wave energy alone, and have been the quintessential "homemade" radio since before the First World War, it is not surprising that at least one serviceman decided to build one during World War II. But crystals for detectors were hard to come by on the beachhead, and so some creative soldier used what was on hand, a razor blade standing in for the crystal and a safety pin for the cat whisker, and made the first foxhole radio.

A razor blade seems an unlikely substitute for a galena crystal, but the soldier who tried it remembered that razor blades, somehow, had been used to make detectors, though perhaps not exactly like this.

The radio worked, but the sound coming through the headphones was fainter than it would have been with a galena crystal. The detector was notoriously difficult to adjust and tended to go out of tune with the slightest jarring. And the only station it was likely to receive, at least at first, was an Axis propaganda station in Rome. But any distraction was welcome during the stalemate at Anzio, and radio especially, an indispensable part of popular culture for many, was one of the few comforts of home, even if much of the music was adulterated with inane propaganda.

The foxhole radio spread, by word of mouth and by newspaper, across Europe and to the Pacific, evolving along the way. Radio amateurs and curious school children were drawn to it because it was an interesting bit of wartime improvisation, and because they had to see for themselves if it would actually work. Over time it became part of radio and childhood folklore.

On the face of it the foxhole radio is an interesting artifact of the war, a testament to the ingenuity of service personnel, a simple project for radio enthusiasts wanting to recreate a wartime curiosity. In the context of the War and the history of radio there is a deeper history, of radio in general, and military radio specifically, of soldier's entertainment and enemy propaganda, amateur enthusiasts and the persistence of lore.

The detector, rather than an arbitrary combination of components, is part of a family of detectors that began in the earliest years of radio, reshaped by amateur lore and half-remembered archaic technology. The razor blade, part of that long line of professional and folk radio equipment, was readily available at Anzio because the shaving of one's facial hair has been shaped by, as much as anything, the military.

A radio receiver is not worth much without something to listen to, and the foxhole radio is part of a story that begins with the military's first tentative steps to adopting radio, the countering of enemy propaganda, and the establishment of armed forces radio stations, some official and some less so.

The name "foxhole radio" also tells a story, of hasty fortifications, First World War trenches, living conditions at Anzio, and words borrowed from the enemy.

Most importantly there are the stories of the servicemen who built these sets, where they were, why they built them, what they listened to. Many were separated by thousands of miles, but they were all connected by their desire to build these strange little radios.

This book traces the parallel stories of military, commercial and amateur radio, and the development of the radio detector, tracing the threads that lead to the foxhole radio, from the earliest years of army radio, to the First World War and an early soldier built radio, the interwar years and the rise of broadcasting and the radio amateur, World War II and the invention of the foxhole radio and birth of armed forces broadcasting, and the foxhole radio's continued evolution in the lore of the amateur.

Though the terms "wireless" and "radio" are both used in this book somewhat interchangeably, they do have different meanings. "Wireless" is the older – though not the oldest - term for transmitting intelligence via radio waves. It is shorthand for "wireless telegraphy" and was in common use in the United States through the First World War, and for longer in much of the rest of the English-speaking world.

"Radio", though occasionally used in early English works on the subject, was the more common term internationally, making its way into American usage with the first international radio regulations of the early 20th century. It was firmly planted in American English by the end of WWI, around the time the wireless telegraph was replaced by the radiotelephone.

Both terms are used here more or less within their historical periods, though there is necessarily some overlap. Where a distinction between *telegraphy* and *voice* transmitted by electromagnetic energy is necessary but not clarified by context, more specific terms such as "wireless telegraphy" are used.

1 A New and Astonishing World

The Old Arsenal Building at Fort Monroe, Virginia replaced an even older building that was destroyed in an explosion and fire on June 22, 1855. That building housed the mechanical shop and laboratory, where an accident while mixing "composite fireworks" triggered the explosion.[1] Of the three men inside at the time Francis M. McKnight, an ordnance artificer, was killed instantly. Another, Henry Sheffis, died three days later from his injuries. Lieutenant Julian McAllister, "very much though not very deeply burnt",[2] survived, and, in his gratitude for what he felt must surely have been divine intervention, championed the construction of the Chapel of the Centurion. It still stands, the oldest wooden American military structure in continuous use for religious service.

The original arsenal building was replaced in 1860 by a long, T-shaped building of "three course English bond brick veneer... glazed wood paneled double doors with masonry stoops and painted masonry jack arches with keystones" and "twelve-over-twelve-light double-hung sash windows with painted masonry sills and lintels".[3] Building 27, the Old Arsenal Building, is the oldest extant army building outside the moat at Fort Monroe. Used today for commercial office space, it originally housed the arsenal's machine shop, manufacturing seacoast gun carriages.

In the 1880s it was converted into classrooms and laboratories for the Artillery School. It was the Quartermaster warehouse through the World Wars and the Post Commissary in 1946. The Signal Field Maintenance Shop moved in ten years later, and by the time Fort Monroe closed in 2011 it was the home of the base's Multi-Media Division and the United States Army Training and Doctrine Command Public Affairs Office.

From 1895 to 1898 the Electrical Laboratory of the Artillery School was there, and there in 1897 the first American military radio, and one of the earliest, if not first, American made radios, was tested, built on site by the gifted young Lieutenant who had established the Laboratory, George Owen Squier.

Born in the waning days of the Civil War on March 21, 1865, Squier entered West Point in 1883 and by all accounts was an exemplary student. He developed a keen interest in physics that would lead to a lifetime of advocacy for scientific research in the army, which was institutionalized by his example during his 36-year career. He founded two of the army's prominent research facilities, the Aviation Research Laboratory at Langley Field, Virginia, and the Signal School at Fort Monmouth, New Jersey, and, while serving as Chief Signal Officer during WWI, he was involved in the army's adoption and development of two of the most important inventions of the era, the airplane and the radio.

After graduating from West Point, Squier was appointed 2nd Lieutenant and assigned to Fort McHenry, Maryland. While there he applied to the graduate program at Johns Hopkins University, earning his PhD in physics in 1893, an unusual achievement for an army officer of the day.

In the summer of 1894 Squier was transferred to Fort Monroe, Virginia where he served as ordnance instructor at the Artillery School, establishing the school's Electrical Laboratory the following year. While there he was given free rein to devote whatever time was available, apart from his duties as instructor, for research.

The Electrical Laboratory occupied one wing of building 27, an unpartitioned space, brightly lit by large and frequent windows. Electrical equipment lay everywhere, in shelves and on wooden tables, beautiful, polished things of brass, glass and varnished wood, functional things built like good furniture, arc lamps, Leyden jars, Wimshurst machines, spark gaps and coils, filling the air with ozone and cracking spark.

The main function of the laboratory, besides instruction, was the investigation of new technology that would benefit coastal fortification. Squier developed remote detonation of underwater mines, installed carbon arc searchlights, electrified artillery fire control, and improved telephony and telegraphy between distant points. He developed electric range finders for artillery, designed equipment for high speed telegraphy, and studied ballistics photographically. And, after a chance meeting with Guglielmo Marconi, he began experimenting with radio, building his own equipment because none was available commercially. By December of 1897 he had "...made a huge Marconi transmitter operated by a Tesla coil, which is a powerful one. There is no trouble in ringing bells, lighting lamps, firing cannon or explosives or starting machinery at considerable distances through the air by Hertzian waves."[4]

Figure 1 Electrical Lab, Fort Monroe c. 1898. Courtesy Floyd Hertweck, CECOM Staff Historian.

In the first few years after they were discovered radio waves were commonly referred to as "Hertzian waves" in honor of Heinrich Hertz, the German physicist who demonstrated their existence in 1887. The term "radio", by itself, was only rarely used. It was space telegraphy, telegraphy without wires, Hertzian telegraphy, radiotelegraphy, spark telegraphy, etheric wave telegraphy, and, most often, wireless telegraphy. All these somewhat poetic names were making the same point - that this was a new system of telegraphy, one that did not require the miles of expensive copper wire used to connect conventional telegraph stations, and one that could fill the gaps where telegraph lines could not reach. It could reach across water, from shore to ship, to moving trains. A few visionaries were already considering the possibility of sending voice by radio waves, but the emphasis was on supplementing if not replacing wired telegraphy.

Radio waves were first theorized by the Scottish physicist James Clerk Maxwell. Born in Edinburgh on June 13, 1831, his natural inquisitiveness was apparent even at an early age, and his father encouraged his scientific interests. He was especially drawn to geometry, and in 1854 he graduated Trinity College second in mathematics.

Maxwell would spend his relatively short life teaching and researching a variety of subjects, in the process establishing himself as one of the most influential physicists of the nineteenth century. He contributed greatly to the study of human color perception and color blindness. He studied the rings of Saturn, concluding that they could only be made up of countless small particles. And in 1861, using a rudimentary tri-color process, he made the first permanent color photograph, appropriately of a Scottish tartan ribbon.

And in 1861, building on the groundwork of Michael Faraday, Maxwell presented a set of equations to the Royal Society which described the relationship between electricity and magnetism.[5] In 1862 he calculated than a propagated electromagnetic field should move at the speed of light, and realized that they must be at least similar phenomena. In 1864 he published *A Dynamical Theory of the Electromagnetic Field,* formalizing his theory that light and magnetism were indeed the same phenomena, and that all electromagnetic disturbances obey the same laws as they travel through space.

To Maxwell and his contemporaries, it seemed logical that a wave, electromagnetic or otherwise, requires a medium to travel through. This reinforced, at least for a while, the already well entrenched theory of a luminiferous aether. Though it conveniently explained the propagation of transverse electromagnetic waves, the aether theory did provoke some questions. It had to be absolutely rigid to carry light waves and yet massless and transparent. In 1897 the Michelson–Morley experiment, which was designed to explore the properties of aether, failed to find it at all, and in 1905 Einstein's special theory of relativity showed that electromagnetic waves can propagate through empty space without an aether to propagate through. Regardless, the term remains firmly planted in the English language, and radio waves are still often described as propagating through the aether.

In 1887 the German physicist Heinrich Hertz performed a series of experiments to prove Maxwell's theories. Maxwell predicted that electromagnetic waves would be created by an oscillating electric spark, which Hertz was able to produce using an induction coil in circuit with two spherical, zinc plated electrodes separated by a small air gap. Such a spark produces a wide range of electromagnetic energy, including radio waves.

Generating radio waves is relatively easy. People had been doing it long before Hertz without realizing it. An electric motor, a sparking streetcar pantograph, even petting a cat can cause tiny sparks that produce radio waves. Detecting them is another matter. Radio waves pass through us without us ever knowing it. Hertz needed some sort of device to translate them into a signal that could be seen or heard.

His solution was simple and elegant. He formed a circle of 2mm thick copper wire, leaving a gap in one side where two spherical electrodes, like those in the transmitter, were attached, facing and not quite touching. Hertz dubbed it the resonator.[6]

When the transmitter was switched on and a sufficient spark was produced, some of the radio wave energy reached the resonator's copper wire, inducing a current sufficient to produce a tiny, faint spark between the electrodes, proving that electromagnetic waves can travel through space.

Hertz went on to measure the velocity of radio waves, which is the same for all electromagnetic radiation, and showed that they could be reflected and refracted. He published his findings in May 1877 and, feeling satisfied that he had confirmed Maxwell's theory, moved on to other things. [7]

The study of radio waves was taken up by other scientists, but for the most part their commercial potential was of little interest to sober 19th century physicists. Sir William Crookes, inventor of the eponymous electrical discharge tube, was an exception. In his article "Some Possibilities of Electricity," printed in the February 1, 1892 issue of *Fortnightly Review*, he appealed to the reader to consider the potential for long distance communication by Hertzian waves. "The researches of Lodge in England and of Hertz in Germany give us an almost infinite range of ethereal vibrations or electrical rays, from wave-lengths of thousands of miles down to a few feet. Here is unfolded to us a new and astonishing world - one which it is hard to conceive should contain no possibilities of transmitting and receiving intelligence."[8]

Crookes understood how it would be done, with a "properly-constituted instrument, and by concerted signals messages in the Morse code can thus pass from one operator to another". And he knew what was needed, a simple device to generate radio waves of desired wavelength, a way to direct the waves, and a more sensitive receiver "which will respond to wave-lengths between certain defined limits and be silent to all others".

The article was the first widely read suggestion of a system of wireless telegraphy. It is significant that it appeared in a popular nonacademic magazine; Crookes was appealing to the amateur to make things happen. Physicist and radio pioneer Sir Oliver Lodge also realized that amateurs could make valuable contributions to radio research. In his 1894 article on Hertz's work he points out that "many of the experiments lend themselves to easy repetition, since they involve nothing novel in the way of apparatus except what is quite easily constructed; many of them can be performed with the ordinary stock apparatus of an amateur's laboratory".[9]

Heinrich Hertz died on January 1, 1894, two years after Crookes' article was printed. There followed a resurgence of interest in his work, and many of his papers were reprinted, in some cases for the first time in languages other than German.[10] Crookes' article and the new accessibility of Hertz's work caught the imagination of amateurs as well as professional scientists, and Hertzian waves became a popular subject for study and public demonstration.

Many of the early radio experimenters used one form or another of the Hertz resonator, which worked well enough as long as the transmissions were sent a short distance. Radio waves, like all electromagnetic energy, are subject to the inverse-square law; that is, their energy is inversely proportional to the square of the distance from their source. If the distance doubles, the energy is quartered. The faint spark of the resonator, already difficult to see in Hertz's laboratory, disappears altogether at any appreciable distance. A more sensitive and reliable detector would need to be developed for radio to be used for communications.

It was a similar story when wired telegraphy was invented. Electrical pulses can be sent down a copper wire easily enough, and someone on the other end may feel a shock if they hold the bare wires. But that would be an inconvenient and unpleasant method for sending and receiving messages, and so the shock needs to be converted into something that can be seen or heard by an operator. All sorts of schemes were tried, and some of the early attempts worked fairy well. Rotating needles, chemically infused paper, and ringing bells were all tested with varying success. Telegraphy truly caught on when Samuel Morse and Alfred Vail developed their Morse code of dots and dashes and the inker, a receiver that recorded the transmitted code on paper tape.

Because early radio was considered analogous to wired telegraphy, development of radio apparatus tended to incorporate the standard components of telegraphy, the sending key and the recording receiver. But instead of closing a circuit to send electricity from a battery through a copper wire, the radio transmitter's key controlled the flow of electricity to a coil and spark gap. And instead of acting on electrical pulses coming directly from a wire, a radio's detector would have to pluck signals from the air and somehow convert them to the mechanical action of a telegraph inker.

On August 14, 1894 Sir Oliver Lodge, demonstrating the work of Hertz for the British Association for the Advancement of Science at Oxford, transmitted radio waves from a spark coil to a receiver placed 180 feet away. His detector was deceptively simple. A glass tube was tightly fitted with two metal plugs, a wire leading from each plug to the receiver circuit. Between and slightly compressed by the plugs was a small amount of metal filings. Normally these filings had a relatively high electric resistance, but if pulsed energy resulting from an electromagnetic wave passed through them, they rearranged and pressed closer together, decreasing their resistance. Tapping the glass tube shook the filings apart, restoring their original resistance. Lodge referred to this as the "coherer effect", and all similar detectors would in time become known as coherers.

Lodge's intention was to make the demonstration of wireless telegraphy clear to a large audience, which would not have been possible with a Hertz style spark gap detector. The new detector made it possible to receive transmissions miles instead of yards away

A well-made coherer is a very sensitive detector, but the coherence action is not directly observable, at least without a microscope. It was used instead as a switch to control electric flow from a battery to other parts of the receiver. At the transmitter, an operator taps out the dots and dashes of a Morse coded message on a telegraph key. Each time the key is depressed, it completes a circuit from a battery to an induction coil, which in turn produces a reciprocating spark. The energy from the spark is fed into an aerial and transmitted as radio waves. The transmitter is either on off, and electromagnetic waves are transmitted only as long as the key is depressed.

At the receiver, an aerial intercepts the radio waves, passing them on to the coherer as pulses of alternating current. The filings cohere, lowering the resistance of the coherer, and allowing current from a battery to reach a device that would indicate that a radio wave had been received, usually a bell, buzzer, or a telegraph inker. At the same time another device is activated to restore the coherer so that it will be ready to receive the next wave. Typically, this was a small tapper activated by an electromagnet. Many early amateur radios used doorbell mechanisms as tappers. Some receivers had their coherer mounted on a vibrating platform that would shake the filings loose.

The coherer effect had a long history before Lodge used it in his receiver. In 1850 Pierre Guitard wrote in *The Mechanic's Magazine* that smoke particles would "coagulate" if a small electric charge passed through them.[11] In 1866 C. and S. A. Varley patented a device for protecting telegraph lines from lightning based on their observations that the resistance of powdered metals sometimes decreased during a thunderstorm. Temistocle Calzecchi-Onesti noticed in 1884 that the filings of certain metals, if packed loosely together, had a very high resistance to electricity. If, however an electric spark was discharged nearby the filings would stick together and the electrical resistance would decrease dramatically. If the filings were then shaken, the resistance would again increase. The French physicist Edouard Branly had been investigating the phenomena since 1890, experimenting with several different powdered metal combinations.

Mostly forgotten today, the coherer was state of the art in the 1890s and made long distance wireless telegraphy possible. Alexander Popov in Russia, Sir Oliver Lodge in England and Nikola Tesla in the United States all used coherers in their wireless experiments. In 1898 Guglielmo Marconi, using a refined coherer based on a design by Branly, demonstrated that electromagnetic waves could be used practically to send the dots and dashes of Morse code over very long distances.

Marconi was born in April 1874 in Bologna. His father Giuseppe was an Italian aristocrat and his mother Annie Jameson was the Irish

Scot granddaughter of the founder of Jameson & Sons distilleries. He had a keen interest in science from his youth, and in 1894, inspired by the recently republished work of Heinrich Hertz, he started to experiment with radio waves, building much of the equipment himself, which he operated in the attic of his family home. Taken piece by piece, there was little new about Marconi's equipment. His transmitter used a coil and spark gap designed by his neighbor and teacher, Augusto Righi, and his receiver was a typical coherer and inker. Marconi however saw the commercial potential in it all, and he set out to perfect and increase its useful range to interest investors.

He found that his system worked better after grounding the transmitter and receiver and switching to a high monopole antenna, and by 1895 he could transmit radio waves over a mile and a half away. He filed a British patent in June 1896 and conducted a demonstration for officials of the War Department and British Post Office the same month. In attendance was William Preece, at the time the Chief Engineer of the British General Post Office, who would become Marconi's strongest supporter in Britain.

Further tests and demonstrations continued through 1897, with Marconi gradually increasing the distance his signals could be received. By the time the Wireless Telegraph and Signal Company, forerunner of the Marconi Company, was formed on July 20, 1897, Marconi was well on his way to becoming synonymous with wireless.

Figure 2 George Owen Squier in 1898. Courtesy Floyd Hertweck, CECOM Staff Historian.

2 This Important Phenomena

In July 1897 George Owen Squier and his research associate Albert Cushing Crehore arrived in England to test and demonstrate their Sychronograph, a high-speed telegraph receiver, on English telegraph lines. The lines were under the authority of the General Post Office, and Squier had been granted access to them by the Chief Engineer of the Post office, William Preece.

After a demonstration for Preece on August 11th, they were introduced to Marconi, "the air telegraph man", as Crehore refers to him in their London journal. Crehore writes they "were then shown Marconi's apparatus by Marconi himself and saw it in operation".[1] Crehore later recalled "I met Marconi in the post office building, and held his original coherer receiver in my hand. I carried two metal strips that stood out like wings on either side, and as I walked through the long halls of the building making a turn around corners so as to be hidden completely from the sender, the bell would ring when the instrument faced certain directions but would not ring when turned other directions".[2]

The meeting apparently made an impression on Squier, and when he returned to Fort Monroe he "immediately began the design and construction of a transmitter and receiver to test its uses for military purposes."[3]

By November 1897 Squier had made a working transmitter and receiver, some of the first radio equipment built in the United States, and certainly the first tested by the military. It was two years before

Marconi would arrive in America to demonstrate his apparatus, and more than a year before the first tests of wireless with the Royal Navy in July 1899.

The army was actively increasing their role in scientific research when Squier began his radio work, much of it influenced by the Board of Ordnance and Fortification.

In 1885 President Grover Cleveland appointed a board to assess the condition of America's coastal fortifications and make recommendations for their improvement. The Board of Fortification, a joint group of army, navy and civilian members headed by Secretary of War William Crowninshield Endicott, painted a grim picture of the state of coastal forts. After years of neglect many were deteriorating and all were outdated. High masonry walls and muzzle loading artillery were state of the art during the Civil War, but technology had changed rapidly in the intervening years and the world's navies were taking advantage. Ships were more heavily armored now, and the new artillery was bigger, rifled, used more efficient propellants that could fire shells further and faster, and could be reloaded quicker and more safely than any gun installed at an American fort.

In their 1886 report[4] the Board recommended 127 million dollars in improvements, mostly for artillery, repairs, and new construction. The amount was more than could be appropriated, but in September 1888 Congress established a permanent Board of Ordnance and Fortification to oversee what improvements could be realistically made.

Advances in technology since the Endicott Board first met meant that much of the work could be done with less money. Fewer pieces of artillery would need to be added because the newer guns were more powerful than the 1886 report anticipated. Endicott era fortifications were built with reinforced concrete and designed to blend into the earth, usually behind a small natural hill or soil parapet. The batteries were fitted with large, rifled, breech loading artillery, made possible by advances in steel technology and mechanical tolerances.

The Board understood that the military needed to take an active role in shaping technology. Section six of the Fortification Appropriations Act of September 22, 1888 reads in part "The Board is authorized to make all needful and proper purchases, investigations, experiments, and tests to ascertain with a view to their utilization by the Government, the most effective guns, including multicharge guns and the conversion of Parrott and other guns on hand, small arms, cartridges, projectiles, fuzes, explosives, torpedoes, armor-plates, and other implements and engines of war; and the Secretary of War is hereby authorized to purchase or cause to be manufactured, such guns, carriages, armor-plates, and other war materials and articles as may, in the judgment of said Board, be necessary in the proper discharge of the duty herein devolved upon them."[5]

The phrase "and other implements and engines of war" was purposely broad enough to allow for any research that may prove necessary for coastal defense, making the Board the first War Department division specifically authorized to fund scientific research.

New and updated forts would benefit from recent advances in electrical engineering, and the Board encouraged research in telephony, lighting, electric fire control for artillery, and any other electrical technology that would aid coastal fortifications. Radio, still theoretical when the Endicott Board met, became a priority with news of Marconi's successes, and any investment in transmitters and receivers, it was hoped, would be less than the cost of seemingly endless repairs of underwater cables.

Breaks were common in telegraph lines that served coastal forts and intersected inland waters. The 1887 Chief Signal Officer's Report laments the difficulties and expense of maintaining a cable connecting Fort Canby, Washington and Fort Stevens, Oregon where it crossed the mouth of the Columbia River.

"This section had just been placed in excellent repair" reported Lieutenant F. R. Day of the Signal Corps, "when, on July 31, 1886, the submarine cable across the mouth of the Columbia River was broken by, it is presumed, a ship's anchor. Several fruitless and expensive attempts were made to recover and repair the cable, which was found to be so deeply embedded in the sand as to resist all efforts made to raise it."[6]

An underwater cable running from Tatoosh Island, Washington to the mainland was damaged on the rocky bottom of the straits in January 1887. "An attempt made to raise the cable with ordinary appliances failed, and it was not until June 25 that successful repairs were made with the assistance of a steamer hired for the purpose and at a heavy expense."[7]

The cable running from Fort Mason, California to Alcatraz Island was especially problematic. By 1887 it had already been repaired several times and had been broken and left unrepaired for a year "due partly to the fact that experience has proven this route to be unsuitable for a cable, owing to the constant danger of injury from ships' anchors."[8] By 1890 the situation was clearly frustrating. "The broken cable between Fort Mason and Alcatraz Island was repaired August 21, at a cost to this Service of $275 for such appliances and skilled labor as could not be furnished by the military authorities. About one and one-half miles of the old cable was recovered at the same time. The cable was again broken on November 7 (for the sixth time), and in view of the evident impracticability of maintaining a cable over that route no further attempts were made to repair it."[9]

The Signal Corps had all but given up on a line to Alcatraz by 1899, keeping 3 1/2 miles of the incomplete section in storage, which, "owing to its liability to being broken by the anchors of vessels, will only be laid as a war measure."[10]

The annoyance of constantly repairing underwater cables with a limited budget and limited resources had reached a boiling point by 1899. "The difficulties under which cables are maintained in the navigable waters of the United States are much greater than would appear possible", wrote the Chief Signal Officer in his Annual Report. "This condition arises largely from an absolute disregard shown by private individuals to the rights of the people at large as represented by the United States Government. To illustrate, the repairs rendered necessary on the cable between Fort Hancock, Sandy Hook, N.J., and Fort Hamilton, N.Y., have aggregated $1,105.05 On one occasion no less than eleven breaks were discovered in this cable, of which three were made with an ax or other sharp instrument. Whenever shipping of any kind ventures on the cable ground, contrary to the tenor of prominent cable signs, it is liable to have its anchor caught. Instead of pulling up the cable and disentangling the anchor, the individual almost invariably disregards his duty to the United States, promptly severs the cable, and thus saves fifteen- or twenty-minutes work. It may be added that our National Government has shown in such matters an indifference unprecedented, although Congress has enacted a law making it an offense punishable by fine and imprisonment to interfere with a military telegraph line."[11]

Radio, as the Board saw it, could eliminate the need for underwater cables altogether. Royal T. Frank, Squier's commandant at Fort Monroe, was also a Board member and requested Squier prepare a report describing his radio work so far.

Squier's report of January 14, 1898 describes a large spark transmitter, the spark produced between two 6 1/2-inch brass balls "designed to be operated by the larger alternating current Tesla coil in the laboratory of the Artillery School."[12] The receiver was built along the lines of Marconi's, using a coherer as a detector. Other than the brass electrodes, which were cast at the Newport News Shipbuilding Company for twenty-five dollars - the bulk of Squier's budget for the project - all of the equipment was constructed in the Electrical Laboratory at Fort Monroe.

Coherer based receivers were complicated and difficult to set up correctly. Radio waves caused individual metal filings to "cohere", decreasing the electrical resistance of the coherer. Electric current from a battery could now flow freely through the coherer and the electric circuit it was part of and continue on to either actuate a solenoid that rang a bell, or, more often, trigger a telegraph inker, itself a complicated mechanical device, to form one dot on a long, thin roll of paper. At the same time, the circuit powered another solenoid that operated a tiny hammer, which struck the coherer and dislodged the powdered metal inside, increasing its resistance and breaking the electric circuit of the receiver, which was now ready to receive the next radio signal from the transmitter. It was a complicated dance and, because of the mechanics involved, limited the speed at which a signal could be received.

Squier, realizing that wireless could profoundly benefit the military, anticipated research beyond the sometimes-difficult coherer-based receiver. "If it can be made reliable" he wrote in his report, "which experiment will show, it is an ideal means of communication between parts of a fortification or between armies in the field. The sender has but to direct his transmitter in the general direction desired and a receiver properly tuned to the transmitter waves will respond. Fog, darkness, even opaque obstacles avail nothing against it. For the navy in carrying on the regular communication between ships in all kinds of weather it would prove invaluable, and the method should be brought to the attention of our Navy department at once." And, of more immediate interest to the Board, it would eliminate the expensive and annoying problem of laying and repairing submarine cables for seacoast fortifications.

By January Squier had transmitted 500 yards, and he saw "no reason why communication at any distance within the range of modern seacoast fortifications is not possible".

Squier also recognized a broader application of wireless than did Marconi and most of his contemporaries. He conducted the first experiments with radio remote control, "lighting electric lights, firing electric primers, fuses etc such as would be used in military operations."[13] And he anticipated transmitting voice by wireless, years before it was practical. "Although not intending to indulge in speculation, I believe it will soon be shown that these Hertzian waves can be used to telephone through space without wires."[14]

Frank's request for Squier's report came after the board received a letter dated December 8, 1897, from Isaac Newton Lewis, another science minded lieutenant who had been closely following Marconi's progress. "In view of the many successful trials made abroad during the past year with the Marconi system of wireless telegraphy, I have the honor to respectfully request the permission and assistance of the Board to make a practical trial of this system between Forts Wadsworth and Hamilton, N.Y.H., using the flagstaff at each post as a support for the terminal wire."[15]

Fort Wadsworth, on Staten Island, faces Fort Hamilton a mile across The Narrows, the tidal straight that connects the Upper and Lower Bays of New York. It was an ideal location for a test. A submarine telegraph cable connecting the forts, originally placed in 1882, was owned by the Baltimore and Ohio Telegraph Company as part of their commercial line, and since the ends landed at the forts, the government was given free use of it.[16] In 1890 Baltimore and Ohio decided to remove the cable, which was replaced by the government at a cost of two thousand dollars.[17] It was deep enough that there was no real danger of it being fouled by ship anchors, but the mile separating the two forts, which was well within the range of Marconi's recent tests, could prove the usefulness of wireless to compliment, if not replace, government owned cables between fortifications where breaks were more likely to occur.

Lewis was already well known for his scientific research when he made his request. He developed the first artillery range and position finder used by the army, revolutionizing fire control in coastal fortifications. He invented or improved the clocks and bells used for artillery fire control, mechanical verniers used to measure small divisions of a degree of an arc, the first plotting board used by gun batteries, and automatic gun sights, all within his first dozen years with the army.[18] He actively sought out new technologies that would benefit the artillery. Twelve years later he would develop the Lewis gun, the ubiquitous machine gun of the First World War.

And, like Squier, Lewis realized that radio would be a boon to coastal fortifications and was an important subject for the Board to consider. In his letter he reminded them that "only last month, an official trial was made in Germany, during which satisfactory communication by this method took place between stations ten miles apart, the terminal wires being supported in air by balloons. Marconi has also repeatedly telegraphed from the Italian forts to vessels of war in the harbor more than five miles distant..."[19] Lewis was invoking national pride - if the Italians and Germans were to have wireless, then the Americans had better not fall behind. Squier would make a similar appeal in his report - "...it is reported that both the English War Office and the Naval Office are investigating the subject for military and naval uses".[20]

Lewis was unaware of Squier's wireless, which had been operating for only a few weeks when he wrote his letter. "So far as I know, there have been no practical tests made in this country."[21] Royal T. Frank would have known of Squier's work as well as Lewis' letter. Consideration of the request, first read before the Board on December 27, was postponed, presumably to allow Colonel Frank enough time to request a report from Squier. When the Board met again on January 20, 1898, they considered "the Marconi system of sufficient importance to warrant the encouragement of both of these officers in experimenting"[22] and requested cost estimates from both Squier and Lewis.

Squier's reply was sent on February 12 and included a detailed description of the equipment and materials needed. He estimated that the coils, batteries, transmitter, receiver, and all the parts and supplies to make a thorough test would cost $1,050.

The transmitter and receiver would be purchased from the United States Electrical Supply Company, who offered the first commercially available wireless equipment in the United States. Incorporated on July 19, 1897, one day before Marconi formed his Wireless Telegraph and Signal Company,[23] they initially specialized in "arc and incandescent lamps, magnet spools for arc lamps, and a very complete line of X-ray apparatus and accessories".[24]

William J. Clarke, the company's founder, was a self-taught electrician and a passionate advocate for research and development of electronic technology. Born in Trenton, Ontario on February 5, 1861, he discovered his love for electricity early and worked in his youth installing door and intercom bells.[25] He managed the electric lighting plant of the Trenton Electric and Water Company, installing the first electric lights in Trenton.

The United States Electrical Supply Company opened shop at 120 Liberty Street in New York, across the hall from the *Electrical World* magazine, which reported on much of Clarke's early work. The building still stands and was the original home of the 9/11 Tribute Center.

Clarke, like Squier, was inspired by Marconi's work and began his own wireless experiments in late 1897. Some of his first transmissions were sent from his office and received at the *Electrical World* office across the hall.[26] On November 24, using equipment he designed and had built by the telegraph manufacturing firm J. H. Bunnell & Co., Clarke gave the first public demonstration of radio in the United States at the home of Jacob Schiff, a prominent banker. *The Electrical Engineer* deemed it a "very pretty and successful test".[27] On December 15, 1897 he demonstrated equipment built by his own company to the American Institute of Electrical Engineers[28], and by late December he was offering wireless equipment for sale.[29]

Clarke's equipment was well crafted, with gold plate and mahogany wood bases recessed to conceal wiring[30]. But there were issues. Despite favorable reviews of his demonstrations, the equipment was not responsive enough to receive Morse code at anything close to an operator's usual speed. This was a problem with Marconi's early equipment as well, but Clarke's receiver lacked the radio frequency shielding of Marconi's, adding instead a multitude of fine adjustments that made his early sets frustratingly difficult to use. Clarke himself considered the equipment experimental. Squier was aware of the problems but intended to use it as a starting point for his own experiments.

Lewis, who submitted his request to the Board on February 13, also knew of the wireless equipment offered by the United States Electrical Supply Co. and had visited Clarke on January 29 to see what was available.[31] He intended to purchase a receiver from Clarke and build a transmitter himself, using a Tesla coil rather than the more usual Ruhmkorff coil to produce the spark.

The estimate Lewis submitted included a shorter and less detailed equipment list than Squier's and was considerably less expensive at $450. Naturally the Board questioned the six-hundred-dollar difference. However, rather than choosing the lower estimate, Recorder of the Board J. C. Ayers sent Squier and Lewis each other's bids and gave them the chance to account for the difference.[32]

Squier explained that he "planned a more thorough investigation of this important phenomena, both along the lines followed by Marconi and also modifications which our experiments here have already shown emerging. I also intend determining to what distance and how reliable this means of communication could be made, not only over water as from shore to ships in darkness and fog, but between parts of an army in the field".[33] And he once again invoked the specter of international competition. "The subject is a new one, and we should not be behind England, Germany and Italy, who are at present spending considerable money on testing this system."[34]

The Board wanted both Squier and Lewis to investigate radio and so split the available budget between them on March 16, allotting six hundred dollars to each, the first money specifically approved by the U. S. government for radio.[35] Neither would have much opportunity to use it.

On April 25, the United States declared war on Spain, retroactive to April 21. Squier was appointed Signal Officer, Department of the East, and transferred to Governors Island, New York on April 27. Lewis had already been reassigned to Washington on April 6 and appointed as the Recorder of the Board of Ordnance and Fortification.[36]

Squier arranged for Crehore to have access to the electrical lab at Fort Monroe so that he could continue work on their rangefinder, synchronograph, and, Squier hoped, make thorough tests of the wireless telegraph that Clarke had shipped in May. The transmitter, coherer and bell receiver were all varnished wood and polished brass, with the meticulous grace of the nineteenth century gentleman's laboratory.[37] Clarke included what were likely the first instructions for a commercial radio, complete with a hand drawn diagram of the equipment.

The "Directions for Operating Wireless Telegraphy Apparatus" begin simply enough. "Place the transmitter upon the table upon your right hand and the receiver upon your left, in such a position that the lettering on the name plates of the apparatus will appear to you right side up." It quickly spirals into a tale of tedious and unforgiving adjustments and calibrations. Clarke, anticipating despair, offers reassurance. "As this class of apparatus is something entirely new, you should not be discouraged if you find it difficult to properly adjust it at first. In fact it might take several weeks before you have properly mastered all the details, and then you will feel that it is indeed an easy matter."[38] Crehore had little time to work with it and did not find it an easy matter. "It is liable to go sometimes and not others... I have an idea that the present receiver is not the thing for the purpose of telegraphy".[39]

In the spring of 1899 the Board sent Lewis to Fort Monroe to experiment with the Clarke wireless, but by then Marconi was conducting demonstrations for the army and navy, and Lewis felt the work was redundant.

Most of the wireless equipment available in 1899, Marconi's included, was not far removed from the lab, much too fiddly and delicate for the rigors of military duty. If the army was going to have domestically made wireless equipment sturdy enough for field use, they would have to build it.

3 With More Perfect Adjustment

"This method of communication, against which darkness, fog, and weather conditions avail nothing", wrote Chief Signal Officer Adolphus Greely in his 1899 *Report*, echoing George Owen Squier, "has already shown itself of value and deserves continuous attention and experiment."[1] And, like Squier, he appealed to national pride, noting that "England, France, Italy and several other European and South American countries are also vigorously taking up this subject for military and naval experiments".

Radio research was picked up by the Signal Corps after the Spanish American War in the spring of 1899. Greely assigned to the task two officers who had already been researching wireless on their own. Captain George Owen Squier, assigned to the Signal Corps since February, had more practical experience with wireless than anyone in the army. Colonel James Allen had been methodically testing and evaluating commercially available wireless apparatus since returning from Puerto Rico, where he installed 100 miles of military telegraph line.

In early April they installed a transmitter and receiver 1000 feet apart at Fort Myer, Virginia, gradually separating them further until messages could be sent across the Potomac to Washington.

On April 15 the equipment was brought to Washington to determine the effects of steel framed buildings on radio waves. The transmitter was placed on the roof of the State, War and Navy Building, later renamed the Eisenhower Executive Office Building, a massive Second Empire structure that still stands west of the White

House. The Washington Monument was considered as a contingency in case the metal structure of the War and Navy Building interfered with the signal.[2] The receiver was set up at the old Naval Observatory Building, three quarters of a mile away.

"It took several hours to adjust the instrument and to perfect connection", reported the *New York Herald*. "When this was done words were ticked off by Colonel Allen which were reproduced by the receiver and read by Colonel Squier. Not all of the words were successful reproduced, but enough to demonstrate that with more perfect adjustment messages could be transmitted."[3]

A few days few days later the receiver was moved to Fort Myer, the transmitter remaining at the War and Navy Building, two and a half miles away. Major Gustave W. S. Stevens, commander of the Signal Corps post at Fort Myer, received the messages.[4] Besides being one of the longest distances so far covered in an American wireless test, it was the first use of the new Wehnelt interrupter, recently invented by the German physicist Arthur Wehnelt, which could produce 2000 breaks per second in the primary circuit, ten times faster than mechanical interrupters.

The tests were reported on in the May 20 issue of *Harper's Weekly*,[5] which included some of the earliest surviving photographs of an American military radio.[6] Who built the equipment is not known, but it was similar to what Marconi was using at the time, a spark gap transmitter with a long antenna operated by a telegraph key, and a coherer and Morse inker receiver with an antenna "stretched from the ground to a height equal to that of the oscillator at the sending end".[7]

General Greely released a statement and his assessment of the tests on May 11 "in view of great public interest and in order to facilitate experiments by other scientists of the United States."[8]

The apparatus, according to Greely, was designed and constructed specifically for the tests. The transmitter, "mounted upon the West elevation of the State, War and Navy Building", used "the present wooden flag pole as the vertical wire for the transmitter". It was similar to the type used by Marconi, except that it used an alternating current coil powered by "a three-quarter horsepower rotary transformer, furnishing 125 volts alternating potential"[9] instead of the usual battery driven Ruhmkorff coil, making it much more powerful. The receiver, mounted onto a wagon at Fort Myer, used a coherer and Morse inker.

Figure 3 Sending a message from the roof of the War Department building. Harper's Weekly, *May 20, 1899.*

Figure 4 Receiving the message and Fort Myer, Virginia. Harper's Weekly.

Greely was skeptical that wireless could replace wired telegraphy. "That there is a field of usefulness for space telegraphy is undoubted, but that it will supplant to a material extent the use of wires for ordinary commercial telegraphy is not believed. Its value for connection between lighthouses and lightships and the shore, at points where cable cannot now be permanently maintained, will be great... at present the radiation proceeds from the transmitter in all directions and the same message can be received at any point within the proper radius at which a receiver is placed. A satisfactory directing reflector, and a receiver of the proper electrical capacity, or, in other words, tuned to the vibration of the particular transmitter, would make a great advance in space telegraphy, and do much toward the extension of its field of practical usefulness... While secrecy of transmission is among the probabilities, the present stage of experiment does not justify its positive prediction."[10]

Spark gaps produced a wide, noisy band of radio energy that could be picked up by any nearby coherer, and Greely realized that transmitters and receivers would need to be tuned and directed if they were going to be secure enough for military use. He was not alone in his assessment. *The Electrical World*, later a champion of radio, saw little utility in its earliest incarnation. "The press, particularly the more sensational part of it, has been teeming for some time past with accounts of recent alleged marvelous inventions for telegraphy without wires. The question naturally arises of what benefit this variety of signaling would be if it were perfected along the lines indicated." To its critics, weight, complexity, and, most significantly, a lack of secrecy made wireless no more useful "than the system of 'wig-wag' signals now in use... the systems recently and widely discussed will be found to have more interest than utility".[11]

Greely and other critics of early Marconi style wireless recognized the same truth – that if wireless was going to succeed, it would need to operate on a clean, narrow and specific bandwidth. Otherwise there would always be the problem of interference between transmitters and lack of secrecy. Radio engineers and enthusiasts called it "syntony", the transmitter and receiver oscillating on the same specific and narrow frequency. Marconi, John Stone Stone, Oliver Lodge and Nikola Tesla would all spend the next several years developing tuned circuits, and later, improved transmitters would make it possible to produce a clean, continuous radio wave.

Despite the current problems, Greely saw the potential of wireless if improved and made it a topic of research at the new Signal School at Fort Myer. He sent Squier to England to learn what he could from Marconi and bought three electric automobiles to test the portability of wireless. And by September 30, 1899 the Signal Corps was confident enough to establish a wireless link between the Fire Island Light Station and the Fire Island Lightship, about ten miles apart.[12]

Other government agencies were also considering wireless. In July 1899 William J. Clarke demonstrated his system for the Lighthouse Board, placing his transmitter on the pier of the lighthouse station, Tompkinsville, Staten Island, and the receiver on the lighthouse tender *Mistletoe*,[13] cruising between Staten Island and Pier 5 of the East River. The demonstration was successful, the bell of the receiver ringing each time a signal was received. The Lighthouse Board was impressed with the demonstration but had no budget for wireless, and so Clarke moved on to other things.

The Weather Bureau was also interested in wireless for collecting data and providing forecasts to remote locations. In 1900 they hired Reginald Fessenden, who at the time was the chair of the Electrical Engineering department at the Western University of Pennsylvania. During Fessenden's time with the Weather Bureau he would begin work that would eventually lead to amplitude modulation and radiotelephony. And he would develop the electrolytic detector, the first serious competition for the coherer.

In England Marconi was enjoying a string of successes. Some of his earliest tests with the British government were with the Lighthouse Board, and his first ship to shore message was sent on December 24, 1898 between the South Foreland Lighthouse and the *East Goodwin Lightship*. In January of the following year the lightship was able to report by wireless when it was damaged in heavy seas, and on April 28 the same lightship, the only one out of four marking the Goodwin Sands to carry wireless equipment, sent the first international distress signal by wireless when it was rammed by the *R. F. Matthews*. The lightship and entire crew were saved.

Good press, success with the Lighthouse Board and the favorable opinion given of the Marconi system by Lloyd's of London, who had witnessed demonstrations in July 1898, led to the Royal Navy requesting tests in the summer of 1899. Three ships were fitted with transmitters and receivers in July and sent and received messages at 74 nautical miles. The following year Marconi contracted with the Royal

Navy to install wireless on 26 additional ships as well as 6 coastal stations.[14]

After successfully reporting on the Kingston Regatta race in July 1898, Marconi was invited by the *New York Herald* to report the 1899 race between the *Shamrock* and the defending *Columbia*, making it the first America's Cup race covered by wireless. The race was also recorded by Thomas Edison's movie camera, and "'Columbia' winning the Cup" was the first event of its kind to be filmed. The *Herald* had originally contacted Reginald Fessenden, but, as his schedule prevented his participation, he recommended Marconi.[15] Though interested, Marconi initially declined, also due to scheduling conflicts, and the *Herald* contracted William J. Clarke. Marconi was later able to rearrange his schedule and attend the races, working with Clarke, each using their own equipment.

Both the Marconi and Clarke apparatus performed well, but because Marconi's was the better-known name he received most of the press coverage. Clarke continued to produce radio equipment for a few years after the race, selling sets to the Signal Corps and at least one to the Weather Bureau. But he was early to the game. The market for radio was small, and by 1902 USESCO had faded. Clarke spent the rest of his years touring as a popular science lecturer. He died in 1909 at 48.

The U. S. Navy, who had sent observers to watch the operation of Marconi's equipment at the America's Cup, were impressed, and arrangements were made for tests on naval vessels. The tests went well, and the Radio Telegraph Board, established specifically to observe and make recommendations on the Marconi system, advised "that the system be given a trial in the Navy".[16]

Marconi, who had hoped to sell sets when he started his company in 1897, soon realized that sales for such a new technology may be too infrequent to sustain business, and the best way, as he saw it, to maintain income was to rent. Marconi offered the navy what he considered a concession, $10,000 for twenty sets plus an annual royalty of $10,000 a year. The navy, who would have preferred to buy sets outright, had no interest in renting, especially from a foreign company, or paying an expensive annual fee, and decided to wait until a time when they could purchase domestically or produce their own sets.[17]

Captain Samuel Reber of the Signal Corps also witnessed the Marconi tests and also recommended that the War Department reject

Marconi's offer.[18] General Greely later announced that "there would be no practical demonstration of the Marconi system of wireless telegraphy in connection with the signal service of the army".[19] The reason given was that the Marconi system was limited to a range of twelve miles over land and thirty over water, no better than equipment currently in use by the Signal Corps. And, like the navy, the War Department was not interested in Marconi's rental scheme. By now the Signal Corps stations between Fire Island and Fire Island Lightship were in service, as well as a station installed by Reber between Governors Island, New York and Tompkinsville, with the goal of "adapting the army apparatus for communication between fortified points and in any other locations where the wireless system might prove superior in practice to the older form of telegraphy. The army is not dependent on Marconi for instruments, having developed a system of its own, and the work will be pushed with vigor when Congress furnishes the necessary means."[20] Disappointed but undaunted, Marconi returned to England to prepare transmitters and receivers for use in the Second Boer War, the first wireless equipment to be used in combat.

The army continued to build and test its own equipment, adding permanent wireless links between forts and shore. On June 30, 1900 wireless stations were installed on Alcatraz Island and Fort Mason,[21] "thus covering parts of the harbor of San Francisco over which it has been impossible to successfully maintain cables."[22]

In the fall of 1901 Marconi returned to New York to once again cover the America's Cup race, reporting as he had in 1899 for the *New York Herald*. This time, however, he had competition.

Lee de Forest, born August 26, 1873 in Council Bluffs, Iowa, knew from an early age that he would be an inventor, lured as much by wealth and fame as scientific curiosity. In 1899, armed with a doctorate in physics from Yale, he set out to make his mark in radio despite Marconi's near monopoly in the field

He developed his first "responder" detector in 1900, the first of several detectors of different designs he would refer to as "responders". It was built somewhat like a filings coherer, with two metal plugs in a glass tube separated by a gap. It was filled with what de Forest referred to as "goo", a paste of glycerin, water, metal filings and litharge, an oxide of lead.[23] Lead crystals formed when a battery was in circuit with the responder, bridging the gap between filings and allowing electricity to flow. Radio wave energy broke the chain of lead crystals, which broke the circuit, producing a click in the receiver's earphones. The lead crystals reformed between radio wave pulses, decreasing resistance and restoring the circuit. Because radio wave energy increased rather than decreased resistance, the responder belonged to a class of detectors usually referred to as "anticoherers".

The responder operated faster than a filings coherer, and by 1901 de Forest felt it had been tested sufficiently to compete against Marconi, who was using a spark gap transmitter installed on the yacht *Mindora* and standard coherer receiving stations on the Navesink Highlands and the Long Island shore.

The American Wireless Telephone and Telegraph Company, formed in 1899, was, ostensibly, the first American radio communications firm. In practice, though they held some important early radio patents, American Wireless conducted only enough real radio business to maintain a façade of legitimacy while promoting overpriced stock to unwary investors.

Despite their unethical business practices and limited attention to real work, they did manage to attract, at various times, some notable radio engineers, including Harry Shoemaker and Greenleaf Whittier Pickard, who would represent American Wireless at the races.

They installed their spark gap transmitter on the *Maid of the Mist*, "an ancient schooner"[24], as Pickard described it, which had to be towed over the course by tug. Like de Forest they would also use a relatively new detector, one with a pedigree that predated Hertz's work. And it was a direct ancestor of the foxhole radio. Steel needles rested on the sharpened edges of carbon blocks, forming a simple carbon microphone. Radio waves passing through the microphone detector produced a tone in headphones connected to the receiver. Because it did not need to be mechanically reset between radio wave pulses, it was considered an "auto restoring" coherer.

Because Marconi controlled the only transmitters present at the 1899 races, there was no problem of interference. But with three spark transmitters at the 1901 race, the interference was even worse than expected. For the first two days of the race. no one, it seemed, could receive a clear message through the constant noise.

Many years later Pickard admitted that much of the interference was caused by the American Wireless transmitter, and that he used it to advantage.

"Realizing that inasmuch as both Marconi and A. W. T. & T. Co. were using virtually untuned systems, we decided to try a special code composed wholly of ten second dashes separated by ten second spaces, the idea being that those long dashes would hopelessly blur or blot out the Morse characters on the tapes at the Marconi shore stations, but could themselves be read regardless of the Morse working. The idea of this code came simultaneously to me and Harry Shoemaker, Chief Engineer of the A. W. T. & T. Co. on seeing a misprinted newspaper in which headline type had been printed over small type. This code working was a brilliant success from the start, and resulted in a nearly complete blocking of the Marconi working for the first two or three days of the races. Unfortunately (as the engineers then saw it) the President of A. W. T. & T. Co. weakened under vague threats of legal action by the Associated Press, and for the remainder of the races, the two companies split time in alternate five-minute periods."

"Our working for the first two days of the races was simple, but effective. At the starting line, we sent the code for *Columbia* – one dash – as the yacht approached the line. When she crossed the line, we sent a dash several minutes long, the operator on shore taking starting time from the beginning of the dash. Then, as the *Columbia* started away from the line, another single dash followed by two dashes gave the code for '*Columbia* on port tack'. By repeating this bulletin until the yacht changed tack or made some other maneuver, we managed to so fill space with our dashes that our competitor got very little ashore, at least in intelligible shape."[25]

"As a result of this transmission from the "Maid of the Mist" the two Marconi shore stations recorded both the short dashes and dots from the "Mindora", and the foot-long dashes from the American Wireless transmission which blotted out some nine-tenths of the Morse characters. At Galilee the operator listened only to the long purr of the dash code, and was not in any way bothered by the short Morse characters."[26]

"At the finish of the first race, we sent the finish time similarly to the starting time, only here we locked the key down for over an hour as our boat was turned back to its birth near Navesink Highlands. Of course, our bulletins were news in highly condensed form, and had to be rewritten and greatly amplified on shore before they were sent to newspapers we served."[27]

The *New York Herald*, who had sponsored Marconi and who blamed American Wireless for the interference, printed an article On October 28 accusing American Wireless of, among other things, purposely causing interference at the races.[28] American Wireless responded with typical bombast.[29]

Lee de Forest, who had been contracted by the Publisher's Press Association, was somewhat forgotten in the back and forth between American Wireless and the *Herald,* but his work attracted investors. In 1902 he started the De Forest Wireless Telegraph Company, the first of many businesses to bear his name.[30] His business partner, Abraham White, was a shady character, more interested in stock manipulation that running a legitimate company. Not that de Forest was above it all. In his diary he wrote "soon, we believe, the suckers will begin to bite. Fine fishing weather, now that the oil fields have played out. 'Wireless' is the bait to use at present. May we stock our string before the wind veers and the sucker shoals are swept out to sea."[31] In 1903 White reorganized De Forest Wireless into the American De Forest Wireless Telegraph Company, freezing stock in the original company.

American Wireless, meanwhile, reorganized twice in 1903, first as Consolidated Wireless, then as International Wireless, before being absorbed by American De Forest in 1904, making De Forest the largest wireless company in the United States. Their claims were still exaggerated, and many of their business practices unethical, but from 1903 through 1906 De Forest made solid and dependable equipment and won several government contracts.

In 1903 the United States Navy was ready to build shore stations and install wireless on at least some ships. By now there were several European and a few American companies manufacturing dependable and rugged transmitters and receivers. Tests were made with equipment from De Forest, Rochefert and Ducretet of France, Braun-Siemens-Halske and Slaby-Arco of Germany, and Lodge–Muirhead of England. The navy deemed the Slaby-Arco equipment most suitable for shipboard use and purchased twenty sets. Radio stations were built along the coast, first at the Washington Naval Yard and the United States Naval Academy, then at navy yards in Portsmouth, Boston, Cape Henry, Norfolk, and Pensacola. Radio schools were set up in Newport, New York and San Francisco. Shipboard radio was installed in specially designed cabins, along with all the needed power cables, antennas, and communications to the bridge.

The navy's Bureau of Equipment printed *Instructions for the Use of Wireless-Telegraph Apparatus* in October 1903, the first manual on the subject produced by any branch of the U. S. armed forces. The twenty-nine-page manual provides instruction for setting up the radio operating room, which was "...about 6 feet square... well ventilated and lighted, dry and close to the earth plates. It should have a glass window or other insulating lead for the entrance of the aerial wire, and should be conveniently near from 60 to 70 feet from the base of the mast. On board ship this room should be on the uppermost covered deck, with leads into it for the aerial wire through hard-rubber or ebonite insulators let into the upper deck. The operating table should be about 6 by 3 feet and 30 inches high, of well-seasoned dry timber, capable of supporting the weight of the instruments, about 500 pounds."[32] The mast, aerials, and installation and operating procedures for the transmitters and receivers were also described.

Meanwhile the War Department continued to pursue equipment suitable for the army, and during the September 1902 Army-Navy maneuvers in Long Island Sound wireless systems manufactured by De Forest, Marconi and Fessenden were tested at Fort Mansfield, Block Island, and on military tugs. The De Forest set was considered superior and the following year was used to replace the broken cable between Forts Wadsworth and Hancock in New York Harbor, ten miles apart.[33]

The need for a workable wireless network in Alaska to connect points where wire could not reach was an incentive for the Signal Corps to develop their own system. Reginald Fessenden had been contracted to connect Fort St. Michael and Fort Davis, Nome, in 1901. After failing to do so, the task was given to Captain Leonard D. Wildman, who began experimenting with a 3 kW system with 140 foot antenna masts linking Forts Schuyler and H.G. Wright, on Fishers Island, in Long Island Sound, 105 miles apart.[34] If it was successful, he would move the whole thing to Forts St. Michael and Davis, which were 125 miles apart, mostly over open water. The Long Island stations were successfully installed in summer 1903 and moved to Alaska in August, becoming the world's longest wireless section in regular service.

Using a minimum of patented devices, and with improved safety and durability, the Signal Corps' wireless system was so improved by Wildman that for a time it was referred to as the "Wildman system".

By 1904 there were enough military, commercial and amateur transmitters operating that some agencies, the navy in particular, were having trouble receiving messages over the steady stream of interference. President Theodore Roosevelt appointed an interdepartmental board to address the interference problem as well as what were considered monopolistic practices by the Marconi companies. The navy felt that wireless should be controlled by one government agency, and since ship to shore communication was, in their view, a priority, it should be them. Roosevelt, who served as Assistant Secretary of the Navy under McKinley, agreed, and stacked the deck in their favor. Three of the five appointed Board members, Rear Admiral Robley D. Evans, Rear Admiral Henry N. Manney, and Commander Joseph L. Jayne, were navy officers, though officially Evans represented the Department of Commerce and Labor. The War Department was represented solely by General Greely, and Willis L. Moore represented the Weather Bureau, the other principal government operator of wireless stations at the time.

The Board's recommendations were the first real attempt at radio regulation in the United States. Commercial stations, they agreed, should be regulated by the government to prevent interference. Control of most government wireless stations was given to the navy, except "that the Signal Corps of the Army be authorized under its chief to establish from time to time such wireless stations as he may deem necessary, and that they do not interfere with the coastwise wireless-telegraph system of the Government under control of the Navy Department; and further, that the Chief Signal Officer be requested to inform the Navy Department what stations of its system may be utilized to transmit messages for the Signal Corps or other bureaus of the War Department, and that representatives of the Signal Corps of the Army and the Bureau of Equipment of the Navy Department be at once requested to draw up such rules as will insure the efficient and harmonious carrying into effect of the above recommendations".[35] The Weather Bureau fared worse and were required to hand over all of their stations to the navy. Both the army and the Weather Bureau could have messages sent from naval stations, but they would be sent by navy personnel at the navy's discretion.

Although the Signal Corps were handed a less than ideal situation after the Board's recommendations, they still controlled most government telegraph lines and were, for the most part, left with the wireless activities they had been concentrating on, connecting sections between fortifications and developing portable field equipment. As Greely stated, the Signal Corps was interested in wireless telegraphy "only as far as relates to equipping its field trains with portable outfits and to establishing such short routes as will insure prompt and reliable intercommunication between coast defenses and cooperating military forces".[36]

Permanent stations, though still being improved, were no longer thought of as experimental, allowing the Signal Corps to develop suitable portable equipment. Though they would have preferred to design and build their own equipment, commercially available sets had improved enough by 1904 that Captain Wildman was assigned to test field sets from Braun-Siemens-Halske, Lodge-Muirhead, Fessenden's National Electric Signaling Company (NESCO), and De Forest, as well as individual components from several companies. None of the commercial sets were found to be altogether satisfactory for army use, having been "developed by their inventors rather from the electrical than from the mechanical side, and as a consequent result laboratory and experimental makeshifts have been placed upon the market as commercial instruments".[37]

Wildman prepared a list of requirements that wireless equipment would need to meet to be suitable for army use.

> 1. Eliminate the necessity for an absolute electrical ground.
> 2. Construct all parts of the apparatus so that in case of destruction of any part from whatever cause, that part can be replaced without elaborate machinery and by intelligent unskilled labor.
> 3. Replace all adjustments which require a knowledge of mathematics, or experience in manipulation, by lettered dials or definite switch positions, so that highly skilled operators shall be unnecessary.
> 4. Reduce the necessary height of aerial wires.
> 5. Produce a receiver that will not only receive the message intended for it, but which can by adjustment also receive any electro-magnetic wave.
> 6. Eliminate wholly or largely disturbances due to atmospheric or static electricity.
> 7. Avoid as far as practible all dangerous high-potential currents at points where there is a possibility of danger to employees.

8. Provide appliances and devices which will protect the instruments and machinery from destructive potentials from whatever cause.

9. Avoid as far as possible the use of patented devices and the consequent payment of large royalties.

10. Devise a system which can be easily transported in time of war and which is capable of transmitting messages under all climatic and topographical conditions.[38]

The practicability of fixed radio stations established, the Signal Corps now looked to making the technology available for communications between units in the field, fulfilling Wildman's requirement that a system should be relatively simple to set up and use, tunable, safe, dependable, rugged, field reparable, and, as much as possible, built by the Signal Corps from Signal Corps designs. And it would all need to fit into a box.

4 What Wireless Will Do

The job of developing portable wireless sets for the army was entrusted to George Owen Squier, whose "theoretical knowledge of the subject is widely recognized",[1] and Leonard D. Wildman, regarded as a wireless expert after his successful installation of the Alaskan stations. "The devices when perfected", wrote Greely in his 1905 *Report*, "will be given thorough field tests before adoption, and it is expected that a wireless set, capable of working 15 or 20 miles, can be transported on a single pack mule and be installed in a few minutes."[2]

Squier was in a better position to build and test portable equipment than Wildman, who had recently received the assignment of Chief Signal Officer of the Department of California. Squier, serving as the Assistant Commandant of the Signal School at Fort Leavenworth, had available the space, resources and willing student body to build and test a variety of wireless transmitters, receivers, and antennae.

The Signal School, separate and distinct from Leavenworth's Infantry and Cavalry School, was opened on September 1, 1905 under direction of War Department General Orders 140 of August 25, 1905. All students were required to complete a thesis and organize a relevant technical conference. These were published by the school and, taken all together, provide an historical outline of the progress of research conducted there. The course of instruction included all manner of field communication available at the time, including wireless.

Among the students and instructors were many notable army officers. Charles McKinley Saltzman, who would spend twenty-three of his thirty-year army career with the Signal Corps, and who would serve as the Chief Signal Officer from 1924 to 1928, was the school's second Commandant. Edgar Russel, later the Chief Signal Officer of the American Expeditionary Forces in France during WWI, served as commandant from 1908-1911. Leonard Wildman, whose design and installation of wireless stations successfully completed the Corp's Alaska Communications System, led the school from 1913 to 1915.

William "Billy" Mitchell, a graduate of the 1906-07 class, instrumental in the completion of the telegraph line in Alaska, and who would later be known for his passionate advocacy of air power, was at Leavenworth both as a student and, for a time, to supervise the development and testing of portable wireless equipment.

Catalogued with Mitchell's papers at the Library of Congress are photographs taken by him during his career, including while he was at the Fort Leavenworth Signal School. Among those are two photographs of the first truly portable wireless set built by the Signal Corps. One shows two wooden trunks, set on the ground in the snow, their lids open, photographed from above. A partition divides the interior of the first trunk into two compartments. In the back, nearest the lid's hinge, and built into a wooden box, is the induction coil. The front compartment holds a simple ball type, open spark gap, mounted flat on insulators so that it is just below the upper trunk edge. A telegraph key is mounted into the lid. The second trunk holds batteries to supply power for the spark, and a small electrolytic detector mounted in the lid.[3]

In the other photograph both trunks are mounted onto the aparejo of a drowsy mule standing in front of one of Fort Leavenworth's brick buildings. A sergeant stands near the mule's head, and another soldier holds open the lid of the transmitter.[4] There is another version of this photograph, taken at the same time, from a slightly different angle and perhaps by a second photographer. It is printed on thick card, and toward the bottom is written in ink "Sig. Corps Wireless made by Sgt King, first ever used by Sig Corps."[5] The set was built under the direction of Squier and Mitchell in the fall of 1905 by Sergeant Thomas I. King of Signal Corps Company A.

The transmitter and receiver, weighing about 250 pounds, were each built into their own wooden trunk so that they could be packed onto an aparejo, a type of packsaddle favored by the army that evenly distributed weight on a mule's back. A pole to raise the aerial would require its own mule.

Figure 5 Early pack set at Fort Leavenworth, likely built by Sergeant King, c. 1905. William Mitchell papers, Manuscript Division, Library of Congress.

Figure 6 Sergeant King's radio at Fort Leavenworth, c 1905. Author's collection.

The transmitter was a simple induction coil and spark, the receiver was built around a De Forest electrolytic "responder". The various parts, essentially the same components that would normally sit on a table in a radio operator's office, were bolted separately and at some distance from each other into the trunks where they best fit and would best function. The set could transmit over 28 miles and receive from a great deal further with a high enough antenna.

It was not, despite what was written on the photograph, the first wireless used by the Signal Corps. But it was the first built by the army small enough to be carried by mule. And it was the first built and tested by Sergeant Thomas I. King, who would be instrumental in the evolution of field wireless from an amalgamation of parts packed into standard issue army trunks to smaller, more rugged, and more tightly integrated sets. His work not only improved the early Signal Corps equipment, it helped to set the standards for equipment that commercial manufacturers hoped to sell to the War Department.

King was born August 9, 1876 in Parkdale (then Poplar Bluff) Arkansas. He worked for some time as a photographer before enlisting in the army in November 1898, serving with the 2nd Infantry, Texas Volunteers, in the Spanish American War. He reenlisted in June 1900 and was assigned to Signal Corps Company F. In 1905 he was promoted to 1st Sergeant and assigned to Signal Corps Company A at Fort Leavenworth.

Commanded by Captain Billy Mitchell,[6] Company A was highly regarded for their efficiency and expertise. Assigned to field work and instruction connected to the Signal School, Infantry and Cavalry School, and the Staff College, they were also the primary unit for development and testing of field wireless equipment.

What had been considered portable before Company A built their first set had to be carried in three wagons pulled by eighteen mules. The new set could be carried in two boxes on one mule, less the antenna.[7]

The antenna was attached to the roof of the Company A barracks for the first test in October 1905, then later moved to the flagpole on the main parade to raise it higher. Messages were received from much further away that they could be transmitted, and by late October transmissions were intercepted from Kansas City, St. Louis, Chicago, and Key West, over 1,200 miles away.[8]

There would be no flagpole in the field, and so a portable pole was built, but because it was large, unwieldy, needed to be carried in a wagon, and never really gave satisfactory results, it was quickly abandoned.

King remembered that Marconi had used large hexagonal kites designed by Baden Baden-Powell, brother of Scouting founder Robert Baden-Powell, for his first trans-Atlantic transmissions, and so began experimenting with kites of his own design. Officially named King Kites in his honor, they would become standard equipment for field wireless units.

The kites were large, seven feet high and five wide, made of 50 yards of white Japanese silk and bamboo, and light for their size, less than two pounds each. Similar to Malay or Eddy kites, they were diamond shaped and bowed, with a rectangular opening in the center, and used singly or in trains of two, three or four. Balloons were also experimented with on less windy days.[9]

Using kites, Company A was able to receive messages from remarkable distances. A message from President Roosevelt was intercepted while he was 2,250 miles away on a ship traveling from New Orleans to Washington, D.C. Another was heard from a ship in the Gulf of Mexico, intended for a station in Galveston. They questioned whether they actually heard a message from the Standard Oil Steamship *Maverick*, which was off the coast of Puerto Rico, until they contacted Standard Oil's office in New York to confirm. The ship was more than 2,500 miles from Leavenworth when the message was sent.[10]

Other uses for wireless were tested. In late October 1905 Billy Mitchell buried a miniature mine, attaching to it a detonator with a simple coherer and battery circuit, echoing an earlier experiment conducted by Squier at Fort Monroe. A short piece of wire extending above the soil served as an antenna to receive the signal from a spark transmitter set up some distance away. The mine exploded instantaneously when Mitchell pressed the transmitter's key, demonstrating that enemy mines could be safely detonated remotely.[11]

Thomas I. King would have a long career with the army. He was transferred in 1910 as a Master Signal Electrician to Fort Omaha, Nebraska with Company D, and in 1917 received a wartime commission as Major serving with the 80th Division Signal Troops, 305th Field Signal Battalion. He retired as a Major in 1932.

Company A continued to build and test radios, including commercially made equipment, up to their deployment to Europe during WWI. Their work directly influenced the development of standard field wireless equipment and the organization of wireless companies for the cavalry. They were called upon for training and demonstrations, and because their feats were frequently covered by the press, they became a public face for the Signal Corps, and drew crowds of onlookers wherever they camped.

They saw a variety of detectors in their ten years of testing, from coherers to crystals. Their first receiver used an electrolytic detector, a device that, using a platinum wire dipped in an electrolyte solution, allowed radio frequency current to flow in only one direction, making it audible in headphones. It was more sensitive, easier to use and less mechanically complicated than the coherer. Despite having to be re-filled and re-calibrated every time the receiver was moved, it remained the army's preferred detector until the First World War, even as new detectors became available.

And this is how it was - new, sometimes better detectors were invented, only gradually supplanting the ones that came before. And occasionally, some nearly extinct detector would be brought back and given a chance to evolve.

5 A Novel Detector

The coherer, the object of praise and scorn that made wireless possible, when faced with more workable detectors, only gradually faded away.

A well-constructed coherer was very sensitive and worked well with noisy spark transmitters. Without it, long distance radio communication would have been delayed by years. But it was difficult to adjust, slow to react, and as likely to respond to atmospheric static as it was to a transmitter's signal. "All was fish to the coherer net", wrote engineer Greenleaf Whittier Pickard, "and the recorder wrote down dot and dash combinations quite impartially for legitimate signals, static disturbances, a slipping trolley several blocks away and even the turning on and off of electric lights in the building."[1]

Sir Jagadish Chandra Bose saw the decohering process as the coherer's greatest weakness. "In order to restore the quickness of response of coherers and detectors in actual practice, it is usual to resort to tapping contrivances; but this expedient besides being crude in conception involves expense in construction, complication of apparatus, and must necessarily be slow in action and somewhat spasmodic."[2]

Some of the dissatisfaction came from the use of homemade coherers. That a functioning coherer could be produced at all in a home workshop was no small feat, but most people simply could not make one to the same high tolerances employed by professionals. In the March 1901 issue of the *Physical Review*, Carl Kinsley, professor of physics at the University of Chicago, tells us that "however much uncertainty attends the use of the wireless telegraph it need not be due to the coherers", which he concludes are not to blame, rather "the scientific experimenter, while presumably impartial, has found coherers unsuited to his purpose, and so by his voluminous writings, has created a popular distrust of an essential part of the wireless telegraph apparatus".[3]

William Eccles, the British physicist who coined the word "diode", was even more to the point. "The coherer's reputation for erratic behavior is wholly due to the performance of samples made in a slipshod manner. Coherers so made might be aptly compared with homemade false teeth."[4]

Despite its defenders, the coherer was unable to keep up with the demands put on it once wireless evolved beyond its experimental stage. Dissatisfaction drives innovation, and many detectors, some based on the coherer, some entirely new, were developed during the coherer's waning years.[5]

Some were ahead of their time, deceptively simple designs that foreshadowed later electronic components. Between 1900 and 1902 Edouard Branly worked with a "tripod" detector, a small bronze disk with three steel or tellurium legs ending at sharpened and oxidized points that rested on a polished steel plate.

In 1902 Marconi developed the magnetic detector, which worked by hysteresis of a magnetic wire. The principal was understood previously, and a detector was developed by Ernest Rutherford and others, but Marconi improved it by using a continuously moving magnetized wire. It was more sensitive than a coherer, and it did not require resetting, and so was able to respond faster. It was the standard detector in Marconi stations until being replaced by the vacuum tube and was the preferred detector on many ships since it was not affected by vibration. The "Maggie", as it was nicknamed by its operators, was too cumbersome for field use by the army, and, although instructions for building one would appear in popular literature, it was sufficiently complex to offer any real advantage to the amateur.

The electrolytic detector, the first real competition for the coherer, was developed by Reginald Fessenden in his early efforts to transmit audio by radio wave in late 1900. His system used amplitude modulation (AM), varying the amplitude of a carrier wave to correspond to the audio being sent.

Open spark gap transmitters produce pulses of damped waves

whose amplitudes quickly decrease over time, making them unsuitable for AM transmission. Fessenden's plan was to use a high-speed alternator to produce a continuous carrier wave with constant amplitude and frequency, inserting a microphone in the transmitter's circuit to introduce audio and modulate the carrier. Such an alternator was still theoretical in 1900, and so Fessenden used a rotary spark gap, which produced a rapid series of damped waves approximating a continuous wave.

A coherer works well as a detector of damped waves, but it is not a demodulator, that is, it can indicate when there is a radio wave, but it cannot extract audio from a modulated carrier wave. Fessenden's electrolytic detector, a fine platinum wire dipped in an acid solution with an applied DC voltage, rectified the AC current induced by the received radio wave, converting it into DC with variations in current corresponding to the audio signal, which was further converted by headphones into sound.

The received audio was distorted but it did prove that it was possible to transmit voice over radio waves. Fessenden had significantly better results after the invention of the Alexanderson alternator by electrical engineer Ernst Alexanderson in 1906, the first device that could produce a truly continuous radio wave. It would be years before the electrolytic detector saw regular service as a demodulator for AM radio, but it also worked well with ordinary spark transmitters, and because it was more sensitive and easier to use than the coherer it was widely adopted and became one of the more common detectors in the pre-vacuum tube years.

In 1903 Lee de Forest, searching for a detector to replace his inelegant "responder", produced the "spade detector", which looked and behaved remarkably like Fessenden's electrolytic detector. Fessenden's company, the National Electric Signaling Company (NESCO), was already selling radios with the electrolytic detector to the navy. The army, unaware of Fessenden's priority, tended to purchase components from De Forest, including the spade detector.

For the army, the electrolytic detector was so highly regarded that it was considered something of a standard, and every new detector introduced before the First World War was compared to it. It worked well with spark gap transmitters in the field and the arcs and alternators of larger stations. It was sensitive, simple to use and reliable.

Dozens of new detectors would be invented before the First World War. Some, like the electrolytic detector, would gain prominence. Some would find niche applications, and some would never leave the lab. Older detectors might be replaced, often gradually, by industry and the military, while new and exotic devices might be rejected outright. But many never disappeared completely, instead they were taken up by the amateur, who would rediscover and reshape them, and sometimes create something altogether new.

Amateur radio was a popular pursuit almost as soon as news of Marconi's exploits reached the press, and transmissions from navy stations and, after 1904, radio time signals made it even more so. The early enthusiasts came from the ranks of "home mechanics", amateurs who devoted their leisure time to building electrical and mechanical equipment.

Commercial transmitters and receivers were expensive, so amateurs usually made their own, at first based on cursory descriptions of Marconi equipment, and later from more detailed plans in books, magazines and newspapers. The January 1898 of the British magazine *The Model Engineer and Electrician* featured "The New Wireless Telegraphy",[6] the first popular article in English featuring details of wireless equipment construction. Even more thorough and influential was an article by A. Frederick Collins on "How to Construct an Efficient Wireless Telegraph Apparatus at a Small Cost", printed in the September 14, 1901 issue of *Scientific American*.[7] By 1902 there were enough books and articles available on the subject to put wireless within reach of anyone with the mechanical aptitude to construct a set.

The first complete wireless outfit marketed directly to amateurs was advertised in the November 25, 1905 issue of *Scientific American*, sharing a quarter of page 427 with ads for Hawthorne & Sheble phonograph sound boxes, Nulite vapor gas lamps, Pettyjohn hollow concrete blocks, Schwartz home furnaces, and Hydrozone, "A Harmless Antiseptic". The Telimco wireless, manufactured by Hugo Gernsback's Electro Importing Company, cost $8.50 and was a "complete outfit, comprising 1 inch spark coil, strap key, sender, sensitive relay, coherer, with automatic decoherer and sounder, 4 ex. strong dry cells, all necessary wiring, including send and catch wires, with full instructions and diagrams" and was "guaranteed to work up to one mile". It was a simple set, crude compared to the professional sets of the day, but it was relatively inexpensive, and it caught the attention of prospective wireless hobbyists lacking the skill or inclination to build their own equipment.

Figure 7 Hugo Gernsback's Telimco Wireless set. Scientific American, *November 25, 1905.*

Hugo Gernsback, born in Luxembourg City August 16, 1884, was drawn to all things electrical from an early age, installing intercoms and buzzers in Luxembourgian homes and studying electricity in school. At nineteen, with a little money in his pocket and a model of a high capacity battery and portable radio he had designed and hoped to sell, he bid his family farewell and moved to New York. He had a steady client, at least for a while, with Packard Motor Cars, which generated enough money for him to build and market the radio he had designed.

Finding there were not yet any electrical supply companies in New York, at least none that sold all the parts to build a wireless set, Gernsback entered the importing business, producing a catalogue of parts and electrical devices. Originally at 32 Park Place, The Electro Importing Company soon moved to their permanent address at 233 Fulton Street in New York, a short walk from the former location of William J. Clarke's United States Electrical Supply Company, in an area that by the 1920s would be known as Radio Row for its abundance of radio and electronic parts dealers.

He sold over 8,000 of his radios, marketed as the Telimco Wireless Telegraph, in 1910. "Every wide-awake American boy and every young man will feel the necessity of procuring one of these outfits", read an advertisement for the Telimco No. 2. Gernsback was prone to bombast, but he recognized the growing market of amateur radio enthusiasts, and he was going to do his best to be at the forefront. In 1908 he started *Modern Electrics*, the first magazine published specifically for the wireless amateur.

In January 1908 a design for a simple radio wave detector was printed in the letters *Modern Electrics*. This "novel detector" was "made of two Gillette razor blades mounted on an insulating base of paraffined wood, and held against a block of wood or hard rubber by two brass springs, to which the binding posts are connected. A piece of pencil lead is laid across the blades. A piece of incandescent lamp filament with a small weight fastened to its center may be used instead".[8]

It was not, strictly speaking, "novel". Detectors from the same family had been used in some commercial receivers, and amateurs were already using variations of the theme. The author, Clark Pettingill, was familiar with a more common version, "one in which carbon knife edges with a steel needle are used, but the steel blades with the carbon across seem to work just as good. It is hard to get a sharp edge on the carbon and the edge chips off very easy, so I thought I would reverse the combination."

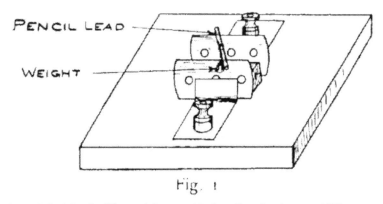

Figure 8 Clark Pettingill's novel detector. Modern Electrics, January 1909.

Pettingill's version was easy to make and used items that were available in most households. Disposable razor blades, sold by Gillette since 1902, were common by 1909, and a wooden pencil could be sacrificed for its graphite. The detector was sufficiently sensitive and required none of the delicate adjustments and maintenance of more complex detectors. And it had a long pedigree.

In 1899, as John Fahie was completing the manuscript for his *History of Wireless Telegraphy*, he wrote to William Crookes to ask him about a passage from his 1892 *Fortnightly Review* article, "Some

Possibilities of Electricity". Crookes had recalled that "some years ago I assisted at experiments where messages were transmitted from one part of a house to another without an intervening wire".[9]

He revealed that the mysterious experimenter was the inventor and professor of music David Edward Hughes, who in 1879 was working on an improved version of his carbon microphone. "I have not ceased since then urging on him to publish an account of his experiments", Crookes wrote, "but if you were to write to him, telling him what I say, it might induce him to publish."[10]

Initially Hughes was reluctant to provide Fahie with his story since he had never published and did not now want to seem to be claiming priority. He changed his mind on April 29, 1899 and sent Fahie a detailed account of the event.

In 1877 Hughes built a simple loose contact microphone, essentially a nail resting on two other nails wired in circuit. He found he could get better results with carbon rods and metal, a discovery that led to the first practical carbon microphones.

The following year he constructed an induction balance, a device with two electrically charged primary coils and two neutral secondary coils arranged so that their currents balance or neutralize each other, used to measure tiny changes in electric charge. He noticed that a loose contact in one of the primary coils was causing a pop in a telephone receiver he had attached to one of his microphones. He continued to hear it no matter how far he moved the microphone and receiver from the induction balance. He found that interrupting the current in any coil had the same effect and adding a battery bias to the microphone increased its sensitivity.

He constructed a coil that could be interrupted by a clockwork mechanism, causing a small spark to form, and left it on his workbench while he took his receiver outside, where he was able to hear the clicks from nearly 500 yards away.

Hughes understood that the phenomenon may have been caused by electromagnetic waves and not simple induction. In December 1879 he invited several noted scientists for a demonstration, among them William Henry Preece, Crookes, Royal Society president William Spottiswoode, and physicist Sir George Gabriel Stokes. Although impressed with the experiment, Stokes said that the results could be explained by induction, but that it was interesting enough that Hughes should write a paper anyway.

Disappointed, Hughes "refused to write a paper on the subject until I was better prepared to demonstrate the existence of these waves."[11] He continued to experiment until Hertz published his own paper. Hughes, feeling Hertz deserved credit, and not wanting it to seem as if he were claiming priority, dropped the subject. He died in January 1900, less than a year after writing his reply to Fahie. His furniture was moved into storage in London, his laboratory equipment, including the microphones and clockwork interrupter, along with it. In 1922 it was rediscovered, still in storage, and is now part of the London Science Museum technology collection.

Though Hughes only had a general idea of the principal behind his discovery, he had made what was almost certainly the first wireless transmitter and receiver, preceding Hertz by nearly a decade. His microphone was a better detector than the coherer, something he was well aware of. "The most sensitive and perfect receiver that I have yet made does not cohere permanently", wrote Hughes in his letter to Fahie, "but recovers its original state instantly."[12]

Fahie published Hughes' letter in the May 5, 1899 issue of *Electrician,*[13] as well as his own *History of Wireless Telegraphy.*[14] As far as Fahie was concerned, he was giving a distinguished scientist his due recognition. For many of the amateurs reading the article, here was presented the possibility of a simple detector that was self-restoring.

Detectors in the heyday of the coherer were naturally described in the context of coherers. "Self-restoring" was a term often applied to detectors that required no jostling after they cohered – if indeed they did cohere - and "auto coherers" was a term often applied specifically to detectors that were similar to the Hughes microphone. The implication was not necessarily that they ever actually "cohered", but that they did not need to be restored after receiving a wave train and were therefore able to respond faster than a coherer.

The Hughes microphone was part of the "imperfect contact" group of detectors, which included most coherers, so called because of their loose contact between metal and carbon or between metal and metal. Specifically, it was a microphone or microphonic detector, and would also function as a microphone in a radio circuit, usually unintentionally.

Carbon and steel detectors were rediscovered by engineers, perhaps taking a cue from David Edward Hughes, working to improve the coherer. Some of the earliest, built by John Stone Stone and Alexander Popov, replaced the metal filings of a coherer with carbon granules.

The detector was not as sensitive as a standard coherer, but it was self-restoring, making receivers far less complicated.

Microphone detectors had a higher resistance than a filings coherer, and a battery was usually added to provide forward bias and make it more sensitive to radio energy.

They were used commercially for only a few years before being replaced by electrolytic and other more sensitive detectors, but in that brief time several variations evolved. Alexander Popov, the French wireless pioneer Eugène Ducretet, and Harry Shoemaker used steel needles resting on carbon supports, similar to the carbon and nail microphones of Hughes. It was this type of detector that Shoemaker and Pickard used at the 1900 yacht race, and four years later they would build one of the most sensitive and durable microphonic detectors, a small brass tube, closed at both ends, containing supports and spacers to hold up two carbon discs, facing each other and supporting several small needles. Small and rugged for a detector of its class, it had "the property of great delicacy and sensitiveness in responding to electrical radiations, and has also the desirable property of regaining its normal condition after the cessation of influence of electrical waves".[15]

Because they were so simple, microphone detectors remained popular with amateurs for years after being retired from commercial stations. Coherer based receivers were beyond the technical expertise or financial means of many amateurs, but microphones could be easily built with readily available materials, usually some variation of a needle straddling two sharpened carbon blocks, or a rod from a carbon arc lamp resting across sharpened steel edges.

In March 1909 *Modern Electrics* printed a letter in response to Pettingill's novel detector. It was written by nineteen-year-old Alfred Powell Morgan, who the following year would write *Wireless Telegraph Construction for Amateurs*,[16] an early classic book on amateur radio. For the next 60 years he would write books on radio, electricity, chemistry, woodworking, model aircraft, and pets, many of which would be standards of elementary school libraries for decades. Between 1954 and 1969 he wrote what would become classics of post-war youth radio lore, *The Boys' First* through *Fourth Book of Radio and Electronics*.

Morgan noted the similarity of the Pettingill detector to an early Shoemaker system, which "employed a microphone detector which made use of steel knife edges bridged by several incandescent filaments, for commercial work, and obtained very good results."[17]

Morgan is referring to carbon filaments; this was still several years before tungsten filament light bulbs were readily available.

"This style of detector is now somewhat out of date," concludes Morgan, "but will prove interesting to those who own a Massie type microphone detector employing carbon edges and a steel needle, or to those who wish to experiment. An amateur can make one of these detectors and it will be more sensitive than the Massie type, for the edges of the knives can be made sharper".[18]

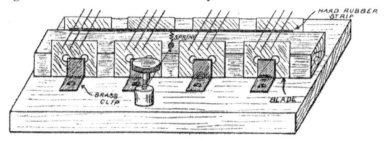

Figure 9 Alfred P. Morgan's "Shoemaker" style microphone detector from the March 1909 Modern Electrics.

The Massie style detector Morgan refers to was made from two small blocks of carbon mounted on a wood or ebonite base and separated by an insulator of hard rubber or wood. The tops of the carbon blocks were filed so that they formed sharp edges, and spanning these edges was a steel sewing needle. It was essentially the reverse of the Shoemaker setup, both variations of the Hughes microphone. The professional version of the Massie detector was built by Walter Wentworth Massie in 1904. Dubbed the oscillaphone,[19] it had the same basic components of the amateur version, along with a magnet mounted just below the needle that could be raised or lowered, keeping the needle in place and allowing for fine adjustment of its pressure on the carbon blocks.

The commercial life of the Massie detector was brief, but because it was so simple to make it became a favorite of amateurs before the First World War. Plans for it were printed in books on wireless,[20] including Massie's own *Wireless Telegraphy and Telephony Popularly Explained*.[21] There were variations, some even simpler, like the setup in A Frederick Collins' *The Book of Wireless* that only required the builder to fasten two pencil leads into brass binding posts, then "take a common steel sewing-needle, about No. 9, and weight it by fastening a lead bullet to the middle of it with a drop of sealing wax and lay it across the leads".[22]

Despite Morgan's preference of the Shoemaker over the Massie detector for its superior sensitivity, Massie's version was the more common, at least in popular wireless literature. Even in the less safety conscious early 20th century, the idea of mounting several exposed razor blades sharp edge up sounded a warning bell for most authors.

A microphone detector using razor blades made at least one final appearance before receding into radio obscurity, in the April 1917 edition of the children's magazine *St. Nicholas*.[23] "Twenty years ago", the article begins, "wireless telegraphy was the marvel of our times. Your father doubtless shook his head in amazement when he heard about the new discovery, and probably wondered by what complicated apparatus the results were obtained. Yet to-day I am going to tell you how to receive wireless messages with almost no apparatus. An old dry-battery, two safety-razor blades having two holes already gut in them, a telephone receiver, some wire, and several odds and ends are all we shall require for our experiments".

The detector was essentially the same as Clark Pettingill's, with two razor blades attached on opposite sides of a small wooden board, a piece of graphite straddling them both. Safety issues aside, better detectors were available by 1917, and the old microphone was a relic. But the idea of making a workable detector entirely from common household items was appealing to amateurs. The razor blade and carbon detector became part of the amateur's lore, if only subconsciously, and would return, half remembered, transformed into something new.

For the amateur, the microphone detector was a stop-gap, a temporary replacement for the coherer, lauded for its simplicity, but with problems of its own – it was easy to knock out of place, had to be readjusted frequently, and often produced a crackling sound in the headphones that drowned out all but the strongest signals.

By the time Clark Pettingill sent his letter to *Modern Electrics* a simpler, more dependable detector had already been found. The crystal and cat whisker, which would for decades be the detector most associated with amateur radio enthusiasts, was sensitive, rugged, and cheap. And because it could demodulate AM, it remained a popular and affordable alternative to the vacuum tube in the early years of broadcast radio, especially in pre-electrified rural areas.

An AM radio wave is modulated by varying its amplitude with the audio signal that is impressed upon it. The simplest way to demodulate the signal, or extract the encoded audio, is to use a rectifier, a non-linear device – one that passes current in one direction only - that converts the AC radio wave signal into DC which in turn is converted back to audio by the receiver's speaker or headphones.

That certain minerals will work as rectifiers was well documented even before Hertz. The first commercially practical radio detectors to use the phenomenon were developed, separately but concurrently, by an engineer and a retired army officer, one almost by accident, the other in a scramble to save a company from ruinous litigation.

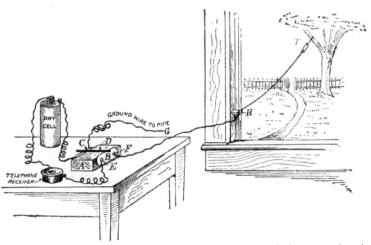

Figure 10 A razor blade microphone radio detector. St. Nicholas *magazine, April 1917.*

6 Materially Clearer

Greenleaf Whittier Pickard, named in honor of his great uncle, the Quaker poet and abolitionist John Greenleaf Whittier, was born in Portland, Maine on Valentine's Day 1877. He took an early interest in electricity, building bells, motors and telegraph circuits. His first paying job was the installation of an alarm bell for a Portland speakeasy, "for which I received the then magnificent sum of $10".[1]

In 1894 he conducted his first experiments in communicating without wires using conduction through a pond at Deering, Near Portland, Maine. He built his first wireless in set 1897, transmitting for a quarter of a mile using a Hertzian oscillator energized with a Wimshurst machine and a filings coherer receiver.[2]

Pickard spent the summer of 1898 taking measurements of atmospheric electricity at the Blue Hill Meteorological Observatory at Milton, Massachusetts. The Smithsonian Institution had taken an interest in radio and asked Blue Hill to experiment with long aerials suspended by kites. "The Smithsonian knew that Blue Hill had an elaborate equipment for air sounding", wrote Pickard, "consisting of many big box kites, ten miles of piano wire, a steam driven reel, etc., and gave us a grant from their Hodgkins fund, for the specific purpose of testing very long and high antennas. As I was at the time in M.I.T., I had no trouble in borrowing from their laboratory a fine big induction coil, with motor driven breaker, and having the Tech machine shop make up spark gaps and other parts."[3] The Hodgkins fund was established in 1893 from a $200,000 donation left to the

Smithsonian by Thomas George Hodgkins, who specified that at least part of it be used for atmospheric research.

Pickard was put in charge of the experiments since he was the only member of the team at all familiar with radio. He used the observatory's kites, which were normally used for meteorological observations, and "soon found that very long, high aerials (we tried some over a mile long and nearly half a mile high) could not be used with our coherer receiver, owing to the enormous amount of static which they collected".[4]

Wireless communication was established between the base and summit of the observatory using a spark gap connected to the ground and a short aerial on the flagpole of the observatory, energized by a 12" spark coil, and a coherer receiver and recorder with 75' antenna and ground at the base, 1.8 miles away.[5] They later successfully transmitted between Blue Hill and Mt. Chickatawbut, three miles away, this time using the flag pole aerial at the observatory with the transmitter and a 100 foot wire held up by a small box kite with the receiver.

In early 1899 Pickard met professor Amos Dolbear, chair of the physics department at Tufts College, and his son Clifton Dolbear who were conducting wireless experiments of their own. The elder Dolbear had invented a system of wireless communication using induction, patented in 1886 and purchased in 1899 by the New England Wireless Telegraph and Telephone Company, part of the American Wireless Telephone and Telegraph Company, who Pickard would later work for during the 1901 yacht race.

Dolbear is also notable for first describing the connection between air temperature and the rate at which a cricket chirps.[6]

Pickard suggested testing their equipment, a German spark gap transmitter and coherer receiver, at the observatory.[7] After the first unsuccessful test in June, a microphone detector and telephone receiver was substituted for the coherer. The receiving station was set up in the Memorial Hall Tower at Cambridge, where they received "recognizable, although mutilated by trolley static, messages from Blue Hill, a distance of 10.8 miles"[8].

His work with Dolbear was his first practical experience with the microphone detector, which, according to Pickard, came into common use in France in 1899,[9] around the time Fahie printed Hughes' letter.

Starting in 1901 Pickard, along with Harry Shoemaker, was an engineer at the American Wireless Telephone and Telegraph Company. American Wireless had unsuccessfully sued Marconi for infringement based on their ownership of Amos Dolbear's 1886 patent, which they felt gave them exclusive control of wireless in the United States and would have effectively made them the American wireless monopoly. The suit was dismissed in 1901 when the court ruled that Dolbear's patent was for an entirely different and, in their opinion, unworkable system.

Pickard and Shoemaker spent the summer of 1901 developing a receiver that would use a microphone detector of their own design, the same receiver that would be used at the 1901 yacht races.

On April 15, 1902 Pickard married Miriam W. Oliver and soon moved into the Amesbury Whittier house, the historic residence of John Greenleaf Whittier. At the request of the residents of Amesbury he agreed to leave the main part of the house a museum, adding on to accommodate the family, and enlarging the bedroom on the western end of the house for radio experiments. He built a 40-foot radio tower in the backyard which the townspeople, already annoyed by the noise from his transmitter, dubbed "Pickard's folly".[10]

In early 1902 American Wireless built wireless stations at Atlantic City and Cape May, New Jersey, and fitted the schooner *Pleiades* with wireless equipment to operate as an experimental station. On May 29 Pickard was testing a new tuning system at the Cape May station, receiving signals from the *Pleiades*, which was about two miles off the coast. He used a microphone detector "consisting of several fine sewing needles, laid lightly across a pair of carbon blocks, and in series with three cells of dry battery and a telephone receiver".[11]

The microphone detector was faster, more sensitive and more reliable than the coherer, but still there were annoyances. Jarring, static, or even a strong radio signal could easily knock it out of adjustment. The contact points would eventually, under normal use, "fatigue", and would need to be readjusted. It tended to live up to its name and acted as a microphone, picking up sounds and vibrations and passing them on to the phones. And, "even if the detector was screened from sounds and jars, it was prone to develop a hissing or frying sound, which overlaid faint signals to their obliteration".[12]

In an effort to alleviate some of the "fry" of the detector, Pickard removed two of the batteries from the circuit. The signals were weaker, but the fry was gone and they were "materially clearer thru being freed of their former background of microphonic noise".[13] Looking over the circuit later, he saw that he had cut out not two, but all three batteries from the circuit, meaning "the telephone diafram was being operated solely by the energy of the receiver signals. A contact detector, operating without local battery, seemed to me so extraordinary, so contrary to all my previous experience, that altho I did not then know the reasons for its operation, I appreciated its possible great value to the art, and resolved at once to thoroly investigate the phenomenon at the earliest possible moment."[14]

His notebook entry from May 29 includes a diagram of the equipment used. To the right, labeled "Sch. Pleiades", is the spark gap, coil, ground, and aerial of the transmitter. A dotted line marked "1.5 to 10 miles" connects the transmitter to the receiver, with its 160-foot aerial, telephone receiver, battery, ground and "Fe/C" microphone detector. "Good signals with battery = 3 v", he wrote, "cutting out battery entirely, faint signals could be heard, even at 10 m. were loud enough to read".[15] Pickard had rediscovered what Hughes knew in 1879, that a carbon and steel detector would work without a local battery.

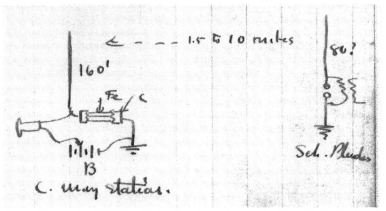

Figure 11 Greenleaf Whittier Pickard's notebook entry for May 29, 1902 when he discovered his microphone radio wave detector would work without a battery bias. George H. Clark Radioana Collection, National Museum of American History, Smithsonian Institution.

A few months later Pickard was employed as an experimental engineer at the Boston Laboratory of the American Telephone and Telegraph Company in charge of radiotelegraphy development. He had at his disposal a rotary spark transmitter capable of over 2000 sparks per second, allowing him to transmit modulated waves. He used the same type of carbon-steel microphone he had used at Cape May for a detector and found that it worked well as a demodulator. After spending some time improving the transmitter, he began to search for a detector that would work like the microphone but without its noise or tendency to be knocked out of place. It needed to meet two requirements: it had to have a "higher conversion efficiency",[16] the ratio of energy in to energy out, and it had to have "increased stability against jars and static. An inefficient detector which goes out of action in the middle of a message is of course of little commercial value."[17]

Pickard had some experience with minerology from work he had done in 1901 at the American Mining and Metals Extraction Company with Clinton Dolbear, inventor of the separation process then in use by the company. And he was aware that some minerals could resist electric current in one direction but less so in the other, potentially making them good rectifiers. Determined to discover which minerals or mineral combinations best met his requirements he resolved to test every sample he could obtain.

He chose magnetite for his first tests, mostly because AT&T already had a supply of it for loading coil cores. On July 25[18] he "broke one of these crystals apart, exposing a small fracture face, made a small area contact thereon with a brass point, and found that this crystal, like the carbon-steel contact, operated well without local battery, but, unlike the carbon-steel contact, did not require a light or microphonic contact for best operation... one of the greatest early stumbling blocks in such development was the old coherer idea that extremely light pressure contacts were necessary. With the carbon-steel microphone this is still true, but I can remember my surprise when I found that many of the minerals worked best with quite high pressure contacts".[19]

Pickard was not the first to notice the unilateral conductivity of certain minerals. Karl Ferdinand Braun in 1874,[20] Silvanus P. Thompson and Oliver Lodge in 1878,[21] and Jagadish Chandra Bose in 1895[22] all published papers on it and would later revisit the phenomenon, applying it to wireless.

Pickard took it further, systematically testing every mineral sample he could get his hands on. It was the first thorough examination of unilateral electrical conductivity of naturally occurring minerals.

Figure 12 Greenleaf W. Pickard's lab. Note the bottles of mineral samples lining the back of the workbench. Courtesy Ben Pickard.

After magnetite he tested chalcopyrite, marcasite, pyrite, and sphalerite,[23] and in 1904 every sample in a "Minerals of Maine" collection given to him by his father.[24]

In June 1904 Pickard set up a laboratory in his house, working nights and holidays testing different minerals and mineral combinations at varying pressures, constructing most of the test equipment himself, including one of the earliest signal generators.

Moving beyond his "Minerals of Maine" set, he ordered vendor's samples of every mineral mentioned in his copy of *Dana's Manual of Minerology*. "After these were received, they were first tested by me for conductivity and those which were found non-conductors were discarded. All of the minerals which showed conductivity which included, I found, the metallic sulphides, sulinides, telinides many of the oxides and some of the negative elements were found conductive. Fortunately, the larger class of minerals such as silicates and in fact all compounds whose chemical names end in 'ate' were non-conductors or insulators. Of the probably 9/10ths of the minerals known as separate species were not in my way useful as crystal detectors".[25]

Minerals that appeared identical would sometimes give dramatically different results, presumably because of "traces of impurities or variations in crystal structure".[26]

A photograph of his lab from the period shows a large group of jars lining the workbench, each containing a different mineral sample. He would spend the next several years, working evenings, weekends and holidays, testing thousands of minerals and mineral pairs, carefully noting signal strength, contact pressure, and effects from atmospheric and physical disturbances. And though he would complete one of the most thorough surveys of naturally occurring minerals as radio wave detectors and would go on to produce some of the finest crystal detectors on the market, he would not be the first to file a patent for one.

7 New and Useful Improvements

In 1901 Sir Jagadish Chandra Bose, physicist, botanist, radio pioneer and an early author of science fiction, filed the first patent for a radio wave detector using a mineral in contact with a metal point.[1] He used several minerals but favored galena and tellurium. Bose used the detector for his research in millimeter length radio waves starting in 1894 and had no interest in producing a commercial radio system.

The first patent for a commercial mineral radio wave detector was filed on March 28, 1906 by General Henry Harrison Chase Dunwoody, retired, U. S. Army, using the relatively new synthetic mineral carborundum.[2]

Dunwoody was born October 23, 1842 in Highland County, Ohio to William Dunwoody and Sarah Murphy. His great grandfather James Dunwoody served as a private in the 8th Company of the Cumberland County Militia during the Revolutionary War. His family moved to Fairfield, Iowa, in May 1849, where young Dunwoody was something of a prankster. Many years after the fact Mr. T. S. Waters, a childhood friend of Dunwoody, revealed to the Fairfield Weekly Ledger-Journal that "the loud noise heard one night some 65 years ago was he and the embryo soldier setting off one of the stumps that in olden days here were set in the streets as crossings for pedestrians. The boys had got hold of some powder and an augur and exploded the stump as a lark".[3]

He entered the United States Military Academy as a cadet September 1, 1862, and was appointed a second lieutenant, 4th Artillery after graduating in 1866. He spent much of his career in weather forecasting with the Signal Office, working as chief weather forecaster and creating a system of distributed storm warnings.[4]

Dunwoody was taciturn and serious minded, considered stern by those who knew him, but still generally well liked. His dedication and innovation endeared him to most of his superiors and made him popular with the press.

One particularly fawning article describes then Major Dunwoody as "strong in nature, 50 years of age, and has piercing steel gray eyes, great shaggy eyebrows, thick, iron gray hair, high intellectual forehead, and the square jaw denoting strength and determination. Although strict in discipline, his rugged honesty and unquestioned fairness have always caused his subordinates to look up to him with a feeling of pride and satisfaction. His is a face which will arrest attention anywhere and in any assemblage on account of the depth of mentality and strength of character there portrayed".[5]

With the outbreak of the Spanish American War he organized the Volunteer Signal Corps, serving as Chief Signal Officer, United States Volunteers, as a colonel, from May 20, 1898 to July 20, 1898, when he retired from volunteer service to return to regular duty in the Signal Corps. He served as Chief Signal Officer in Cuba from 1898 to 1901, overseeing the construction of telegraph lines on the island.

Dunwoody's first direct involvement with wireless came in August 1901 while he was Acting Chief Signal Officer, Washington state. Along with Captain Edgar Russel and Captain Samuel Reber, Dunwoody oversaw the installation of wireless stations along the Pacific coast.

In August 1902 while serving as the Signal Officer, Department of the East, Governors Island, New York, Dunwoody accepted a bid from the De Forest Wireless Telegraph Company for connecting Forts Wadsworth and Hancock by wireless, replacing the cables connecting the forts and headquarters on Governors Island.[6]

The first tests were made on March 11, 1903 with Dunwoody manning the transmitter at Fort Wadsworth, and C. G. Tompkins, general manager of the De Forest Company, in charge of operations at Fort Hancock. The De Forest receiver used a microphone detector made of two aluminum rods with a steel needle laid across them. Despite damp and rainy weather, the results were "regarded as highly satisfactory".[7]

Figure 13 Henry Harrison Chase Dunwoody. U. S. Army Signal Corps Photograph 111-SC-90959. National Archives at College Park, College Park, Maryland.

On October 21, 1903 Colonel Dunwoody left the office of Chief Signal Officer and assumed command of the signal post at Fort Myer. He was promoted to Brigadier general July 6, 1904 and retired, at his request, the following day.

On July 26th Lee de Forest and Abraham White of the American De Forest Wireless telegraph Company, while meeting with representatives of the Navy Department regarding a contract for wireless stations to be erected in Cuba, Key West, Puerto Rico and Panama, announced that Dunwoody "would be in charge of the Washington office as vice-president and a director of the company, and be the personal representative of the company in its future dealings with the government".[8] Lee de Forest had a good working relationship with Dunwoody appreciated the advantage of hiring someone well connected to the War Department and with knowledge of the military bidding process. He also felt he was rewarding Dunwoody for his role in securing lucrative army contracts.

The question of ethics regarding Dunwoody and de Forest's arrangement came up at least once. An article in the *Pittsburgh Daily Post* questioned the appropriateness of a retired army officer taking a position with a company that was conducting business with the government, especially, in Dunwoody's case, when "it was largely on his recommendation that the Government finally adopted the De Forest system for its own use."[9] The War Department was apparently unconcerned about any perceived impropriety and continued to award contracts to de Forest.

In March 1906 de Forest teamed with Alexander Graham Bell to test the raising of aerials using Dr. Bell's kites. Bell had been working with tetrahedral kites since the 1890s with hopes of applying them to flying machines and wrote an article for *National Geographic*[10] about them that was read by de Forest.

Bell and his team were set up with a De Forest receiver and a 230-cell tetrahedral kite with a 400-foot antenna at Bell's experimental station near Arlington, Virginia. Dunwoody sent messages from the United States Naval Station at the Washington Navy Yard, then from the De Forest station at Galilee, on the New Jersey coast, and finally from a steamer 100 miles from New York, over 350 miles from the receiver.[11]

On April 6, at Glengarriff Harbor, County Cork, Ireland, using a kite loaned to him by Bell, de Forest received a wireless message sent

3000 miles across the Atlantic from the 40 kilowatt De Forest station at Manhattan Beach, Brooklyn, New York. The transmission was sent at 20 words per minute and clearly received.[12] It was a coup for de Forest - Marconi was still struggling with transoceanic wireless, over four years after his first transmission across the Atlantic.

The celebration did not last long. The next day the De Forest Company lost a nearly three-year legal battle with Reginald Fessenden's NESCO, receiving a fine and an injunction against using their most important detector.

Though he used a microphone detector in some stations, most De Forest receivers at the time used his "spade" electrolytic detector, which worked well, but was remarkably, and not coincidentally, similar to Fessenden's electrolytic detector. NESCO sued De Forest in 1903 for patent infringement, and, sensing that he would not win the case, Lee de Forest scrambled for a new detector. He had made some progress on the audion vacuum tube, a modification of John Ambrose Fleming's vacuum tube rectifier, but it was not yet ready to be used commercially. He needed a detector that would be simple to construct, reliable, cheap, and had no chance of being challenged for copyright infringement. Fortunately, he already had one.

In early 1906 Henry Harrison Chase Dunwoody discovered that the synthetic mineral carborundum would rectify and work as a detector. An extremely hard compound of silicon and carbon, carborundum was first produced by Edward Goodrich Acheson in 1890 during his attempts to make artificial diamonds. Naturally occurring silicon carbide is known as moissanite and is rare, most of it found in small amounts from certain meteorites. Carborundum has been produced commercially since 1893 and is used mostly as an abrasive.

If either de Forest or Dunwoody kept notes of the events leading up to the discovery of the carborundum detector, they have been lost. An avid reader of scientific journals, de Forest likely knew of Braun and perhaps Bose's work with unilateral conductivity of minerals, and may have noticed an article in the November 1905 issue of *Science Abstracts* announcing that silicon had been produced in the electric furnace, and that "its specific electrical resistance is high".[13] Silicon was difficult to get in 1906, but the article also mentioned that graphite and carborundum may have similar electrical properties. Graphite will work as a detector, but it is brittle and requires a light touch. Carborundum, on the other hand, is rugged stuff.

Whether Dunwoody decided on his own to test carborundum or de Forest suggested it to him is unclear, but it was Dunwoody who filed the patent on March 23, 1906.[14] He proved that carborundum would work as a detector, but his design did not produce the sensitive, stable detector de Forest needed.

The patent drawings describe twelve different configurations, and the differences are not subtle. Three are variations on the electrolytic detector, with the carborundum suspended in a cup of electrolyte. Two are like the Massie microphone, complete with needle and magnet. The rest are simply chunks of carborundum in contact with metal plates, wires, or another piece of carborundum. Dunwoody claimed that all the variations worked, but the multiple patent drawings betray a lack of confidence in the design. All of Dunwoody's carborundum detector designs – the electrolytics aside – used a light contact, which may have worked, but not well. Most contemporaneous detectors used a light contact point, so it is understandable that Dunwoody would have assumed the same for carborundum.

The version Dunwoody found that worked best "consisted of a few turns of copper wire, wound around each end of a small, irregular mass of carborundum crystals... This was mounted for protection in a fibre shell with brass ends, just like a tubular fuse, so it was one of the early fixed crystal detectors".[15] Only one in ten worked at all, and not very well. The De Forest operators despised them.

Hoping that a properly configured carborundum detector might save his company, de Forest asked the one person he knew who had already been working with minerals for detection, Greenleaf Whittier Pickard.

They first met in 1904 at the Louisiana Purchase Exposition in Saint Louis. De forest was there with his company's exhibit, a grandiose, brightly lit 300-foot radio tower with observation decks and large, illuminated letters spelling out "DEFOREST", its 10-kilowatt station transmitting daily news reports to the *St. Louis Star* and the *Post-Dispatch*, five miles away.

Pickard had installed a new model of photophone at the AT&T exhibit and was overseeing its operation. Curious about the only wireless exhibit at the fair - Marconi dropped out when he found out that de Forest was going to be there - Pickard struck up a conversation with de Forest. Knowing his employment history, it is likely de Forest knew of Pickard's role in the 1901 America's Cup, but, for the sake of business, he was willing to overlook it and hired Pickard as an expert witness for patent litigation, including the electrolytic detector case with Fessenden. And in April 1906 he asked Pickard to evaluate and, if possible, improve Dunwoody's detector.

Pickard knew from experience that it was best to mount one end of the crystal on a wide base of solder and use a very small point of contact on the other end. With carborundum, he found that point of contact worked best with relatively heavy pressure applied. His carborundum detector patent of September 1907[16] specified a high-pressure contact and a one to three-volt electrical bias, greatly improving it as a detector.

In his tests of carborundum, Pickard concluded that it was not as sensitive as electrolytic or even magnetic detectors, but in practical use the differences were negligible. The high-pressure contact could not be easily dislodged, making it popular with shipboard wireless operators, who would refer to it simply as "coal".

Around the same time Dunwoody was making his first carborundum detector, 13-year-old Franklin Malcom Doolittle, who in 1922 would found Connecticut's first commercial radio station, WPAJ, was making one of his own.

His father one day brought home a small crystal, "unknown alike to himself and me. I took it to my room and there tested it to ascertain the degree to which it would conduct electric waves. I found it very sensitive, and from it I constructed a little receiver."[17] After bringing the crystal to Yale, where a professor identified it as carborundum, he built a larger receiver with a new carborundum crystal that worked better than any had had used before.

A nearby commercial station, likely one owned by Deforest, had installed a new receiver that, "because the patent was not perfected, kept it under lock and key, allowing no one but their operator to see it," recalled Doolittle. "Meantime, I kept using mine in communication with them and other stations. When they had received their full patents and allowed those interested to see their newly purchased receiver, I went to look at it. It was made of carborundum, but was more crude than my own. We had made the discovery simultaneously."[18]

Pickard made his first truly functional carborundum detector on May 6, 1906,[19] and installed it at the United De Forest station at 42 Broadway, New York, on May 25. The operator was so pleased with it that Pickard had difficulty getting it back, and it remained there through October.

Using Pickard's improvements, de Forest designed new carborundum detectors that could easily replace the patent challenged detectors of his current production receivers, "in other words, the carborundum detector is made interchangeable with the electrolytic detector, which it has superseded."[20]

Because payments were, at best, late while Pickard had worked for De Forest as an expert witness, his wife Miriam warned him that he should ask to be compensated before completing any work with the carborundum detector. But Pickard, hopeful and in need of the money, took the job anyway. He was never paid. It was "just as I had expected"[21], Miriam Pickard would later testify.

On September 8, 1906 de Forest sent a letter to *Electrical World*, giving credit to Dunwoody and publicly stating priority for his own company's use of carborundum as a detector. He writes that it "lies in sensitiveness between the electrolytic and magnetic detectors, being somewhat more sensitive than the latter", and that it "is emphatically not an 'imperfect contact' receiver, and cannot properly be classed as an auto-coherer or a microphone".[22] He is reacting to an article by H. J. Round, published in the same journal in August, which implied that, like a microphone detector or coherer, carborundum was an imperfect contact detector, and "to whom its use was originally due could not be ascertained".[23] In November Pickard responded with an article of his own, detailing his research.[24]

The improved carborundum detector worked well, and the company was saved, but the Fessenden injunction was costly. The board and Lee de Forest had been at odds for some time, the board frustrated by de Forest's multiple patent infringements, and de Forest annoyed by what he felt was a lack of support for his research. Whether or not it was entirely his decision, de Forest parted ways with American De Forest in November 1906, taking with him $1000 and his patent for the audion vacuum tube, which the board thought useless. Within a decade it would help de Forest reestablish his fortunes.

American De Forest was reorganized as The United Wireless Telegraph Company, becoming for a time the largest wireless company in the United States. Dunwoody resigned soon after, and Pickard continued for another year as a patent consultant. The carborundum detector, unlikely to be challenged in patent court, was used in most United Wireless stations. It was as good as any detector of its day, and any company that controlled it should have remained on top, if that company had not been United Wireless.

8 Stable and Sensitive

Between 1903 and 1906 Greenleaf Whittier Pickard tested over 250 minerals, most natural, some products of the furnace, in 31,250 combinations to determine how well they would work as radio wave detectors.[1]

Many of the mineral-mineral and mineral-metal pairs made sensitive detectors, but most "would now and then go out of adjustment, which defeated one of my objectives; a fixed contact detector which would be stable enough to be put up in a cartridge form, like a fuse".[2]

He recalled that the microphone detector used the element carbon, and, referring to the periodic table, he found that the carbon group also included silicon, germanium, tin and lead. Since elements of the same group tend to have similar physical properties, he reasoned that silicon and germanium may also make good detectors. Unfortunately neither of these were available in pure form in any sizable quantity.

In November 1905 Pickard read in *Science Abstracts* that silicon had been produced in the electric furnace, and that "its specific electrical resistance is high"[3], reinforcing his belief that it might make a good detector. The same article, which de Forest also likely read, mentions other products of the electric furnace, among them carborundum. "I am inclined to believe that I did not then observe that carborundum was specified, because if I had I would doubtless have procured some, as it was easy to obtain it at that time, infinitely easier than silicon."[4]

In early 1906 AT&T moved their offices from Boston to New York. Not wishing to relocate, Pickard left AT&T and opened a consulting office in Boston, devoting the remainder of his time to developing mineral radio wave detectors.

In June 1906 he wrote Dr. Henry Noel Potter, an engineer at Westinghouse[5], who had recently prepared pure crystalline silicon in an electric furnace. Potter provided him with a sample, which made an excellent detector, resistant to electrical and mechanical jarring.[6] "I decided that I had found a commercial, stable and sensitive detector which would operate well under noncritical adjustments, that is, one could be placed in the hands of an average operator."[7]

He considered silicon with a "blunt metal point pressing fairly lightly against it" the best mineral detector of all he tested and decided to patent.[8]

He contacted Philip Farnsworth, a New York attorney he knew through his work as an expert witness, to help patent the silicon detector. Farnsworth suggested that not only silicon but all detectors in the same class should be protected and formed a fifty-fifty partnership with Pickard to produce and market them.

Pickard brought the silicon detector to Harry Shoemaker, now chief engineer at the International Telegraph Construction Company, in hopes of bringing him on as an engineer with the new company. Shoemaker was working on perfecting new equipment of his own and was not interested in taking on a detector he did not own or control. He did however offer to show it to engineer John Firth, who in turn showed it to the army and navy, who were enthusiastic about it.

In March 1907 Pickard and Farnsworth received their first order for 50 silicon detectors at $30 each from the Signal Corps.[9] Soon after, the Wireless Specialty Apparatus Company was established, with John Firth as president, general manager and sales manager, Pickard as vice president and chief engineer, and Philip Farnsworth as patent counsel and treasurer.

After a year of successful sales of their silicon detector to the army and navy, WSA introduced a series of detectors that used a combination of minerals, usually zincite and chalcopyrite, in firm contact with each other. They named the new detector the "Perfect Pickard Contact", shortened to "Perikon", for the "perfect" or firm contact between the minerals, as opposed to the loose or imperfect contact of coherers, microphones, and similar detectors.

Figure 14 Greenleaf Whittier Pickard. Courtesy Mary Ann Hoffman, Archival & Web Services Manager, IEEE History Center

The Perikon detectors sold well, but carborundum for a time remained the most common mineral detector, mostly because of the great number of United Wireless stations. According to *The Mineral Industry* for 1907, "carborundum detectors are used in approximately 130 out of 145 wireless telegraphy Stations erected in the United States or installed on vessels plying its waters".[10] The article describes which carborundum crystals work best, and takes the opportunity to disparage silicon. "The green variety of crystals is preferred and is found more sensitive than the blue or black crystals. Well defined crystals are required and fragments of close, dense masses are not sensitive. Silicon is also a very sensitive detector but unlike carborundum it is difficult to hold in place after the party sought is found, because when pressure is applied its sensitiveness is lost."[11]

Carborundum was used extensively in commercial and some amateur equipment, but was not so readily accepted by the government, other than on two Revenue Cutter Service vessels that were using De Forest wireless systems. The Bureau of Equipment of the Navy Department tested carborundum detectors but found them "not as efficient as those already in use and they were dropped".[12] The army, favoring the electrolytic and WSA's Perikon, never embraced carborundum.

By 1910 the United Wireless Telegraph Company was suffering from legal trouble, mostly from stock fraud and questionable business practices. Already bankrupt, they were sued by the Marconi Company in 1912 for patent infringement and lost. Their assets, including the carborundum detector, were transferred to American Marconi, who used the detector in some of their first permanent transatlantic stations.

The demise of United Wireless came when other mineral detectors were starting to gain prominence. Galena, a readily available, sensitive detector, became a favorite of amateurs, pushing out microphones and the few remaining homemade coherers and electrolytic detectors. It was used with a fine wire or "cat whisker", a fine wire, usually of phosphor bronze.

The first use of the term "cat whisker" and of the flexible wire contact itself is unclear. Radio historian George H. Clark, consulting with Pickard and other radio pioneers, thoroughly researched the subject in the late 1930s and never reached a definitive conclusion. Pickard experimented with a #24 phosphor bronze wire contact in 1906 with his first tests of silicon. In 1910 Benjamin Miessner filed a patent for a detector using iron pyrite and a 30 gauge wire "fine metallic point".[13] Miessner, a naval radio operator, wondered if reaching the small nooks and crannies of a crystal with a fine, sharp wire would make a more sensitive detector than crystal-to-crystal or crystal-to-blunt contact, as in the Pickard detector, which only reached the outer projections of the mineral.

In Miessner's estimation it was a more sensitive detector, and he sold his patent to Pickard, who made several variations. Sometimes the wire was straight, sometimes it was coiled into a spring, and sometimes multiple wires were bundled together. George Clark supposed that, since the bundled wires so resembled actual cat whiskers, the term may have come into being at the same time, although neither Miessner nor Pickard used it.[14] Clark was not altogether convinced in his theory, and only a week earlier he had written "that the term came from amateurs is quite probable, in that only books and magazines for amateurs make use of the term".[15]

Plans for radios using crystal detectors appeared in popular works by 1909[16], and the term "cat whisker" was already known to amateurs by September 1913 when *Popular Electricity* referred to it in a brief article describing the construction of a detector that could hold several minerals in a six-cup carousel.[17]

Pickard may not have coined "cat whisker" but he did claim first use of "solid state". "When I introduced this term in 1909, there were already liquid rectifiers, gaseous rectifiers and vacuum rectifiers, all of which had been used in radio. Solid was therefore the natural term for a device which was constructed entirely of solids."[18]

Pickard continued to develop detectors, tuners and accessories for Wireless Specialty Apparatus, using the bedroom of the Whittier House as the company's research lab.[19]

He would work for Lee de Forest again in 1915, this time regarding the first litigation on the vacuum tube. In his long career he made several notable contributions to the radio art, developing a radio compass, new types of antennae, and systems for atmospheric noise suppression. He retired from WSA in 1931, working as a consultant and continuing to develop radio equipment. He died in 1956.

After leaving United Wireless, Henry Harrison Chase Dunwoody, along with a few of his retired military associates, established the Aztec Copper Company in Organ, New Mexico. He spent winters in Las Cruces at the Amador Hotel[20], overseeing production in mostly played out mines that his company was able to acquire inexpensively. In retirement he was an active inventor, filing several patents for armaments, telephones and a cycloidal propeller.

Dunwoody died on January 1, 1933 at Interlaken. General Douglas MacArthur, at the time Chief of Staff of the United States Army, sent a letter of condolence to Dunwoody's son, Halsey. "General Dunwoody exemplified those fine professional and personal qualifications", he wrote, "which earned for him an enviable reputation as a Signal Corps Officer of rare scientific accomplishments and a gentleman of high character and ideals. The records bear ample testimony to the eminent success he attained in his chosen field of endeavor."[21]

Several of his descendants had distinguished military careers. His son Halsey was Assistant Chief of the Air Service during WWI, later becoming one of the first Vice Presidents of the newly formed American Airlines. His grandson Brigadier General Harold Dunwoody served in WWII, Korea and Vietnam, and his great granddaughter Ann Dunwoody was the first female four-star general in the history of the United States armed forces.

Pickard met Dunwoody only once, in the summer of 1906, and "after a half-hour talk found that he knew little about radio, but had discovered by pure accident that carborundum would act as a detector"[22]. Pickard may have been judging too harshly. Lee de Forest, not one for flattery, would later write that "General Dunwoody never did get full credit for his invention of the carborundum detector. It is a pity".[23] Well into his eighties Dunwoody remembered enough about radio to show his grandson Harold how to build a crystal set.[24]

For military and commercial uses, the crystal detector supplemented rather than supplanted the electrolytic, and they both existed side by side for a while. Crystals were easy to work with, there was no electrode to replace, and those that required firm contacts were less likely to be jarred out of adjustment. Electrolytic detectors, on the other hand, were less likely to be knocked out by a strong spark and were generally regarded as being more sensitive.

Although the electrical properties of crystal detectors were well documented by Pickard and others, how they worked was not well understood. It was generally believed at the time that rectification was due to a thermal reaction, that is, the junction between two dissimilar minerals or a mineral and metal cat whisker heated slightly in the presence of radio waves, and that this relatively hot junction somehow acted as a one-way door for electrical flow. From 1907 to 1909 physicist George Washington Pierce, who would later have a long career as a beloved professor at Harvard, made an exhaustive study of mineral detectors and proved that whatever was happening was not thermal.[25] It would take semiconductor theory and quantum physics in the 1930s and 40s to finally explain what was actually happening.

Crystal detectors were cheap and easy to use, making them especially popular with amateurs. Receiving sets with cat whisker detectors could easily be made by those with even modest skills. The crystal made radio accessible to the masses. Newspapers devoted columns to the growing hobby, publishing building tips and serialized plans for more complicated sets. Popular books and magazines by the likes of Alfred Powell Morgan and Hugo Gernsback flourished and brought radio to a new audience. An industry grew around the selling of radio parts and inexpensive crystals. It was easier and cheaper now to make home equipment, especially receivers, and with the proliferation of military and commercial stations there was more to listen to.

Much of the popular literature was aimed at children who, with little money available, learned to improvise what they could and scrounge or substitute for the rest. Newspaper and magazine articles featuring young people operating their own wireless stations inspired others to try it for themselves. In 1906 Charles Fielding, a messenger working for the postal telegraph company, built a wireless station in his back yard at Newport, Rhode Island, mostly to monitor navy transmissions, but soon he was communicating with naval radio operators. His work so impressed the navy that, although he was two years under the age requirement, he was offered a job as an electrician.[26] And Malcolm Doolittle, who at 12, and possibly before Dunwoody, first discovered that carborundum would work as a detector, was at 13 invited to Yale to discuss his wireless experiments.[27]

By the time crystal detectors were available, there was a connected community of radio amateurs, and their word of mouth dissemination of obscure radio knowledge and improvisation, along with radio books, magazines, and clubs all contributed to a rich lore of amateur radio, where ideas and devices, long after being abandoned by professionals, often resurface in different and sometimes bizarre forms. Because the lore is active, all parts of the radio, detectors especially, are likely to reappear, some for nostalgia, some because they are especially simple or especially challenging to make.

Rather than becoming static museum displays, the detectors, antennae, circuits, all that enters the lore, continues to be shaped, transformed, and blended. Improvisation, napkin scribbles, half-remembered instructions all reshape the bits and pieces, subtly and dramatically, successfully and not, often leading to something brand new. Some of the output of the slow cooker of an active lore become almost legendary because of their strangeness, like the potato electrolytic detector that appeared in a 1915 issue of *The Electrical Experimenter* that consisted only of two needles stuck in to opposite sides of a potato.[28]

Even the coherer was occasionally featured in amateur articles, long after simpler detectors were available. The first radio article in the Boy Scouts of America's magazine *Boys' Life*, printed in February 1912, featured a coherer-based receiver, long after its heyday.

Detectors that were relatively simple and worked as rectifiers were more likely to not only be part of the lore but also remain viable alternatives for the casual amateur. The microphone was such a detector, appearing in the popular literature well into the age of the crystal and even the vacuum tube. It would disappear for a while, then return, reshaped in the muddy foxholes of an Italian beachhead.

9 A Pure, Sharp Wave

While Pickard and Dunwoody were developing their detectors, the Signal Corps continued to work towards lighter, stronger and more rugged radio equipment.

Early equipment was difficult to transport. Transmitters and receivers were built into trunks and were easy enough to pack on a mule, but the antenna pole – 60 to 90 feet tall – was more of a challenge. Henry W. Daly of the Quartermaster' Department, the army's Chief Packmaster, was chosen to standardize packing and transport of field radio equipment.

Daly's career as a packmaster began in the 1860s with pack mules carrying supplies to mining camps in Canada. After serving in the Spanish American War he went to Washington where he made improvements to pack train operation and pack saddles. In 1899 he developed an improved version of the Mexican *aparejo*, which became the standard mule pack saddle for many years. In 1900 he was sent to West Point as packing instructor, where in 1901 he wrote the army's first manual devoted specifically to pack transportation,[1] intended for cadets at West Point, and later revised and expanded for general military use.[2] It was revised several times and remained the standard work on the subject through the First World War. He was considered by the army the greatest authority on mules and packing, the "last of the old-time packers".[3]

He was stationed at Fort Leavenworth from 1902 to 1909 where he perfected several packing systems for wireless, redesigning it as equipment evolved. From 1909 to 1917 he oversaw pack train inspection in Washington, D.C. and was appointed a wartime commission as Captain in the Quartermaster Corps July 10, 1917 and promoted to Major the following year. He retired in 1919.

Radio was much improved by 1905 but it was not quite durable or portable enough to be considered field ready. Tuning, where there was any, was rudimentary. Transmissions could be intercepted and were prone to interference. Telefunken of Germany made durable sets that performed well but they were wagon sets and were considered too heavy and too foreign, though a few were purchased for testing.

The firsts standardized sets built from American equipment - a three-kilowatt set for transports and stations, a one-kilowatt portable gas-powered set for tugboats, wagons, or stations, and a battery powered 125-watt field set to be carried by mules – were developed in 1906.[4]

On September 28, 1906 Tomás Estrada Palma, the first President of Cuba, resigned after accusations of election fraud led to a revolt of the opposing party. Secretary of War William H. Taft, already in Cuba to intervene and acting under article III of the Platt Amendment, established himself as Provisional Governor. The revolt ended peacefully when the Marines arrived. The army arrived on October 6 and would spend most of their time building roads and lines of communication, gathering intelligence, and protecting citizens of the United States living in Cuba.

For the Signal Corps, it was an opportunity to test radio for the first time in a military operation. Major Charles McKinley Saltzman, formerly the Commandant of the Signal School at Fort Leavenworth, was made Chief Signal Officer of the Cuban Expeditionary Forces. Under the direction of Captain Billy Mitchell, Signal Corps Company A organized all radio communication.

The field wireless platoon at the time consisted of two squads, each with "three noncommissioned officers and six men. A noncommissioned officer and four men of each section are mounted. Each section is accompanied by an instrument wagon, which carries the equipment, instruments, and rations. The men who are not mounted ride on the wagon."[5] The unit operated and was equipped like a cavalry platoon, "except that a machete is carried in place of the saber".[6] Each wagon carried a Telefunken set, complete with transmitter, receiver, antenna, tools, and a bicycle driven electric generator. Weighing 430 pounds, the equipment could be carried by two mules when it was necessary to travel where wagons could not. With a little experience the squads were able to set up their stations in half an hour or less, sending messages 25 miles.

Wireless in Cuba was considered a success, and was the first practical use of portable systems visible to most officers outside of the Signal Corps. It was now out of the experimental stage and had proven "that a General commanding an army in the field can now keep in touch with his cavalry screen without going to the trouble of building flying field telegraph or buzzer lines. This will save an enormous amount of work and will also lessen the transportation for the Signal Corps, as less material for construction need be carried".[7]

Figure 15 U.S. field radio station, Guanajay, Cuba, 1907. Photo by George A. Wieczorek, author's collection.

Because it was so successful, Chief Signal Officer James Allen ordered fifteen more sets to be used "at various posts in this country",[8] including one set already installed on the artillery district boat at Fort Monroe, Forts Totten and H. G. Wright, New York and Fort Hancock, New Jersey for coast artillery and militia exercises.

In 1907 the army installed wireless on several of their transport ships. "The transport Thomas was equipped with wireless instruments before leaving San Francisco for Manila on June 5, and the system was at once put into successful operation. Three messages were received by the navy station at Mare Island before Honolulu was reached, the last one when the vessel was 700 miles out."[9] Sets would also be installed on transports Logan, Sheridan and Sherman. The sets were "designed, assembled and furnished by the signal corps" and represented "the latest improvements of Maj. Edgar Russel". 1907 was also the year that the army purchased its first radiotelephone equipment, tested under direction of the Artillery Board at Fort Monroe.

Sergeant King's kite was now standard issue, slightly modified so it could fly in a slight breeze or stronger wind and be easily broken down and packed. Two varieties, six or seven and one-half feet high, were available. The cord used to fly it was composed of 42 strands of phosphor-bronze wire woven around a hemp center.[10] King's design was used, or at least available, as late as the 1920s, the two sizes renamed type KI-2, 6 feet high and 6 feet wide, and type KI-3, 7 1/2 feet high by 7 1/2 feet wide, the bamboo now replaced by "spruce supported by a rim of No. 32 B. & S. gauge heavy stranded wire" covered with "light slate-colored percale".[11]

There was a type KI-1 kite, obsolete by 1920, a "folding Malay kite" 60 by 60 inches, its maximum width eleven inches below the top, with a cloth cover and a spruce frame reinforced by brass wire and waxed thread.

Signal Corps radio equipment was nearly standardized by 1907. Five sets were available, with improvements added as they were produced. The field wireless set, pack, was a 450-pound set that could be packed on three mules. The field wireless set, 1 kilowatt, wagon, a thousand-pound, wagon mounted set with a 100-foot antenna and a gasoline driven alternating current generator, had a range of 75 to 100 miles. The same equipment mounted on a desk instead of a wagon was designated the station wireless set, 1 kilowatt. The station wireless set, 3 kilowatts, with a range of 200 to 300 miles, was designed for installation in a permanent station. And the transport wireless set, 3 kilowatts, was installed on army transport ships, the generator usually mounted in the ship's engine room, the transmitter and receiver in a room on the upper deck, and the antenna strung between the masts.[12]

The 1908 field radio fit snugly into two sixteen-inch chests weighing 130 pounds. Power came from two batteries or a 120-pound hand driven dynamo. Six 80-foot antenna wires radiated from the top of a

60-foot sectional, hollow, reinforced spruce mast with a counterpoise instead of a ground, six wires radiating from the base six feet above the ground. The mast and raising device were in 12 sections, each 6' 8" long.[13]

In 1911 Sergeant King, now with Signal Corps Company D at Fort Leavenworth, was still making improvements to Signal Corps transmitters, receivers and antennae. He designed a 90-foot sectional pole that could be "put up and the entire outfit made ready for work in a minute and a half", a task that would have taken ten men twenty-five minutes to do when experiments began at Leavenworth five years earlier. Transmission range was also improved, and messages could be sent 40 miles or more under ideal conditions.

King felt wireless was past the experimental stage and advocated for its use in the field. "If the Civil War had been fought with the present modern equipment and with the wireless," he said, "it would have lasted four months instead of four years."[14]

Commercially available equipment had improved enough that it was suitable for field use. Pack sets built by National Electric Supply Company were purchased by the navy. The Signal Corps used equipment from Wireless Specialty Apparatus, Lee deForest and others, and in November 1911 Company D was issued a Telefunken wagon set, one of two owned by the signal corps. Although it could send messages 250 miles or farther, four horses were needed to pull the heavy wagon.

Field wireless equipment was more formally standardized as its manufacture moved gradually from the Signal Corps to commercial contractors.

The 1910 set had an open spark gap, silicon or Perikon detector, and was packed in two trunks. Four mules were used, the "generator mule," the "chest mule," the "mast mule," and the "kit mule."[15]

The 1913 set had a quenched spark gap, more efficient than an open spark gap because it allowed for greater dampening of the oscillation of the spark. The transmitter and receiver, with its mineral detector, were now one unit, and everything could be packed on two mules. It was powered by an 18 pole 250-watt 110-volt hand generator.

The 1915 set was similar but with a more efficient hand cranked generator that required less pull and was less tiring on the operators.

Figure 16 A typical pre-WWI "trunk" radio set in the field, this one operated by the U.S. Marines. United States Marine photo, author's collection.

All these new sets required instructions. Aside from various handwritten or typed operating instructions and notes, starting with the instruction sheet given to Squier by Clarke in 1899, the first official wireless manual was issued by the navy. *Instructions for the Use of Wireless-Telegraph Apparatus*[16] was printed in 1903, the year the navy first installed radio on ships as part of their regular equipment. The manual described the installation of aerials and the Slaby-Arco equipment then in use, but was, "in the main, applicable to any system of wireless telegraphy employing an induction coil for transmitting and a coherer with relay for receiving".[17]

It was replaced in 1906 by the *Manual of Wireless Telegraphy for the Use of Naval Electricians*,[18] a larger work that included more theory and general practice than its predecessor. It was printed in several editions, sometimes retitled to accommodate technological and nomenclature changes, and was the standard manual for navy through the 1920s.[19]

The army used commercially available manuals at first, favoring *Maver's Wireless Telegraphy*, one of the most thorough early works on the subject.[20] Several lectures on wireless were printed at the Fort Leavenworth Signal School, but these were seen mostly by students at the college and not necessarily intended for field use.[21]

In 1909 Lieutenant George A. Wieczorek's *Notes on Wireless Telegraph Stations* was printed, specifically for the operation of the test station at Fort Wood, New York, but with the intention of becoming a more general manual for "enlisted men in charge of permanent stations, or operating in the field with semi-permanent or portable sets".[22] The twelve page manual covered the basics of station placement, antennae and general maintenance, but nothing about specific equipment.

Wireless was covered in the 1909 edition of *Regulations for United States Military Telegraph Lines*,[23] but, as the title indicates, the emphasis was on regulations and little is mentioned of operation. By 1911 wireless was well enough established that it was included in the *Drill Regulations for Field Companies of the Signal Corps*. The focus was on the organization of wireless sections, but it also included brief instructions for operating a transmitter and receiver. A diagram is included, dated January 4, 1910, of a "Field Wireless Set – Pack – Wiring Diagram of Trunk Type, Set No 43". 43 was not so much a model number as it was a series number, a direct descendent of that first set built at Leavenworth, though it is unclear which set was counted as number one. The set was technologically advanced, with integrated components, inductively coupled coils and a silicon or Perikon detector.[24]

The first generally distributed army manual specifically on wireless was the 1914 edition of *Radiotelegraphy, Circular No. 1*.[25] Radio theory as well as operation of equipment currently in use by the Signal Corps were covered. Reprinted each year through 1917, it was the standard manual until the United States' entry into World War One. Conspicuously missing from the manual, other than a mention of Pickard's W.S.A., was the word "wireless".

Paragraph VI of War Department General Order 15, 1912 specified that "in conformity with international usage, the word 'radio' will be used to designate 'wireless' and the word 'radiogram' to designate 'wireless telegram' and 'wireless message'".[26] The order did not have an instantaneous effect, and both "radio" and "wireless" were used interchangeably through the First World War. The army, through habit, slipped "wireless" into official documents years after the order. Much of the English-speaking world would continue to use "wireless" for decades. But "radio" was universally understood, the word used in international radio law since 1910.

The order came, not coincidentally, after the Radio Act of August 13, 1912, the first major American legislation, after the earlier and narrower 1910 Ship Act, that specifically used the words "radio" and "radiogram".

The 1910 Ship Act required all ships leaving American ports and carrying fifty or more persons carry a radio capable of transmitting at least 100 miles. The 1912 Act, reacting to the sinking of the Titanic several months earlier, expanded on the 1910 act by requiring ships to monitor for and give priority to distress signals, and formally adopted S.O.S. as the standard distress signal, as agreed to in the International Wireless Telegraph Convention of 1906. It required for the first time that all stations operating in the United States be licensed. And it required that all transmitters produce a "pure" and "sharp" wave, effectively banning open spark gap transmitters.

The 1912 act did not instantly end the use of spark. Military transmitters, especially those used in the field, still used quenched spark gaps through the First World War, and some amateurs continued to use spark until the 1920s or later. Spark even outlasted the coherer, which, replaced by simpler, more sensitive detectors, was essentially extinct by 1912.

The coherer would reappear occasionally, though not as part of a radio receiver. In 1955 Japan's oldest toy manufacturer Masudaya, founded in 1724, introduced the first radio-controlled toy, the streamlined Radicon Bus, available in grey, red or blue. Each press of the single button on its remote control would cause the bus to move forward, stop, turn right or turn left. Within the tin body of the bus was a coherer to receive the signal from a battery-operated spark generator housed in the remote control.

Coherers were still the standard detector during the Second Anglo-Boer War of 1899-1902, the first use of radio during wartime. The South African Republic ordered six sets from the German electrical company Siemens and Halske in August 1899, but by the time it arrived in Cape Town war had been declared and the equipment was confiscated by the British.

The British meanwhile rented five sets from Marconi which had to be modified and carried by wagons for field use, where they proved nearly useless. Because they were designed for installation in a fixed station, there were no portable antenna masts. Bamboo poles were used, which soon cracked. Kites were tried as well but the wind was too inconsistent, and the transmitting and receiving stations only rarely were able to raise their antennae at the same time. The South African climate was not ideal for the equipment, and frequent lightning storms played havoc with the coherers. The sets themselves were not designed for field use, and the importance of grounding was not yet understood. Eventually the British Army gave up on them, and the radios were installed on ships with better results.[27]

Radio was more successful during the Russo-Japanese War of 1904-05, where it was used by the navies on both sides, and in the First Balkan War of 1912-13.

For the United States, radio had its first thorough test during the Mexican Revolution. In 1911 troops were sent to the border of Texas in response to raids by Carrancista rebels. The "Bandit Wars" were part of the larger Border War which continued through most of the Mexican Revolution. In February 1911 Signal Corps Company A, under the command of Captain William Cruikshank, arrived in west Texas from Fort Leavenworth to establish wireless telegraph stations between Eagle Pass and Minera, Texas.[28]

Wireless was used again in the 1914 occupation of Veracruz when Signal Corps Company D constructed temporary stations to communicate with the navy.

In March 1916, in response to a raid by the *División del Norte* on Columbus, New Mexico, Brigadier General John J. Pershing assembled an expeditionary force to pursue the group's leader, Pancho Villa.

Pershing was sent two Telefunken wagon sets, a tractor set, four pack sets and mules along with their detachments, as well as part of Signal Corps Field Company I and two extra pack sets assigned to them.[29] The pack sets were used by the cavalry, where Pershing felt they proved "of little value", and recommended larger sets with greater range.[30] The wagon sets fared better, working "almost constantly" at over 300 miles, though hampered by mountainous atmosphere and often out of repair. It was impossible to get spare parts for the sets since Germany was now embroiled in the First World War. Pershing considered wireless essential to a modern army and warned of the shortage of parts and equipment.

There was a "lack of appreciation of the limitations of the pack radio sets",[31] wrote the Expedition's Signal Officer, Charles deForest Chandler, and they performed poorly mostly because they were used beyond their intended range of 30 miles "during favorable atmospheric conditions". The cavalry in Mexico was moving sometimes more than twice that distance in a day. "They should not have been expected to operate over the area covered by the Punitive Expedition."[32] The range of these sets was increased when "communicating with a larger set", or when using a larger antenna, which was done at El Valle and Dublan while the 2 kw sets were temporarily disabled.

The Expedition also saw the first use of airplanes in an American military operation. Eight machines in all were used for reconnaissance. Already old and in poor condition, they did not perform well in desert conditions. Their pilots however were a determined bunch, and several important missions were accomplished. By the end of the Mexican Expedition all the planes were either wrecked or scrapped.[33]

In Europe, where two years of war had rapidly shaped their evolution, the airplane and radio, only moderately successful in Mexico, had become indispensable.

10 Hell Tore Loose

On October 11, 1918, somewhere in the woods near Dombasle-en-Argonne, France, the same day someone stole his brand new pair of boots, Lieutenant George Bennett Ferree lost the stem to his Illinois pocket watch.[1] It would have been an annoyance on a normal day, but this was the third week of the Meuse-Argonne Offensive, and every barrage of the 1st Battalion, 124th Field Artillery was started by the time of that watch. He repaired it using a piece of wire, which worked well enough until he was able to replace it with a proper stem.

Ferree commanded the radio section of the HQ Battalion, and it was their job to relay information from observation aircraft to the artillery batteries, and to synchronize the batteries' watches before each barrage. Ferree's watch, a high school graduation gift he had carried since 1915, kept the official time. Normally, it would have been synchronized by telephone with HQ's clock, which itself was synchronized with time signals broadcast from the Eiffel Tower. Ferree valued accuracy and would have preferred to synchronize his watch with the Eiffel Tower directly. But the radio section's receiver, designed to receive Morse signals from small spark transmitters in reconnaissance aircraft, could only receive wavelengths up to 650 meters, not the 2,200-meter broadcasts from the Eiffel Tower.[2] So Ferree used what was on hand and built a receiver that could.

Twenty years old and a student at the University of Illinois when the United States declared war on Germany in April 1917, Ferree enlisted, against his father's wishes, in Troop B of the 1st Illinois

Cavalry in July 1917. In September Troop B became Battery B of the 124th Field Artillery, training at Camp Logan in Houston. In March 1918 Ferree, now a Sergeant, was transferred to the radio section of HQ Battery, where he was offered a ride in an airplane so that he could see how its radio transmitter operated. There was professional interest, since one of his primary roles as a radio operator would be to relay messages between observation aircraft and firing batteries. But, more importantly, Ferree "wanted to ride in an airplane in the worst way". Soon after taking off, the "Jenny" side slipped and crashed. The plane was wrecked, the pilot unhurt, and Ferree walked away with only a black eye.

Figure 17 George B. Ferree's Illinois pocket watch. Courtesy Eddie Ferree.

A month later, while being examined for promotion to 2nd Lieutenant, Colonel Horatio B. Hackett asked Ferree how long after the crash it had been before he flew again. When Ferree answered that it was two days, Hackett remarked to the other interviewers "I guess he has nerve enough".[3] Ferree was promoted to 2nd Lieutenant on the 8th of May, and on May 14 the 124th Field Artillery left Camp Logan for Camp Merritt, their last brief stay before heading overseas.

They crossed to England on May 26, along with the 108th Field Signal Battalion, on the transport S.S. *Melita*. The remainder of the

58th Field Artillery Brigade sailed in the same convoy, the 122nd FA, the 108th Trench Mortar Battery, and the 108th Mobile Ordnance Shop on the *Kashmir*; the 123rd FA on the *Scotian*, and the 108th Ammunition Train on the *City of Poona*.[4] The convoy, escorted by the USS *Texas*,[5] reached Liverpool on June 8. They trained at the Second Corps Artillery School at Camp Valdahon, France, for two months before heading for the front.

From Valdahon they marched to Besançon, by train to Pagny-sur-Meuse, and, on September 5, they reached their forward position at Bouconville-sur-Madt. It was in a dugout at Bouconville on September 10 that Ferree built his radio.

Almost every part of it was picked up in the field. It was built in a 1905 model German telephone battery box, used with the *Armeefernsprecher alter Art*, an old-style field telephone used throughout the war, despite being updated in 1913 by the more secure *Eiserner Armeefernsprecher*, the "iron army telephone". Over a foot wide, six inches high and three and three quarters inches deep, the *Sprechbatterie alter Art* was larger than more recently made battery boxes, giving Ferree plenty of room to work with. It was built solidly of varnished, honey colored wood, finger joined, with a deep, hinged lid secured by a heavy latch. A leather carrying handle was attached to the top, next to a small weatherproofed card listing the German phonetic spelling alphabet, "Adolf" through "Zacharias".[6]

The tuning coil had previously been the spark coil of a shot-up Ford ambulance. Electrical contacts came from a German field phone. The brass rods holding the coil and tuning slider were cut from a rifle ram rod that had belonged to a doughboy killed nearby. Headphones were from the French receiver issued to their unit, and the detector was a spare galena crystal from their supply.

It was a simple, tuned crystal set, ruggedly built using a screwdriver, pliers and a hack saw, the only tools Ferree had on hand. Properly grounded and with a long antenna, it could receive signals from radio station FL transmitting from the Eiffel Tower. For Ferree, building the radio was well worth the effort, and he took great satisfaction in the accuracy of his section's watches. "Before every barrage", he wrote in his diary, "the watches of the batteries are all corrected. We, at the radio station, checked our watches each day with FL and as a result we were never off more than a few seconds".[7]

Figure 18 George Bennett Ferree's radio, built into a German telephone battery box. Cat. # MON 1622.1/CCN: 277040. Courtesy the Museum Support Center, Ft. Belvoir.

Figure 19 Ferree's radio open, from the top. Cat. # MON 1622.1/CCN: 277040. Courtesy the Museum Support Center, Ft. Belvoir.

The Eiffel Tower was completed in 1889 for the Paris World's fair and was, at the time, the tallest man-made structure in the world. Parisians were slow to warm to it, and some considered it a blight on the landscape. The permit issued for construction specified that the tower could stand for twenty years, and in 1909 ownership would revert to the city of Paris, who planned to dismantle it. Hoping to save his beloved tower from being scrapped, engineer Gustave Eiffel encouraged scientists to take advantage of its great height for scientific experiments. Eiffel himself conducted meteorological observations and wind resistance experiments.

In November 1898 Eugène Ducretet, a manufacturer of scientific instruments and the first person in France to successfully transmit and receive radio waves, installed a spark gap transmitter in the third floor of the tower, transmitting to the Panthéon, two and a half miles away. In 1903, realizing that the military was now actively researching radio for their own use, Eiffel contacted Captain Gustave-Auguste Ferrié, who oversaw radio research for the French Army.

Ferrié installed an antenna on the first floor of the tower, later moving it to the top floor, and set up a spark transmitter and electrolytic detector receiver in a wood shack near the southern pillar. The tower became the central hub for radio communications with military bases around Paris, and the following year with those in eastern France on the German border. A more permanent station was installed in 1906.

In 1908 the tower station was able to transmit 6,000 km, and in 1909 the station was moved underground. Because of the strategic importance the tower now held as a radio station, Eiffel's contract with the City of Paris was renewed in January 1910, temporarily saving it from demolition. The station was assigned the call letters "FL" after the International Radiotelegraph Conference of 1912, which assigned the prefix "F" to all French stations.

The station served as the main communications link for the French and other Allied armies during the First World War, and intercepted many enemy messages, exposing spies and German military plans. The war made the Tower a symbol of national pride, saving it from the scrap heap.

Much of France set their clocks by the Eiffel Tower's time signals. The United States Navy was the first to broadcast time signals by radio in 1903 using the reference clock at the United States Naval Observatory. A series of dots and dashes alerted the listener to the actual time signal, sent at a predetermined time, and usually indicated by a long dash.

Time signal transmissions from the Eiffel Tower began in 1910, the time signal being automatically sent by the closing of a relay attached to the main clock of the Paris Observatory. By 1913 they were sent as a regularly scheduled service, uninterrupted for the duration of the war, which could be heard across the Atlantic in Canada and the United States. The signals were intended to be used by ships at sea to adjust their chronometers, but they were also used by railroads and by individuals to adjust their own clocks and watches. In 1910 Horace Hurm, a pioneering radio inventor living in Paris, developed the Ondophone, one of the first "pocket sized" portable crystal radios. It was later marketed specifically as a receiver for Eiffel Tower time signals.

The Eiffel Tower station changed frequencies a few times in its early years, and by the start of WWI it was transmitting at a standard frequency of 2,200 meters. Time signals were also standardized by the beginning of the war, transmitted three times a day, at 10 A.M., 10:45 A.M. and 11:45 P.M. At 9:55 AM an attention signal — • — • — was sent three times. At 9:57 — • • — eighteen times, followed by three dashes, the last dash marking 9:58. Then — • five times followed by three dashes at 9:59. Finally two dashes and a dot five times followed by three dashes, the end of the last dash marking exactly 10 AM. The same plan was followed for the minutes leading up to 10:45 and 11:45 PM.[8]

Synchronizing all the watches in a regiment using these signals was somewhat complicated. Most of the smaller units did not have radios capable of receiving the 2,200-meter signal from the Eiffel Tower station, and so the job fell on the radio operator at regimental headquarters. The first step was to adjust the receiver to the Eiffel Tower's frequency a few minutes before the signal would be sent. The operator would then note the exact time on his own watch when the final dash of the time signal was received. If he now attempted to correct his own watch, he would likely over or under adjust, and the accuracy would be lost. Instead, he corrected a second watch to the difference between what his own watch says and the time signal time. If, for example, his watch had said 10:00:12 when the 10:00 time signal completed, he would set the second watch twelve seconds behind his own, correcting for the twelve seconds his is ahead. All the local watches would then be corrected to the second watch.

Figure 20 George B. Ferree during the First World War. Courtesy Eddie Ferree.

All of the other units - the artillery batteries, the radio section, anyone not having a radio capable of receiving time signals - would now synchronize their watches by telephone. The telephone operator, now equipped with a watch showing the correct time, calls each unit and tells them he will give the correct time at a specific time. Ten or fifteen seconds before that time he announces "Attention", and then, at the exact moment the minute changes, he announces "top". The telephone operator receiving the messages notes the time on his own watch, the difference is calculated, and all the unit's other watches are synchronized.[9] There was plenty of room for error, a point not lost on George Ferree.

On September 11, a day after finishing his makeshift receiver, two aviators met with Ferree and his group to work out how they and the radio section would communicate with each other during battle. They were preparing for what would be the first and only offensive led solely by the American Expeditionary Forces, the Battle of Saint-Mihiel.

"At 1:00 A. M. hell tore loose", wrote Ferree in his diary. "It was a beautiful sight. You could see the flashes and light from the guns up and down both sides of the line".[10] The front was a wall of fire from mostly American artillery. The Germans, knowing they lacked the firepower to defend against the allied offensive, had begun pulling back days before the attack and lacked the organization to return effective artillery fire. At dawn the infantry moved in, quickly overwhelming the German forces. By the afternoon of September 13, the Saint Mihiel salient, held by the Germans for four years, collapsed, freeing much the American forces for the Meuse-Argonne Offensive.

On September 15th the 124th began a five-day march to the Argonne. For the remainder of the war they would take whatever shelter they could, and at Récicourt they found a "nice, deep dugout". They were evicted the following day by a division who had already claimed it and were forced to take a less welcoming dugout. "Oh boy", wrote Ferree, "what a mess of cooties were mixed in with the straw in the bunks".[11]

Ferree's group only had a radio receiver, not a transmitter, for communicating with reconnaissance aircraft, which only had spark transmitters. Messages were communicated to the airplanes from the ground using large cloth panels. Special black and white panels identified units, and patterns made with long rectangular panels, usually white, but black on snowy days, were used to send instructions.

To communicate with their guns and with battalion headquarters, the radio section used wire.

Telephone and telegraph were by far the predominant means of communication during WWI. Wire was preferred where it could be run, and the Signal Corps strung 22,692 miles of it and operated another 27,585 miles of French wire while in Europe.[12] Flags, heliographs, rockets, Very pistols, runners and pigeons were also used, each having specific applications.

Radio was not nearly sophisticated nor secure enough to handle the massive amount of communication moving through telephone and telegraph wires. But there were some places where it was more practical – places where wire could not be strung, where it was constantly shot or shelled, between moving units, in tanks and other vehicles, and between the ground and aircraft flying reconnaissance missions. For all of these, radio needed to be smaller, more nimble, simpler to set up and use, and less likely to cause interference with neighboring sets.

11 Small Favors

At the beginning of the First World War the British and French, like the Americans, had bulky pack and wagon sets that were difficult to transport, setup and adjust. And, although tuning had improved, they were still too noisy to not interfere with other sets at the crowded front.

In Britain the Admiralty took control of the Marconi factory in Chelmsford, working with Marconi engineers to rapidly advance the technology. Radios for point-to-point signaling at the battlefront were developed, but the real emphasis was on communication with tanks and aircraft artillery spotters, signal interception, and direction finding. Radio direction finding made it possible for the British to track raiding German airships and intercept them, and by 1917 was instrumental in the location and sinking of U-boats by the allies.

The French concentrated much of their research toward improving and efficiently mass-producing vacuum tubes for radio detectors, amplifiers, oscillators, and modulators to add voice to radio. This flurry of research and development was led by the same officer who had installed the first military radio in the Eiffel Tower a decade earlier, Colonel Gustave-Auguste Ferrié.

Ferrié was now in charge of the *Radiotelegraphie Militaire*, whose job it was to oversee all military radio research in France. The similarities between Ferrié and George Owen Squier are striking. They were close in age, Squier born in 1865, Ferrié in 1868. Both were scientifically trained, Ferrié as an engineer at the *École Polytechnique*, Squier receiving a PhD in physics from Johns Hopkins. Both were scientist-soldiers, advocating scientific research and development within the military.

Both would receive the Franklin Medal for engineering, Squier in 1919 and Ferrié in 1923. Like Squier, Ferrié was directly involved with early radio development in his country and shaped the direction of military radio. And both were in leadership roles during WWI, Squier the Chief Signal Officer since 1917, and Ferrié the director of French military communication.

Ferrié understood that, if it was going to be practical for the military, radio had to be less noisy, more portable, rugged, secure, and simple to set up and operate than prewar radio had been. He saw in the vacuum tube the potential to do all of this and made it a priority to improve and manufacture them on a massive scale.

In a war that produced hundreds of technological advancements, the vacuum tube was one of the most significant. "Varied as are the applications at present", George Owen Squier wrote in his Annual Report of 1919, "the uses, actual and potential, growing out of war-development work have proved that the art of vacuum-tube engineering and the application of its products to radio engineering, telephone and telegraph engineering, and particularly to electrical engineering in general, are still in their early infancy. That vacuum tube in various forms and sizes will, within a few years, become widely used in every field of electrical development and application is not to be denied."[1]

Tubes at the beginning of the war were relatively rare and expensive, mainly things of the laboratory. The Allies would need millions. In 1914 engineers Michael Péri and Jacques Biguet developed a vacuum tube based on de Forest's audion, but simpler, with components assembled concentrically, a cylindrical anode surrounding a spiral tungsten grid and a straight filament anode. To simplify construction, it was designed like a lightbulb.[2] Ferrié turned to E.C.& A. Grammont, a manufacturer of lightbulbs, to produce the new tube under the trade name "*Fotos*". Grammont was unable to keep up with demand on their own and to make up the difference Ferrié turned to the *Compagnie Générale des Lampes*, who had already manufactured a few copies of the Fleming valve and the de Forest audion under the trade name *Métal*. The *télégraphie militaire* or, more commonly, Type TM bulb, was the first mass produced vacuum tube, with over 100,000 produced initially. The British copied the design as their standard Type R valve.

When the United States entered the war in 1917 Squier made the development of vacuum tubes one of the Corp's priorities. Tubes were manufactured for the military by General Electric and De Forest, who produced "De Forest type" bare filament tube, and by Western Electric, who produced coated filament tubes which were considered superior by the Signal Corps.[3]

Several tubes were developed for the Signal Corps during the war. The most common were the Western Electric 203A, designated by the Signal Corps as the VT-1 and by the navy as the CW-933, used primarily as an amplifier and detector, and the Western Electric 205A, the Signal Corp's VT-2 and the navy's CW-931 oscillator and modulator. Over one million American tubes were produced for the Signal Corps alone by the end of the war.

The United States Army Signal Corps had at the beginning of the war only 55 officers and 1,570 men,[4] and were still using bulky spark sets, not much changed since the earliest pack sets. Some of the first transmitters and receivers to arrive in Europe were the very same already aging sets Pershing took to the Mexican border in 1914.

American sets in production at the beginning of the war were primitive compared to those already in use in Europe. There were some promising new radios being tested, but none were ready for production at any meaningful scale. It would be many months before the Signal Corps could develop and build their own battle-ready transmitters and receivers, and so they looked to temporarily adopt French and British equipment. Because they would be working in French sectors and their equipment needed to be compatible, they found French radio to be more suitable. At least one British radio was preferred to its French counterpart, the "Sterling", a small, rugged, and relatively safe spark transmitter for aircraft.

Airplanes at the beginning of the war were used mainly for reconnaissance. Planes from both sides, carrying a pilot and an observer, flew across lines to locate the enemy and report back on their positions and strength. At first the observer would take notes and make sketches. Cameras were later used to make clear and detailed images for analysis, improving over time with longer focal lengths, sharper lenses and stereoscopy. Over half a million aerial photographs of the front were taken by both sides during the war and were indispensable for evaluation of enemy movements and activities.

Planes from opposing sides would often meet in the middle, at first cordially, the pilots often exchanging smiles and waves. Eventually both sides realized that it was in their best interest to prevent their opponent from completing their mission. Rocks were thrown, pistols fired, some even resorted to ramming in attempts to knock the enemy from the sky. Machine guns were added and faster, more nimble aircraft developed.

In mid-1915 the Germans introduced their first dedicated fighter airplane, the Fokker *Eindecker*, armed with synchronized machine guns that could be fired through the propeller. Maneuverability, superior guns, aggressive tactics and the psychological advantage of aircraft widely believed to be unbeatable by the Allies assured German air superiority. The introduction of the French *Nieuport* 11 and the British DH.2 broke what the popular press referred to as "The Fokker Scourge" in 1916. The war was now in the air, and the age of the dogfight had begun.

The combined use of airplanes and radio for artillery spotting so improved the accuracy of artillery units that both sides did their best to shoot down the other's aircraft at every opportunity. Air superiority in World War I was sought not for support of ground troops or aerial attacks as much as it was for the direction of artillery fire.

Artillery spotting airplanes in the first months of the war used a variety of visual signals or dropped messages to communicate with their artillery units. Radio transmitters were installed by 1915, first by the French and British, improving the speed a message could be sent and the likelihood of its being received. Radios had been used in lighter-than-air craft even before the war. Airships carried large transmitters and receivers, though they had to be designed and installed carefully to avoid a catastrophic meeting of spark and hydrogen gas. The small airplanes used for observation could not take on much extra weight, and so were equipped with the lightest and most compact transmitters that could be produced. They had no receivers, relying instead on visual communications from the ground.

Most portable transmitters still used spark, which could potentially ignite stray gasoline fumes. The No 1 "Sterling" Spark Transmitter, designed by the Royal Air Service and manufactured by the Sterling Telephone and Electric Company, was a masterpiece of compactness whose quenched spark was sealed safely away in a metal housing.

Because it was easier to use and considered safer than French transmitters with an open spark, the Sterling was the preferred transmitter of British and American aviators. Powered by a propeller driven generator mounted to the airplane, the 30-watt set, capable of transmitting up to ten miles, was attached to a 120-foot retractable, trailing antenna wire that fed through the floor of the airplane. It was one of the few British sets adopted by the American military, and was copied as the American SCR-65 and later as the improved SCR-65 A. At 7 7/16 by 6 3/8 by 3 1/4 inches the SCR-65 was one of the smallest transmitters built to date.[5]

Since airplanes only had transmitters, artillery radio sections were usually only equipped with receivers. The preferred receiver was the French A-1, a sophisticated and durable crystal set with precise tuning. Adopted by the Americans, it was officially dubbed the "Receiving Set, Artillery Type A-1, Complete, French"[6] and was the standard French and American receiver for air to ground communications. The British Mark III receiver was similar and used a carborundum, galena or Perikon detector.

Small and rugged, the A-1 featured a primary and secondary circuit coupled inductively, both tunable by variable capacitance and inductance. It used a crystal detector of galena, silicon, or antimony, with a steel wire cat whisker. Two types of detector stands were available, one with a hard rubber base and screw clamp to hold the crystal, the other with a glass tube "in order to prevent the wind and moisture from interfering with the spring or crystal".[7] Built compactly into a small wooden chest, it had the look of a military radio, its dials arranged neatly and clearly marked. It could receive wavelengths from 75 to 650 meters,[8] roughly from 4000 to 460kHz, and included a built in "buzzer" to help find a good spot on the crystal for detection, the buzzer "itself a feeble sending set, and the oscillations emitted by it are sufficiently strong to induce like oscillations in the secondary circuit strong enough to be heard in the receivers"[9]

The receiver could be connected to the "3-ter" amplifier, a three tube amplifier of French design. The amplifier could be used with only two of its tubes, freeing one to be used as a detector in the receiver when there was damage to the crystal or else wind or dampness prevented the crystal from operating. However, as one early instruction sheet stated, "the crystal detector and three lamps is a better combination and will usually give better results in the hands of the average operator."[10]

In practice, the A-1 was a general-purpose receiver for smaller units, but its main function was receiving transmissions from artillery spotting aircraft. It was the 124th Radio Section's receiver for the duration of the war.

Artillery spotting airplanes, protected both from the ground by anti-aircraft guns and by accompanying fighters, first had to locate the batteries and radio section they were working with, marked by large cloth panels. The pilot then flew back and forth between his artillery and the target, while the observer calculated distance and angle. Officially it was the observer's job to operate the radio, but in practice it was often the pilot tapping away at the key, maintaining control of a fragile aircraft in a hostile environment while simultaneously sending coded messages in Morse. "Radio is the science", according to the 1918 Ellington Field Yearbook, "whereby a pilot, in the leisure seized in the quiet moments of combat with eighteen enemy planes, while under a rattling archie fire, communicates to his commander the complexion, civil occupation and beer preference of a Hun 15,000 feet below."[11]

The pilot and observer watched where the artillery's shells landed, calculated the distance and direction for corrections, and transmitted them back to the radio section. They used a "clock code" to indicate how far and in what direction the last shell fell from the target, which was at the center of the clock. North was 12 o'clock, east 3 o'clock and so on, and the distance was given by a letter code, each letter representing a concentric circle surrounding the target at a specified distance.

George A. Wieczorek, who had written the early army wireless manual *Notes on Wireless Telegraph Stations* in 1909, and who was now Signal Officer of the 35th Division, made a pencil sketch while at the Second Corps Signal School showing the cooperation of an airplane and the artillery's radio group. It also illustrates just how dangerous the pilot's job was. Two jagged lines, representing trenches, run diagonally down the page. To the left are the guns of the battery and the radio set, complete with antenna. To the right, across the enemy line, looking like smashed spiders but actually shell craters, is the clearly marked target. And between the trenches, above no man's land, a single airplane flies in a figure eight, its regular pattern making it an easier target. Besides enemy aircraft and ground fire, pilots also had to avoid being struck by their own artillery's shells, something that did occasionally happen. The figure eight is sketched in dashed line, "observe here" written where the path crosses itself, "send radio msg here" labeled at the loop nearest the radio.[12]

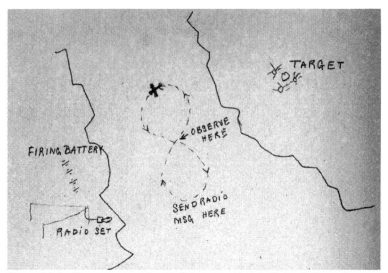

Figure 21 Artillery spotting aircraft flying over No Man's Land. From George A. Wieczorek's WWI Signal School notebook, 1918. Author's collection.

Besides reconnaissance and artillery spotting, bombing and ground attacks, airplanes were used for dropping printed propaganda onto the enemy. Aerial dispersal of propaganda dates to as early as 1806 when Captain Thomas Cochrane of the Royal Navy used kites to drop messages on the coast of France during the Napoleonic Wars. In 1870 the French used balloons to scatter leaflets over the Prussians during the Siege of Paris. The Italians were the first to drop propaganda from airplanes in 1912 during the Italo-Turkish War, offering each Arab soldier who surrendered a sack of wheat and a piece of gold.

The first large scale use of airplanes for distributing propaganda was during the First World War, where millions of leaflets were dropped by both sides. The British, to protect their pilots, eventually switched to balloons, but the Germans continued to drop propaganda from airplanes for the duration of the war. "German airplanes came over again today and dropped some literature" wrote George B. Ferree on October 27, 1918. "They were sheets of paper about 8 x 10 inches, printed in English. They advised the Americans to come over and give themselves up and be free boarders for the rest of the war."[13]

The leaflets were dropped onto a nearby hill, attracting souvenir hunting American soldiers. The Germans, seeing the distracted troops in the open, took the opportunity to shell the hill.

Any area where soldiers gathered was potentially a target for enemy shelling. Mess lines and rest areas were especially vulnerable. On the same day the souvenir hunting men were shelled on the hilltop, Ferree witnessed the effects of a German artillery barrage on an infantry company that had "stopped to rest in the scant shelter of the three foot stone wall around the cemetery" at Romagne-sous-Montfaucon.[14] The stretcher bearers were already carrying away the dead and injured when he arrived, "some were screaming, some moaning and some just silent bundles of meat". A shell landed in the engine of an ambulance arriving to pick up the injured, killing the passenger and the driver, who was "slumped over the wheel, his head completely gone".

Close calls from bullets or shells were common. On the morning of October 27, a dud shell dropped through the roof of the room adjacent to the one Ferree and his men were occupying. It landed "between the legs of a soldier who was lying on a bunk. He was so scared that he couldn't move for a minute. He said he just lay there waiting for it to explode, then he came to and tore out of there".[15]

Ferree himself had several close calls, some from machine gun fire, and one from a shell that landed "about ten feet away. Whether I stumbled or the concussion knocked me down, I don't know, I know that I could feel the air rush by my pants and I went down. They say that you will never hear the shell that gets you but that isn't true. I heard this one. I was just plain lucky, had I been just inches to one side or the other I wouldn't be here. Dick was telling me afterwards that he saw me go down and thought 'My God, they got Ferree'."[16]

Surrounded by devastation, imminent death, and the miserable stagnation of the trenches, morale was where one found it. What was provided by the army was nearer to propaganda, designed to instill fighting spirit and to warn of the dangers of bottle and brothel. More successful were soldier-led efforts, like the weekly *Stars and Stripes* newspaper which, though sanctioned by the army, was produced by and for servicemen.

Several charitable organizations set up huts or tents, providing what comforts of home they could. Most popular were the fresh doughnuts and hot coffee from the Salvation Army. But the huts were far from the front and could only serve soldiers who were able to make the journey to get there. "Parm and I tramped six kilos to a Y.M.C.A to get some sweets", wrote Ferree, "and all that they could sell us was a package of cookies and a bar of chocolate. However, we were thankful for small favors."[17]

Books, when available, were prized, as were letters from home. Many soldiers, Ferree included, kept journals. Gambling, a pastime of soldiers since there have been armies, was everywhere in the trenches. Sports were played where space was available and a ball could be found.

Soldiers created trench art, transforming spent shell casings and other discards into intricately crafted ashtrays, flower vases and other *objets d'art*. Ferree's radio, besides being useful, was itself trench art, something crafted from the detritus of the battlefield for distraction and morale.

The simplest luxuries of home were relished. "Got six letters today", wrote Ferree. "One was from Gladys Campbell and there was a stick of gum in it. The gum lasted seven days before I finally lost it."[18]

Music could provide some solace even in the trenches. Men brought or made musical instruments, and some even formed bands. Recorded music was available, though usually in rear areas or on ships. The Edison Company produced a phonograph built into a rugged, crate-like case for military morale. The Army & Navy Model Diamond Disc Phonograph was intended for shipboard and rear area use, though some units did carry them further, abandoning them only, like the 314th Field Artillery, just before reaching the front. "...we took our last bath and disposed of surplus equipment, and this included our much admired Army and Navy graphophone, which would be of no service to us in the days that we were to move on our own motive power into the unknown."[19]

Though not used in the field, WWI saw the first use of radio for morale, providing music and news for American soldiers hospitalized in France. Because some patients required or preferred quiet, it was impossible to play a phonograph for the ones that would benefit from it. The solution was to attach a phonograph, located in another part of the building, to a radio transmitter, then locally broadcast to a series of small receivers placed between the beds. The soldiers who wanted to listen in only need to put on the headphones at their bedside.[20]

Figure 22 The famous Salvation Army doughnuts. A phonograph is playing in the
foreground. Postcard from the author's collection.

12 Unbelievable Silence

President Wilson's Executive Order 2605A of April 30, 1917 ordered that "radio stations within the jurisdiction of the United States as are required for Naval Communications shall be taken over by the Government of the United States and used and controlled by it, to the exclusion of any other control or use; and furthermore, that all radio stations not necessary to the Government of the United States for Naval Communications may be closed for radio communication and all radio apparatus therein may be removed therefrom."[1]

The navy took it a step further, banning the amateur ownership of working transmitters or receivers for the duration of the war. Rather than stagnating, amateurs occupied themselves with theory and design, planning for the eventual lifting of restrictions. Improved equipment and, most intriguing, cheap vacuum tubes would be available after the war, and amateurs wanted to be ready for them.

The Signal Corps recruited radio professionals and amateurs as operators and trainers in France. The Women's Wireless Corps, founded within a week of the United States' entry into the war by Edna Owen, trained hundreds of women as radio operators to replace men sent overseas. Many of the newly licensed women in turn taught radio to recruits, and some worked as testers and researchers in the Signal Corps Laboratory.

The navy, through the Girls' Division of the United States Junior Naval Reserve, had been training women in radio since 1916.[2] In March 1917 the Navy Department authorized "the enrollment of women in the Naval Coast Defense Reserve in the ratings of yeoman, electrician (radio), or in such other ratings as the commandant may consider essential to the district organizations".[3]

While female radio operators remained stateside, the Signal Corps did recruit, at General Pershing's request, 450 female telephone operators fluent in French and English to serve in the Signal Corps Female Telephone Operators Unit. Nicknamed the "Hello Girls", 223 of them were sent to exchanges in France and Britain where they maintained telephone communications for the American Expeditionary Forces.

Despite wearing army uniforms, being subjected to army rules and being awarded citations typically awarded only to those serving in the army, after the war the switchboard operators were denied veteran status until, after a long fight led by former operator Merle Egan Anderson, it was finally granted to the surviving eighteen women in 1978.

Fort Leavenworth was the only United States Army signal training school operating before the war. In May 1917 three new training centers were established, at Camp Samuel F. B. Morse near San Antonio, Texas, at the Presidio in California, and at Camp Alfred Vail in New Jersey, which in 1925 would be renamed Fort Monmouth and become the center of Signal Corps research until the 1970s. In 1918 a radio school was established in College Park, Maryland, an electrician's and buzzer school at Fort Leavenworth, and a new signal school at Camp Franklin, near Camp Meade, Maryland, where the "Hello Girls" were trained.

Corps level signal schools were opened in France at Gondrecourt-le-Château, Châtillon-sur-Seine, and Clamecy, along with several division level schools where students received instruction in all forms of communication including wire, rockets, pigeons, and radio, with an emphasis on French equipment.

French sets were not immediately intuitive to American operators, and vacuum tubes were unfamiliar to many of them. French equipment manuals were translated and distributed as "Radio Apparatus Descriptive Bulletins" to help students learn the new apparatus.

Examples of French transmitters, receivers and amplifiers were sent to the newly established radio lab at Camp Alfred Vail and the Signal Lab at the Bureau of Standards where they were analyzed, copied and modified for American use, then tested in the field in France before being mass produced.

Figure 23 Women training to be radio operators during the First World War. Author's collection.

The popular French A-1 receiver was copied in 1917, with minor modifications, as the AR-4, and was tested in the field by Captain Edwin Armstrong, inventor of the regenerative radio circuit who would later develop the superheterodyne receiver and the first practical FM system.

For the most part Armstrong considered the A-1 and the AR-4 equal, preferring the control panel board of the AR-4, which was made of Micarta, a composite material developed by George Westinghouse, to the hard rubber board of the A-1. Both sets used wooden spools to wrap the primary and secondary coils, which Armstrong advised against because of their tendency to shrink, instead favoring Micarta or Bakelite-Dilecto, a material made of layered paper saturated with liquid Bakelite and hardened. He suggested oiled linen sleeving to protect wire connections instead of the rubber tubing used in both radios. He took greatest issue with the telephone jack, realizing it would fail to make good contact with the plug after continued use.[4]

Most of Armstrong's recommendations were incorporated in the SCR-54 and the later SCR-54A, a minor update, the main difference in the latter being the relocation of the test buzzer to the main panel of the radio instead of mounted inside the lid. Both were produced in the thousands under contract with De Forest Radio Telephone and Telegraph, Liberty Electric, Wireless Specialty Apparatus, American Marconi, and General Radio. Like the A-1, there was an optional vacuum tube detector available, the DT-3-A, which incorporated a VT-1 tube.

By the time it was designed, improved, and mass produced the SCR-54 arrived too late to be widely distributed, and many divisions continued to use French receivers for the remainder of the war, including Ferree's 124th.

Thousands of SCR-54 and SCR-54-A receivers remained unshipped when the war ended, some retained for training, many more sold as surplus, becoming a favorite of amateurs, many of them still functional after nearly a century.

Figure 24 The US Army SCR-54, modeled after the French A-1, the workhorse of artillery radio groups. Photograph No. 111-SC-33262; "Receiving set box, Type SCR-54." June 1918; Records of the Office of the Chief Signal Officer, Record Group 111; National Archives at College Park, College Park, MD.

The Signal Corps developed dozens of new transmitters and receivers during the war, based on French or British models or else completely new, as well as a profusion of new amplifiers, meters, tube testers, interphones, telegraphs, direction finders and other equipment.

Simple descriptive names were sufficient when the army had only a few types of transmitters and receivers. Early sets were referred to by their model year. An illustration in the 1914 edition of Radiotelegraphy, for example, is labeled "field radio pack set, model 1914".[5] A more flexible naming scheme was needed during the war to catalog the fast-growing inventory of parts and equipment.

Some components were assigned an alphabetic type designation before the war, like the type D and F sectional masts described in the 1914 *Radiotelegraphy*.[6] The 1915 edition specified that "radio pack sets will hereafter be accounted for as 'Radio pack sets, complete'."[7] This was refined in the 1916 edition, which noted that pack radios should be referred to as "'radio pack sets, complete', giving year and serial number".[8]

By January 1918 the Signal Corps established a numbering system to catalogue all its equipment, usually a one, two, or three letter code identifying the component type, followed by a one, two or three-digit numerical code for the specific model. Updated versions of existing equipment were often appended with a final "A".

SCR stood for "Set, Complete, Radio", though it was later popularly interpreted as "Signal Corps Radio". It comprised all the components issued as part of the set, including, for the SCR-54, the BC-14 receiving set, the DC-1 crystal detector, the TL-2 screwdriver, the P-11 telephone headset, and all the bags, batteries, and antenna equipment.[9]

Prewar equipment that remained in inventory, though usually considered obsolete, was given a number based on the new nomenclature system. The SCR-40 through SCR-50 were all pre-war sets that were used before and during the war, either for training or in the field.

By 1915 the navy had its own nomenclature system, The United States Navy Type Number System, a series of letters and numbers devised by George H. Clark, at the time a civilian radio engineer working for the navy.[10] Type numbers usually began with "SE" for parts made by the navy's Bureau of Steam Engineering, or "C" for commercially made parts, followed by a letter code for the manufacturer, for example, "CN" identified a part manufactured by the National Electric Supply Company. The part number itself was essentially consecutive. The army and navy would maintain separate nomenclature systems until WWII.

On October 26, a little over two weeks before the Armistice, Ferree's radio section was issued a vacuum tube amplifier, likely an SCR-121 low frequency amplifier set, and a DT-3 vacuum tube detector. The amplifier was welcome, but they continued to use the galena crystal already in their receiver rather than the vacuum tube detector. It was common for radio operators to prefer crystal detectors, which they found more sensitive, clearer, and easier to deal with than vacuum tubes. George Owen Squier came to a similar conclusion, and in his 1919 Report he wrote that although initial tests were favorable, "it was concluded that the crystal detector was sufficiently sensitive".[11]

On the same day Ferree's radio section received their new amplifier, a message was intercepted on his crystal set "saying that peace may be signed soon. But we didn't believe it, not with all of the shelling that was going on around us. A German shell landed about 50 yards away and a fragment cut our aerial down."[12] The Allied commanders had met the previous day at the headquarters of Marshall Foch, the Supreme Allied Commander, at Senlis to discuss terms of the armistice with Germany who, no longer seeing any possibility of winning the war, had first contacted the United States in early October to open discussions.

The situation was rapidly disintegrating for the Central Powers. An armistice was signed by The Ottoman Empire on October 30, followed by Austria-Hungary on November 3. Germany was now dealing with revolution at home, and the Kaiser was considering abdication. On November 7 a German delegation, riding in automobiles, crossed the lines and were led by French officers ten hours across France to the the *Forêt de Compiègne* where they were read the terms of the armistice in Marshall Foch's private rail car.

Their crossing fueled Allied rumors of a cease fire. Ferree recalled "rumors that a big, white German car was going through the lines",[13] and realized that it meant the war was ending soon.

At 5:00 AM November 11 the Germans delegation, hearing that the Kaiser had abdicated, and realizing there was no chance of negotiating more favorable terms, agreed to the armistice. By 5:20 all the delegates had signed.

At 5:45 A.M. Corporal Dwight Isaacs heard the general call from the Eiffel Tower transmitter while on Ferree's crystal set. "CQ CQ de FL FL"[14] it began, followed by a message from Marshall Foch.

"Les hostilités seront arrêtées sur tout le front à partir du 11 Novembre 11 heures heure française. Les Troupes Alliées ne dépasseront pas jusqu à nouvel ordre la ligne atteinte à cette date et à cette heure."[15]

Isaacs understood enough French to realize what it meant. He woke Ferree, and they both listened as the message was repeated at 6:45 A.M., this time in English.

"CQ, CQ, de FL FL. Hostilities will cease on the whole front from the 11th November, 11:00 o'clock, French o'clock. The allied troops will not cross until a further order the lines reached in that date and that hour. Marshall Foch, Commander in Chief."[16]

The news was already spreading by the time Ferree relayed the message to Major Frank Rearden at Battalion headquarters, although official word would not arrive for another three hours. "Early that morning", reported the *Stars and Stripes*, "from the wireless station on the Eiffel Tower in Paris, there had gone forth through the air to the wondering, half-incredulous line that the Americans held near Sedan to the Moselle the order from Marshall Foch to cease firing on the stroke of 11".[17]

As Corporal Isaacs was copying the armistice terms, a German shell landed, severing the radio's antenna. The shelling would intensify for the next several hours.

"About ten o'clock a German shell came over and landed in a mess line around one of the kitchens of one of the batteries and killed several men", wrote Ferree. "Then the guns started up again and kept it up until three minutes of eleven."[18] The artillery intended to carry back as little ammunition as possible, and every battery wanted to say they had fired the last shot. Little regard was given to aim. Frank P. Sibley reported in his history of the 26th Infantry Division that "the guns weren't pointed anywhere in particular; they were just headed in the general direction of Germany and turned loose as fast as they could be fired."[19] The indiscriminate shelling would take a toll, and over ten thousand casualties were reported on both sides during the final hours.

"As the hour approached", Sibley continues, "officers and men of the artillery gathered at the batteries all eager to fire 'the last shot in the war.' In one battery each man took a shell and waited in line for his turn to fire the gun. In another battery, five officers took hold of the lanyard, and all fired the last shot together. In still another, a long rope was made fast to the lanyard of each of the four guns. Some two hundred men got hands on each rope, and one man, with a watch, went out forward. At the hour, he dropped a handkerchief. A thousand men sagged back on the firing ropes; four guns barked simultaneously, and a thousand Americans let out a yell that must have been heard in Bocheland."[20]

There were many "last" shots of the war. SF 1st Class James A. Kaffka of Naval Railway Battery Number 4 was selected to fire the navy's official last shot at 10:59 a.m. near their position at Charny.[21] The honor of firing the last official Allied artillery shot of the war was given to Battery E. of the 11th Field Artillery, attached to the 89th Division, fired from a 155mm howitzer nicknamed "Calamity Jane". The official time, commemorated in the 11th's regimental motto "On Time", was 10:59:59.[22]

"When the last shell was fired", wrote Ferree, "I was sitting on a log of a tree that had been shot, holding my watch in my hand to get the time when the last shell went over. *Finis la guerre.* I looked up at the sky and said 'Thank you, God'."[23]

There is some disagreement about when the last official shot was fired. Ferree claims it was several minutes earlier.

Robert Casey, in his anonymously published diary of the war, *The Cannoneers Have Hairy Ears*, entered for "ten-fifty-nine A. M. - The 11th has just fired its last shot. The guns are so hot that the paint is rising from them in blisters."[24]

Ferree, in his heavily annotated copy of Casey's book, disagrees. "Wrong", he wrote and circled, an arrow pointing to Casey's Ten-fifty-nine. "10:57 A.M. I had official Radio time watch by which all barrages of Batterys A B & C started. I checked time twice daily from Eiffel Tower in Paris and I say the last shot fired by the 11th Field Artillery was fired at 10:57 AM 11 Nov 1918. 2nd Lieut. George B. Ferree, 124 F.A."[25]

The official History of the 89th Division also questions the timing of the last shot, wondering if "somebody's watch was slow, and, according to the photographer, actual time was 11:05!"[26] Undoubtedly the news of the armistice reached some batteries late, and there were shots fired after 11:00. By who and when the last shot was actually fired is lost. But aside from a few stray rumbles the entire front fell at once silent.

"On the stroke of 11 the cannon stopped, the rifles dropped from the shoulders, the machine guns grew still", reported the *Stars and Stripes*. "There followed then a strange, unbelievable silence as though the world had died. It lasted but a moment, lasted for the space that a breath is held. Then came such an uproar of relief and jubilance, such a tooting of horns, shrieking of whistles, such an overture from the bands and trains and church bells, such a shouting of voices as the earth is not likely to hear again in our day and generation."[27]

This is how it was in the cities and towns, crowds cheering, music, and champagne. But the experience of the soldier at the front was very different. This may only be temporary, after all. "The silence is oppressive" wrote Robert Casey. "There is some cheering across the river – occasional bursts of it as the news is carried to the advanced lines. For the most part, though, we are in silence."[28]

"It might be supposed", wrote George English, historian of the 89th infantry, "that wild scenes of jubilation occurred along the front, such as took place throughout the countries of the Allies. But the contrary was true. Except for a little cheering by our troops in Stenay, no demonstrations were manifest. The silence of the guns seemed to invite sober tranquility and quiet joy. There was audible the sound of celebration among the Germans, detachments of whom were still in Cervisy and Inor. But among our own troops silence reigned."[29]

In 1919 Ferree entered the University of Indiana, leaving after two years to seek his fortune in California. He went to work for a car dealership and was one day given the task of teaching a customer how to drive the car she had purchased. The customer was a palm reader and offered to read Ferree's palm after her lessons. She told him that he was in the wrong line of work and should be working as a school teacher. Ferree did not take much stock in palm reading, but the encounter did make him consider teaching. Two years later he graduated from the University of Indiana and took a job in Beardstown, Illinois as a teacher and coach.

In 1928 he was hired by Chenoa High in Chenoa, Illinois. He remained there for 25 years, a respected educator and one of the most successful coaches in Illinois high school athletics. During his first year he coached the Redbirds to win the Illini Conference title. He continued as head football coach for a total of seventeen seasons, with an overall record of 93 wins, 41 losses and 9 ties.

He taught three math classes, Chemistry, Physics, and Physical Education. He coached not only football but all sports that Chenoa competed in. Under his guidance the 1948-49 basketball team, often playing much larger schools, nearly made it to state finals. Number 81 on that team was Stan Albeck, who would later coach the San Antonio Spurs, the New Jersey Nets, and the Chicago Bulls. In 1977 Chenoa High School named their athletic field in Ferree's honor, and in 1980 he was inducted into the Illinois High School Football Coaches Hall of Fame.

Though Ferree was well above the draft age when the United States entered the Second World War, his desire to serve led him to enlist in the Army Air Corps. The newly commissioned Captain Ferree was put in charge of the physical training program at Jefferson Barracks, Missouri. "There is no game or conditioning process to prepare men for actual warfare that is in the same category as football" he said. "It teaches men to think and act quickly and those are the two major requisites of a fighter."[30] He was discharged in 1946 with the rank of major and continued to teach at Chenoa until his retirement.

In December of 1974 it occurred to him that the army may be interested in the old crystal radio he had built half a century earlier in the Argonne Forest. He affixed a plaque to it that reads:

"This little crystal set was made in the fall of 1918 in World War I, during the Battle of the Argonne, from material picked up on the battle fields. The contacts of wire are from German field telephones, the brass rods are from an American doughboy's rifle ram rod, killed near our battery positions. The condenser is from the spark coil of a shot-up Ford ambulance. The head phones are from our French issue radio set.

The set was made by Lieut. George B. Ferree, 0-220195, Radio Officer, 124th Field Artillery, in order to receive radio signals from Eiffel Tower in Paris. The news to cease firing 11 Nov 1918 was received at 6:00 A.M. on this set, three hours before the order came down thru military channels. Here is the message as it was received: 'CQ CQ de de FL FL to the commander in chief. Hostilities will cease on the whole front from the eleventh November eleven o'clock French o'clock. The allied troops will not cross until further order the line reached on that date and that hour. Marshall Foch.'"

He offered the radio to West Point, where his colonel during the war, Horatio B. Hackett, had attended. Officials there suggested he contact the Army Signal Corps Museum in Fort Monmouth, New Jersey.

The museum sent a delegation to Ferree's home, and in an informal ceremony on February 21, 1975, he donated the crystal set and other communications equipment he had brought home from the war. Accepting the equipment were Sergeant First Class William Grace, station commander for Bloomington-Dewitt County, and Sergeant James Vaughn. Ferree was certain that the set would still work despite some of the components being brittle with age.

Ferree retired from Chenoa High in 1954, keeping busy for the remainder of his life, collecting and polishing stones, fishing, and occasionally hunting for uranium. He died on June 16, 1982 at the age of 85.

The radio spent the next 36 years at the Army Communications and Electronic Museum at Fort Monmouth, New Jersey. For a while it was in a glass display case, a cardboard sign with Ferree's description propped in front of it, later in storage, part of a massive collection of communication equipment from the earliest days of the Signal Corps. It was relocated after Fort Monmouth closed in September 2011 to the Museum Support Center at Fort Belvoir, Virginia.[31]

Figure 25 George Bennett Ferree donating his radio to the Army Communications Museum, February 1975. From the Bloomington IL Pantagraph archives, used with permission from David Proeber.

13 Into the Air Again

On April 15, 1919, the Secretary of the Navy lifted wartime restrictions on amateur receivers "other than those used for the reception of commercial radio traffic".[1] The ban on transmitters ended October 1, mostly due to the lobbying efforts of the American Radio Relay League, who had formed in 1914 as a network of radio operators working in cooperation to relay radio messages across long distances. By 1917, with over 1,000 members, they reorganized formally and opened membership to all amateur radio enthusiasts. A few weeks later all their members and every other radio amateur in America were ordered off the air.

When the restrictions were lifted, amateurs across the country brought their equipment out of storage, set up their stations, built and tested the things they had designed and dreamed about for the last two years.

"The removal of the restrictions", reported *QST*, the magazine of the ARRL, "is going to be felt in every line of business from the lumber yard to the instrument maker. The Old Man's electrical supply store will have to order soldering paste by the barrel."[2]

Getting back on the air would take some work. All amateur licenses had to be re-applied for, and new technology made much of the old equipment obsolete. Most amateurs welcomed the challenges and looked forward to trying newly available equipment. "The days of real sport are at last with us", encouraged *QST*. "Come on, fellows, and get into the air again."[3]

Some, because of frugality or loyalty, held on to the old technology for a while, and spark transmitters, electrolytics, microphone detectors, even coherers continued to operate in scattered ham shacks for years after their heyday. The old equipment became part of the lore of radio, especially as new amateurs, curious about how the old timers had done it, from time to time built their own.

But it was the vacuum tube that changed everything. Because they were mass produced, they were cheaper and more readily available than before the war. And they were more specialized. Transmitting tubes generated continuous waves for clear broadcasts of voice and music, and detector and amplifier tubes made it possible to build broadcast receivers that could fill a room with sound. Of course, if people were going to buy these new radios, there had to be something to listen to.

Broadcast radio took its first tentative steps before the First World War with the transmission of news and election results in Morse code. On November 2, 1920, from a small shack perched on the roof of a building in Turtle Creek, Pennsylvania, a 100-watt radio station operating under the call sign 8ZZ broadcast the results of the 34th presidential election between Warren G. Harding and James M. Cox. The station was owned by Westinghouse, who in effort to grow their commercial radio receiver business, decided earlier that year to set up radio stations to provide regular programming. The public would buy radios, it was reasoned, only if there was consistent quality programming available.

What the military considered radio's greatest weakness, that it transmitted in a wide arc, and not point to point, was the most appealing thing about it commercially. Westinghouse vice president Harry P. Davis realized "that the efforts that were being made to develop radio telephony as a confidential means of communication were wrong, and that instead its field was really one of wide publicity, in fact, the only means of instantaneous collective communication ever devised".[4] Broadcast radio made immediate mass communication possible across cities, states, potentially the entire nation.

The Westinghouse station, operating as KDKA after its first few broadcasts, switched to a daily schedule on December 21. Encouraged by their success, Westinghouse opened additional stations in Newark, Springfield, Massachusetts and Chicago.

First broadcasting mostly music and news, the stations gradually expanded their programming. KDKA was the first station to broadcast a live major league baseball game, between the Pirates and Phillies, on August 5, 1921.[5]

By the mid-20s the initial novelty of broadcast radio was starting to wear off, and broadcasters responded by creating original content and tracking how many people were listening. Variety shows, serialized dramas, comedies, and live news reporting brought listeners back. More stations opened across the country, from one in 1921, to thirty in 1922, and 556 in 1923.

In 1926 the Radio Corporation of America, formed in 1919 from a merger of American Marconi and General Electric, purchased two AT&T owned stations, WEAF and WCAP, and merged them with their existing stations to form NBC, the first major radio network. CBS formed the following year, and both expanded across the country through the 20s and 30s. It was now possible for listeners on opposite coasts to hear the same concert, the same news, the same variety show. Radio was on its way to becoming a national experience.

Still, radio was out of reach for many families who were financially less well off or who lived in rural areas not yet electrified.

Receivers, especially in the early 20s, were expensive. A mid-level RCA cost $70 to $120 or more in 1922, at a time when the average annual income was just over $3,000.[6]

Less expensive receivers were available, like the Crosley 51, which originally sold for $18, but adding on the separate amplifier and speaker made it closer to $50, not including the replacement cost of tubes and batteries. It was not a casual investment.

Besides the expense, a lack of electricity made owning a radio difficult for many living away from cities. Forty nine percent of the American population lived in rural areas in 1920. Of those living on farms, fewer than eleven percent had electricity before the creation of the Rural Electrification Administration in 1936,[7] making it inconvenient or impossible to operate a vacuum tube receiver. Most early sets ran on batteries, but these had to be recharged, which meant frequent trips into town.

The Wincharger, a small and dependable wind generator designed to charge radio storage batteries, was introduced and marketed to farmers and other rural residents. Zenith, who owned a share of the Wincharger company, offered the complete generator and tower for $15 with the purchase of a Zenith farm radio, which itself was $40 or more, a significant investment. Whether urban or rural, for a less expensive option, many looked to an old technology, the crystal radio.

A commercially manufactured crystal receiver could be purchased for $10 or less. A homemade set cost even less. Often the only equipment that needed to be purchased were the headphones and crystal. Everything else could usually be found at home, or else salvaged from broken equipment.

Building a crystal set was elementary for experienced radio enthusiasts, but for most casual broadcast listeners it was less familiar. They may have at some time used or even built a simple crystal set, but to make a more sophisticated and selective receiver they would need instructions.

In 1922 the Bureau of Standards issued their Circular 120, *Construction and Operation of a Simple Homemade Receiving Outfit*, providing clear and complete instructions for building a simple, well designed and tunable crystal receiver. The whole thing, including antenna, could be made for ten to fifteen dollars, one third to one half the total cost being the headphones.

How many of these were built is unknown but sets based on the design were common between the world wars. Two pieces of wood were used for the chassis, one laid flat for a base, the other attached to the first, upright on its long edge. The base held the tapped coil, cat whisker, crystal and phone connections, while the upright piece was the control panel, with two tuning controls, antenna, and ground connections. The coil was wrapped around a round cardboard oatmeal box, which is still a common form for crystal radio coils and a part of crystal radio lore.

Newspapers in the 1920s featured amateur radio sections, and these frequently covered crystal and other non-powered radio receivers, usually with a "do it yourself" approach, using, for the most part, repurposed or homemade components. Because many new radio enthusiasts, especially in the 1920s, had only a rudimentary if any knowledge of how a radio worked, the articles often featured measured drawings and detailed descriptions. They appealed to and were often specifically written for children, and a simple crystal radio receiver was for decades a rite of passage for grade school children.

Along with the standard galena and cat whisker, old detectors, like the coherer, magnetic, electrolytic and microphone, reappeared from time to time. There were strange hybrids, and some of them hinted at the foxhole radio.

Because they were common in most households, razor blades were used in many home science and engineering projects, including radio. One article suggested solving the problem of disposing of used razor blades by using them as the rotors and stators of a variable capacitor "for sharp tuning".[8]

Razor blades were used in amateur versions of microphonic detectors at least since 1909 when Clark Pettingill wrote his "Novel Detector" article.[9] He followed up in 1911 with a different configuration, still using the razor blade, but this time with its edge pressed against a piece of carborundum.[10] A sufficiently strong signal could actually cause vibrations in the blade, producing an audible tone for each dot and dash received. Superficially it looked like a microphonic detector, but the contact was tighter. The blade functioned more or less like a cat whisker. Hugo Gernsback noted a similar crystal and razor blade arrangement in 1953 where, if everything was properly adjusted, the received station could be heard faintly through the vibrating blade.[11]

The idea of using razor blades as part of a detector persisted and evolved over time. Microphone detectors were mentioned in amateur articles throughout the 1920s and later, both the Massie type, where a needle straddled two pieces of carbon, or the Shoemaker type, with a pencil lead on two upturned razor blades.[12] In 1921 *Radio News* described a receiver that use a razor blade as a cat whisker, its edge in contact with a galena crystal.[13] The blade was used not because it substituted for a more expensive part - cat whiskers cost only pennies - but because, unlike the cat whisker, it could not be easily jarred out of position. It was a common enough arrangement that another variation appeared in the September 1922 issue of *Popular Science*,[14] this time with the point of the blade in contact with the crystal. In 1925 *Radio News* described an "emergency" crystal detector, a strange hybrid microphone and mineral detector, where "two razor blades (Gillette are preferable as holes are already drilled in them) are mounted on a block of wood which is about 3/8 or 1/2 inch wide... for a crystal a piece of coke, carborundum or pyrites will serve very well. The crystal is moved about until sensitive spots are found, when balanced as shown on the edges of the razor blades".[15]

Most printed descriptions of microphone detectors were clear. Two razor blades were mounted, side by side, so that their long edges faced up, a piece of carbon straddling the edges. Some newspapers ran condensed radio sections with less thorough descriptions. An amateur new to radio could interpret "a detector made of the lead of a broken pencil and two safety razor blades"[16] a number of ways. Someone who has seen a cat whisker and crystal but has no idea what a microphone detector is might assume the pencil lead acts as the cat whisker and the blade substitutes for the crystal. And it would likely work. A pencil-lead-as-cat-whisker was a common setup in the 20s. "A pointed piece of pencil lead", reported a column in 1925, "held tightly against a crystal by means of a binding post makes an excellent 'cat-whisker' for a silicon or galena crystal".[17]

A letter in the July-August 1975 issue of Elementary Electronics confirms that at least some amateurs in the 1920s made the razor-as-crystal leap. "My grandfather tells me that he used a safety razor blade as the crystal detector in a radio in 1925", writes R. T. in Wichita, Kansas. "Is he kidding me?"[18]

More common in radio columns were another element of foxhole radios, safety pin cat whiskers. Their shape and springiness made them an excellent substitute, almost as if they had been designed for the job. They were usually mounted upright and open, their pointed end resting on the crystal. The descriptions were purposely inexact. "No dimensions are given", reported the syndicated "Radio Experimenter" column in 1922, "as this is left to the experimenter, and whatever materials he has on hand".[19] And this was the appeal, to make something useful out of whatever odds and ends happened to be lying around.

Galena, inexpensive and reliable as a detector, is the mineral usually associated with amateur crystal radio. It was the most readily available crystal between the wars. Silicon, pyrite and other mineral detectors were also available. Some more experienced radio operators still preferred carborundum. It produced a clear tone, was reliable and, because contact was made with higher pressure, could stand up to most bumps and vibrations. In 1925 The Carborundum Company of New York released a self-contained carborundum detector, a small tube with electrical connections at each end and a small piece of carborundum sealed inside, held under pressure between two metal plates.

Vacuum tube receivers gradually replaced crystal sets through the 1920s and 30s, even in rural areas. Less expensive sets were available, as were improved console sets and smaller tabletop receivers that offered some portability.

Meanwhile the Signal Corps and the military as a whole were hampered by dramatic post war budget and personnel cutbacks. The 2,712 officers and 53,277 enlisted men of the war time Signal Corps was reduced to 1,216 officers and 10,372 men by June 1919. In 1926 there were less than 300 officers and 2,200 men. Their budget decreased from seventy-three million at the end of the war to two million in 1923.

Despite cuts, the Signal Corps was able to make some significant advances in research and development between the wars. In the 1920s that still mostly meant wire. "Telegraph and telephone lines constitute the basic means of signal communication", stated the 1923 *Field Service Regulations*, and "other means of communication supplement and extend the service of the telegraph and telephone lines".[20] Wired communications research was conducted mainly at the Signal Corps Electrical Laboratory at Washington and at the lab at the Bureau of Standards.

Most radio research was moved to Camp Alfred Vail, New Jersey when the Signal School was relocated there from Fort Leavenworth in 1919. Renamed Fort Monmouth in 1925, it became the center for Signal Corps research. A new laboratory was dedicated there in 1935, named in honor of George Owen Squier, who had died the previous year.[21]

New sets for field use were developed, with an emphasis on signal strength, ruggedness and portability. The SCR-194 and later SCR-195 "Walkie Talkie" were 25-pound transceivers that could be carried as a backpack. Tank, transport and aircraft radio were greatly improved, especially after the adoption of FM. Radio beacons and radio compasses allowed aircraft to fly "blind" without visual ground signals.

Arguably the most important interwar research at Fort Monmouth was in radar. In 1936 Colonel William R. Blair successfully designed and tested a system of pulsed radio signal detection of aircraft that led to the SCR-268, the United States military's first radio position finding system - the term "radar" was coined in 1940 - for controlling searchlights and antiaircraft guns.

The military had little direct involvement with broadcasting before the Second World War, other than cooperation with the Office of the Coordinator of Information in providing war related news information to American shortwave stations. The COI, formed in July 1941 to coordinate the efforts of several government intelligence agencies, were tasked with creating programming to counter the effects of Nazi radio propaganda, an effort that led to the creation of the Voice of America in 1942.

For the civilian population, broadcast radio was an indispensable part of life by the 1930s. The radio receiver took on a special place in the home, and blocks of time were set aside to listen to favorite programs, baseball games and special events. Radio sales increased from 100,000 sets in 1922 to 550,000 in 1923 and 4,428,000 in 1929. Even in 1933, during the worst period of the Great Depression, Americans bought 4,157,000 radio receivers. As demand grew, mass production drove costs down. By 1941 over eighty percent of households had at least one set, and on December 7, 1941, 24 million of those were tuned to hear President Roosevelt announce that war had been declared on Japan.[22]

14 That Damned Anzio

In April 1944, while sitting in a foxhole on the beachhead between Anzio and Nettuno, Italy, Private Eldon Phelps built a simple crystal radio from battlefield scraps. Lacking only the crystal, he remembered that safety razor blades could somehow be used as detectors. Rather than using two blades to make a microphone detector, he used one, fastened flat to a board, and probed it with a safety pin cat whisker.

The radio worked, to the astonishment of nearby soldiers, and Phelps was able to hear stations from Rome and Naples most nights. Back home it would have been met with passing curiosity, another odd contrivance of a creative radio amateur. But in the simultaneously dull and terrifying stalemate at Anzio, it was a godsend.

Winston Churchill suggested a landing at Anzio in December 1943 to bypass the Gustav Line, a German defensive line that ran across the Italian peninsula through Cassino, where Allied troops moving up from the south had been locked in stalemate with German Field Marshal Kesselring's forces. Either, it was assumed, Kesselring would pull troops from the Gustav Line to defend against the invasion, thereby opening the possibility of an Allied breakout, or else Allied troops from Shingle would move inland and take Rome.

On January 22, 1944, 36,000 soldiers from the United States 3rd Infantry Division, 6615th Ranger Force and the British 1st Infantry Division, commanded by Major General John P. Lucas, landed on the beaches surrounding Anzio and Nettuno, meeting little resistance. Thirteen Allies were killed on the first day.

Lucas, lacking confidence in the plan and realizing that he was currently outnumbered by Germans, decided to strengthen his defenses on the beachhead before advancing.

Kesselring, having anticipated an Allied landing, quickly moved available divisions from the Gustav line to surround the beachhead. Meanwhile additional Allied forces arrived, including the United States 1st Armored Division and the 45th Infantry Division, bringing their total number to 69,000 men.

After a series of disastrous and inconclusive assaults and counterattacks resulting in nearly 20,000 casualties on both sides, Allied and Axis commanders realized that they would need to wait until spring to launch an effective offensive and took advantage of the relative lull to build up their forces.

The stalemate lasted from March to early May, both sides improving their defensive positions, patrolling, and exchanging artillery fire. For over two months men sat in muddy holes praying the next shell would not be a direct hit. Many of the Germans were positioned in the nearby hills and all parts of the beachhead were vulnerable to their artillery. Two Krupp K5 rail guns, each firing 283mm shells, aimed mostly for the ships in the Anzio harbor, and the roar of the 255kg shells passing overhead was by all accounts terrifying. Named "Robert" and "Leopold" by their crews, the Allies called them Anzio Annie and the Anzio Express, the latter because the shells sounded like freight trains as they passed. Smaller artillery was focused on the beachhead.

There was no rear area at Anzio. "I don't mean to suggest that they kept every foot of our territory drenched with shells all the time, for they certainly didn't," wrote journalist Ernie Pyle. "They were short of ammunition, for one thing. But they could reach us, and we never knew where they would shoot next. A man was just as liable to get hit standing in the doorway of the villa where he slept at night as he was in a command post five miles out in the field."[1] "Anzio was a tough one, and any survivor was lucky", recalled Leroy D. Good of the 434th Antiaircraft Artillery. "Cooks and clerks were as endangered as front line infantry."[2]

Hospitals were considered by many the most dangerous areas on the beachhead. Though well behind front lines and surrounded by sandbags, they were vulnerable to artillery and to the guns of German aircraft. Patients would often sneak away early, feeling they would be safer at the front. At least there they would have a gun to defend themselves. Many patients, doctors and nurses were wounded or killed by bullets and artillery fire in the area that became known as Hell's

Half Acre.[3]

The beachhead was small, only fifteen miles wide and seven miles from sea to the front line. There was no natural cover, save a small grove of trees where troops were sent for occasional 48-hour breaks, though even that place was far from safe.

Sergeant George A. Mackie, who passed through Anzio three months after the Allies finally broke through the German line, was "really surprised to see how small an area Anzio is. How they stood out for such a long time is beyond me. All of the towns around there, including Anzio, are totally destroyed. Just a wall standing here and there, the rest of the towns are laid flat. The same goes for Cassino and all the town around it, also. It is hard to believe unless you actually see it. You wouldn't think it possible, to wipe out a town so completely. For miles around all you can see is bomb craters and fox-holes. The boys that were there really went through hell."[4]

With little cover on the flat, featureless beachhead, troops began digging in almost as soon as they arrived.

"I guess it will be O. K. to tell you about my living quarters", wrote Bill Bakersmith of the 582nd Signal Aircraft Warning Battalion. "Before I went to the hospital we were living in tents. Well, when I came back I thought that the outfit had moved out. All the tents were gone. Then suddenly heads started to pop out of the ground. All of the fellows have dug in. Mostly living singularly, but some had dug in together. Well there was no hole for me. So Sal and Bert hopped in and helped me make my dugout. It is four ft. by seven ft. by four ft. I have a roof about one ft. of dirt on top of boards. It makes a swell shelter. I have now put lights in it. It is much quieter and warmer than sleeping on top of the ground. Of course I have my folding cot in it."[5]

Many of the first foxholes were miserable things, cold and wet from the rainy winter. The sandy soil would often cave in, and some soldiers were lost in foxholes with unsupported sides. Many more were casualties of hypothermia and trench foot from perpetually wet dugouts.

More miserable were the front-line infantry, lying in muddy slit trenches, the water table too high to allow for a deeper hole. And there was always the mud. "We are having another bout with the rain", wrote Robert Albro in late February, "mud and mire all over. This is all a flat reclaimed marshland, and it doesn't take much of a rain to make it 'soupy'".[6]

As the stalemate persisted, the beachhead resembled the static trenches of the First World War. Spring brought drier ground, and soldiers took the opportunity to improve their foxholes, enlarging and reinforcing them. The landscape was honeycombed with foxholes, gun pits and trenches. "Viewed from the air", reported the army's history of Anzio, "the beachhead created the illusion that thousands of giant moles had been at work".[7] Sturdy covers were built from logs or wood scavenged from abandoned buildings, piled with as much dirt as could be managed to protect from shrapnel and antipersonnel bombs. Doors, shutters and beams from ruined buildings, wood from broken crates, even large wine vats were used to reinforce and cover foxholes.[8]

Some grew larger and more elaborate over time. Walls were lined with cardboard from ration cases, and some had lighting, furniture, and even decorations salvaged from battle damaged buildings. Foxholes nearer the front were not nearly as comfortable, but they were made safer by being reinforced with wood salvaged from packing crates and sand filled cardboard tubes used to ship artillery shells.[9] Everyone who could, hospitals, kitchens, artillery, all dug in, spending most daylight hours underground, hoping to avoid sniper fire and shrapnel from exploding shells.

"I hope we never see another Anzio beachhead again", wrote Private William Purdy. "Oh dear Lord, you have no idea how we sweat and prayed every time a shell flew over. I just about wore out the bible reading it. Talk about war nerves. We all had them."[10] Don Welling of the 3rd Infantry Division summed it up. "That was a meat grinder, that damned Anzio. It was bloody. Bloody as hell".[11]

Soldiers were rotated out of the front as often as possible and sent to "The Pines", an area of forested dunes three miles east of Nettuno, for rest, bathing, entertainment and additional training. No place on the beachhead was out of range of German artillery or gunfire, "The Pines" included, and no one was ever far from a foxhole.

Entertainers were only able to visit the beachhead after the Allies broke out of the beachhead in late May. Marlene Dietrich was the first and had the opportunity to announce the D day landings on June 6 to the troops remaining at Anzio. Scheduled to move on to Rome after June 6, she was delayed at Anzio for several days, which she spent visiting hospitals and performing. Humphry Bogart, Lauren Bacall and Irving Berlin all visited after the breakout. Before that, it was up to the troops to provide their own entertainment.

Regimental bands formed, traveling rear areas and playing big band music.[12] The Americans and British occasionally exchanged bands, and

Figure 26 Photos of foxholes at Anzio taken by Mert Walcott. From top left "111 Inside Dug-out"; "119 Dug-Out Sam & Tom"; "110 Dug-Out Mert & Phil". Author's collection.

the 5th Division Pipers were especially popular with the Americans, who wanted more music by "those guys in skirts".[13]

Several underground movie theaters were built. Two were made by the 1st Armored Division, large, covered, and heavily reinforced holes where 200 soldiers could sit in relative comfort on wooden crates and happily watch whatever movie was available.[14]

Figure 27 Underground theater at Anzio. Photo by George Glidwell. Author's collection.

Figure 28 Soldiers watch a movie at the Fifth Army movie house, Anzio.

Baseball games were played on improvised fields, with baseballs provided by the Special Services Division. Shirts served as bases, which were always near foxholes in case the enemy tired of watching the game and decided to hurl artillery at the field instead.

Figure 29 Baseball at Anzio, May 1944. Photo by Sam Goldstein.

Thursday May 11 saw the first and only annual running of the Anzio Derby, the brainchild of Sergeant Bill Harr, a racing editor and handicapper from Baltimore. Harr acted as technical advisor for the event, which was promoted by Corporal Joseph P. Boyle. At first suggested as a joke, it became a major event after an Anzio Racing Commission was formed. Racing programs were printed, and an official photographer, veterinarian, announcer, and "four pretty nurses from the hospital on hand to congratulate the winners" were selected.[15]

Originally scheduled to be run on Saturday, it was moved up two days due to persistent rumors that the invasion in France was imminent, which would likely put a stop to the whole thing. The course was built in haste over a softball field, a quarter mile track marked with white engineer's tape.[16]

The Derby, preceded by three preliminary races and a twelve-piece band who performed "O Solo Mio", was won by an eight-year-old bay mare named Six-by-Six, who covered the quarter mile in thirty-one seconds. The winner finished ahead of six other horses and one less than willing donkey named George, who crossed the line in a brisk four minutes nine seconds. The prize for winning jockey Bill Schmit was a two-pound box of chocolates. Six-By-Six was awarded a floral wreath.[17]

The race proved so popular that it was announced that a second race would be run the following Saturday. Crews quickly disassembled the track so that softball games could resume, only to build it again two days later for the Anzio Preakness.[18]

The British soldiers preferred racing the black beetles that seemed to be everywhere. Small trenches were dug to catch them. The trenches soon filled with beetles, and from those the fastest were chosen.

They were painted with their owner's colors, put in to glass jars, then, after being paraded before the crowd, were placed, covered with their opened and inverted jars, in the middle of a six-foot diameter circle drawn in the sand. Bets were placed, the start was sounded, and the jars lifted. The first beetle to cross the ring was the winner.[19] According to Dennis Spencer of the British 5th Infantry Division the races were "complete with bookmakers stands and boards. Quite a lot of lira changed hands during these meetings".[20]

Some beetles gained a reputation. The fastest were traded and sold, sometimes at a premium. One group pulled their resources to buy an especially successful beetle for the wild sum of £40.[21]

Gambling was widespread, and impromptu dice and poker games sprang up across the beachhead. Some units built large special purpose foxholes for their nightly poker games. It could be an expensive night of entertainment, as Sergeant Darl Abshere could attest, when he was obliged to "take in laundry to make up for his losses at five card draw".[22]

The Italians left most of their wine behind when they evacuated, and the GIs were glad to find it. Where there was no wine, soldiers from places familiar with moonshine built stills, using the copper tubing from downed German aircraft, though not always with the best results. At first they used the wine from the cellars of Anzio to make an infamously strong brandy. Once the wine was depleted they distilled anything that would ferment, producing, as author Feed Sheehan described it, an "especially virulent brand of raisin-jack".[23]

In some areas soldiers took up farming, planting fresh vegetables and tending to livestock left behind by the evacuated citizens of Anzio and Nettuno. Cows were fed and tended for fresh milk. Chickens were especially prized, once soldiers learned they had more value as layers than as fricassee.

Figure 30 Gambling at Anzio. Photo by George Glidwell. Author's collection.

One especially charmed hen was on the verge of being fried by an artillery unit when a German shell struck the building they were housed in, knocking a wall down, setting the house on fire and sending the soldiers running. Once the dust settled, someone remembered the chicken. They found her, unharmed, with a fresh egg laid during the barrage. "The boys decided they preferred eggs often to fried chicken once" and Lucky the hen was spared.[24]

Chickens lost in enemy attacks were mourned. Myrtle, who provided her regiment with six eggs a week, died on Easter Sunday and was "given a military funeral by the regimental medics and a little white cross to mark her grave".[25]

Though not officially permitted, some soldiers became amateur photographers. One of the most active was Mert Walcott, who documented the details of soldier life on the beachhead and beyond. Printing in a small collapsible darkroom built on the beachhead, he catalogued, numbered and sold his own photographs to soldiers who wanted mementos but had no camera of their own, and processed the film of those who did.

Figure 31 Mert Walcott's beachhead darkroom. Photo number 139. Author's collection.

On a beachhead filled with bizarre and extraordinary sights, one of the more unusual was The Baron, scurrying in the middle of the night, often dodging gunfire, from one outpost to another, dapperly dressed in a tuxedo, carrying linking rings and accompanied by a duck. A vaudeville magician in civilian life, Private Roland Ormsby was drafted "off the runway of a vaudeville theater in upstate New York".[26] Recognizing he would be more valuable to the army as an entertainer, he was placed in the Special Service Company of the 15th Infantry, where he served as master of ceremonies for other entertainers as well as performing as a comedian and magician. He was well liked, and his show was so popular that he was soon entertaining much of the Fifth Army across the beachhead, in whatever building or large enough dugout was available, performing for hours at a time as small groups of soldiers took their turns as audience.

Figure 32 "The Baron" in later years, still performing. Courtesy Bevery Leffler.

Don Robinson, news editor of the 45th Division News, was happy to share quarters with the Baron "but he needn't have brought the duck. It was a big white one, weighing all of ten pounds, and the noisiest duck any of us had ever encountered. Since it was too cold outside for the duck, we kept it in the office. Visitors were always startled when the duck scurried out from under my desk when I sat down. I got more interest aroused in it than the Baron did. No one knew how to give a duck a bath, so it went unwashed and became smelly. When we told Major Gilstrap he could have a duck or a Press Section, the issue hung in the balance a while, but he finally decided in favor of the Press Section."[27]

What little is known about Roland "Ron" Ormsby after the war reveals an adventurous life. He worked for some time as a model for British hunting clothes. In Bangor, Maine he built a log cabin by hand, and owned an old time themed bar near Fresno, California where he played piano for the patrons. He retired to northern Arkansas, still performing his magic act for schoolchildren until his death in 1997.[28]

The army had little direct involvement with morale or entertainment before the early 20th century. For the first 120 years or so only the basic necessities were provided and any additional goods available for troops to purchase were supplied by army approved merchants, though this became something of a monopoly. The army periodically attempted to counter corrupt practices with regulations. General Order 46 of 1895 established the first army run post exchanges,[29] and the 1903 Army Appropriations Act expanded the 1895 order by setting aside $500,000 annually "for the construction, equipment and maintenance of suitable buildings at military posts and stations for the conduct of the post exchange, school, library, reading, lunch, amusement rooms and gymnasium to be expended in the discretion and under the direction of the Secretary of War"[30]

An Army Morale division was established in 1918, mainly to set a moral path for soldiers, steering them clear of brothels and hard drink. Most real "morale" came from the hot coffee and donuts provided by the Red Cross, YMCA and other private charitable groups.

Other morale related departments, such as the Library and Motion Picture Services, were established between the wars. By the time the United States entered WWII the various service departments were organized as Special Services, which by 1943 also included the Army Exchange Service. Special Services provided troop shows, sporting equipment, books and other recreational materials.

Each Special Service Company carried several kits, large crates packed with equipment for specific types of activity. Kits "A" and "A-1" contained baseball, basketball, boxing and football equipment, as well as cards, dominos, horse shoes and other gaming supplies.

Intended to provide "AEF members with homelike music, news, and commercial radio programs",[31] Kit "B", designed in January 1942 by the Joint Army and Navy Committee on Welfare and Recreation, included a phonograph, a collection of ten-inch records, twenty-five half-hour radio broadcast transcription records, music books, and a portable radio. New radio transcriptions were recorded and delivered continuously for the duration of the war.

Kit "B-1" included a PA system and generator complete with microphones, an electric phonograph, and a radio receiver.

Kit D was the music kit, and it came with music books, guitars, mandolins, ocarinas, ukuleles, and a small upright piano. Everything needed for a theatrical production was included in Kit "E" - scripts, costumes, makeup, wigs and props. Kit "J" had a projector, screen, sound system, and spare bulbs to equip a small movie theater. Kit C was a library of 100 hard bound and 1,900 paper bound books, and Kit "I" included typewriters, mimeograph equipment, and other paraphernalia needed to publish a unit's weekly news sheet.[32]

Most divisions and camps seemed to have a newspaper. Anzio alone had nearly 30, printed underground on mimeograph machines, with names like *Sea Horse, Red Devil, Braves' Bulletin, Flacky Wacky, Beachhead News,* and, with the widest circulation, the *45th Division News.*[33]

The *Stars and Stripes* returned during WWII, with editions printed in every theater. First published as an eight-page weekly during the First World War, it was revived in 1942 with more than twenty-five editions reaching 1.2 million readers.

YANK, a weekly, army produced, soldier written magazine with twenty-one editions in various areas of operation, was read enthusiastically by nearly three million soldiers, sailors and airmen.

Most of the activities and materials provided by Special Services were only available to troops in rear areas. Reading materials were often the only distraction available to a soldier in a foxhole, and books were prized and eagerly read. "Our entertainment consisted of paperback books, when available," recalled George Anthony Avery of the 84th Mortar Battalion, "and the Army newspaper *Stars and Stripes.*"[34]

Letters and care packages from home were also a boost to morale, and mail handling at the beachhead was efficient and among the most expedient in the European theater.

Radio by the beginning of World War II was an established part of everyday home life for many Americans. Having for the most part grown up with it, troops longed for music and news from home. Some found phonographs and small radio receivers in the abandoned shops and villas of Anzio and Nettuno, and a few dugouts even sported large

Figure 33 Special Service B-Kit. Photograph No. 111-SC-170572. 1944; Records of the Office of the Chief Signal Officer, Record Group 111; National Archives at College Park, College Park, MD.

Figure 34 British soldiers receive radios provided by the Nuffield fund, 1940. British Army photo, from the author's collection.

console radios in polished wood cabinets, something that would have been a luxury in a well-appointed home, let alone in a foxhole.

Anthony D'Angelo recalled that "at that time I had a radio given to me by a family I became friendly with at Anzio, and who had to leave when all civilians were being taken off the Beachhead. As I was responsible for the electrical equipment and the generator, I had my radios hooked up to it and listened to the radio at night in the dugout. Some of the programs that came in were 'BBC London Calling', Berlin Sally playing American songs and saying 'you boys will never go home, come to our side and we will take care of you'. There was also an American station broadcasting from Naples."[35]

Private organizations provided thousands of broadcast receivers, mostly for training camps and rear areas. The Nuffield Trust donated portable sets to British forces early in the war,[36] and radio drives in the United States and elsewhere sent receivers to military recreation facilities.

Figure 35 Radio in a dugout, Anzio. Photo courtesy Anthony S. D'Angelo.

The army and navy also made efforts to distribute radios, both to hospitals, a practice that started on a small scale during the First World War, and to training and recreation areas using various "morale sets", receivers that were selected for their durability and portability. At least 6,000 receivers were distributed as part of the Special services B-Kit. The SSD1 and SSD2 were reconfigured commercial sets, treated to resist fungus and placed in a rugged cabinet. Both were five-tube, standard broadcast AM and shortwave sets, and could run on AC or battery, 110 or 240 volts. It is unknown exactly how many of the sets were produced but 6 to18 thousand SSD1 receivers were ordered along with an additional 90,000 SSD2 sets. The SSD2 was included late in the war in the last of the Special Service B Kits.[37]

The R-100/URR "Morale Builder" receiver, which had bands for standard broadcast AM as well as shortwave, was ordered in 1945 from several radio manufacturers including Zenith, Majestic and Espey.[38] It was a relatively large table top set and was intended to be used in recreation centers and other places where troops gathered. Built late in the war, many ended up in the surplus market, giving it the appearance of being more common than it was. How many were produced is not clear, but there were far fewer than the SSD2.

Other sets were either designed or produced by the War Department or else and purchased and modified to withstand various environments. North American Phillips produced 100 or so sets similar to the B-Kit set for troops in North Africa. The navy ordered several morale sets of their own for use on board ships. And in 1943 General Eisenhower purchased 750 receivers from the British, with hundreds or possibly thousands more loaned the following year.[39]

Some standard issue army radios could receive broadcast bands. Norris J. Dupre, a radio operator with the 45th Reconnaissance Troop, recalled that his "transmitter wasn't worth a damn. But the receiver was. And I was able to listen to foreign broadcasts, especially the BBC. That was our outlet to news other than what we could get through the grapevine."[40]

One artillery unit produced their own "radio" programs, "broadcasting" their own musical and comedy productions, news and daily menus across telephone lines to an audience of foxhole bound troops, complete with commercials. "Men, war is hell", began an ad sponsored by Pfc. Birdie Dale Matson for his laundry service, "No longer do we have the time to soak our undies in Lux. But there's no reason for your combat suit to stand up by itself. Don't see your first sergeant. See Dale's One Way Laundry. Dale is anxious to take the spots out of your pants - especially the five and ten spots!"[41]

Most radio sets distributed by the military were intended for rear area or shipboard use. For the most part, sets that made it to enlisted men in the field were either appropriated from the enemy, purchased locally, abandoned civilian sets, or soldier-built from salvaged parts. Of the soldier-built sets at Anzio, the simple crystal set with a radio blade detector was by far the most common type, and during the stalemate they seemed to be everywhere.

"We went on patrols at night", recalled Don Welling, "and one night we went out and we got to another CP that was underground, and some guy had on some earphones, and he was tapping his foot. I said 'what the hell are you doin'?' And he showed me he had a crystal set set up. I said heck, I made those years ago. And he said, 'do you want to listen to somethin'?' I said yeah. So he took the earphones off and gave 'em to me and I could hear 'String of Pearls' by Glen Miller. So then we moved on, of course. During the day we didn't have a heck of a lot to do except sleep and read. So I went back and I got the equipment together and I built me one of those things. It had a set of earphones. And 'course that's about all you needed was earphones, you know… we had razor blades, we had safety pins, and add some wire. I made one, we used it, and then, well another guy wanted one, and of course I started makin' 'em. I would tell them the equipment they needed to give me. And then we ran out of earphones."[42]

Chancing upon on even a crude radio would have been extraordinary to a soldier spending weeks or months isolated in a muddy hole in the ground.

"I was walking up in the front lines one time and I was walking by a foxhole and this old boy had a radio," recalls Bryan Compton of the 45th Division. "Well, I stopped to listen because he had music a-goin' and gee, music! I hadn't heard a radio play in months and months."[43]

There were several types of foxhole radios at Anzio, and there may have been more than one "first", but the novelty of their design suggests a single origin, at least for the razor-as-crystal model. Goldie Phelps, who was married to Eldon Phelps for 53 years, believed her husband invented it.[44] And it was Eldon Phelps who was first sought out by the newspapers to describe it.

Eldon I. Phelps was born August 8, 1919 in Clinton, Oklahoma, the second oldest of Royal and Ione Phelps' five children. Louisa Sperle, a childhood friend and neighbor of Ione, walked half mile from her farm through a pasture to the Phelps' home to serve as midwife when Eldon was born. The Phelps relocated to Kansas soon after, losing contact with Louisa and her husband Chris.

Two years later the Sperle's third child and only daughter, Goldie, was born.

In 1941 a family friend of the Sperles, seeing a potential match between her nephew and Goldie, encouraged Goldie to write an introductory letter. The nephew wrote back, and soon they were corresponding daily. Before having a chance to meet in person, Eldon Phelps, the young man Goldie had been corresponding with, shipped off to Europe with the 45th Infantry Division. The correspondence continued almost daily during the war. Louisa, realizing that her daughter had been corresponding with the boy she had helped deliver, encouraged Goldie to tell Eldon her true feelings.

After Goldie tore up her first letter, her mother encouraged her to write a second one. She sent it the same day that Eldon sent a similar letter from Italy. They finally met face to face after the war and married shortly after.

Eldon Phelps' interest in radio started early. His older brother Vernon, a radio amateur in his youth, would make a career of it, building radio systems for aircraft. Eldon took an interest in his brother's hobby and grew well versed in radio lore.[45]

In January 1944 Phelps came ashore at the Anzio beachhead, part of Operation Shingle, the third of four invasions he would participate in.[46] Weeks later, drawing on his knowledge of radio lore, he built a crude but functional receiver from what was available to him.

He described it to a United Press reporter, and the story was carried by newspapers across the United States. "Stick a razor blade in a piece of dry wood. Attach a coil to the wood and connect it to a ground. Attach an aerial to the blade. Move a cat's whisker antenna coil against the flat surface of the blade to tune the station. It's the same principle as the old crystal set."[47]

As incomplete as the instructions were, anyone with a rudimentary knowledge of radio would have recognized this as a simple crystal set, albeit lacking a capacitor.

The story was picked up the following week by the *Stars and Stripes*. "Yank ingenuity has reached some kind of a climax with the invention of a 'foxhole radio' made with wire, wood and a razor blade. It works, honest! The genius who made it, Pvt. Eldon Philps, [sic] Enid, Okla., gets Rome and Naples on it every night. It works on the principle of the old-time crystal sets except that a razor blade is used instead of a crystal. Here are the directions, if you want to make one, as many fellows on the beachhead already are doing—attach aerial to razor blade, do same with one wire from earphone, put a fine wire through one end of your coil. The other end of the coil is grounded. The other wire from the earphone also is grounded. The razor blade is tacked to a dry piece of wood or some other piece of insulating material. To tune the radio, just move the fine wire around the flat surface of the razor blade."[48]

Although they misspelled his name, *Stars and Stripes* did credit Phelps as the inventor. And now the contraption had a name, the "foxhole radio". Letters followed, from the beachhead and beyond, requesting more details.

"In the May 6 issue, you carried an article about a small 'foxhole radio' constructed by Pvt. Eldon Philps, Enid, Okla., which was made with wire, wood and a razor blade. The directions for making one of these 'foxhole radios' were published. I've followed them carefully but achieved nothing. I should, therefore, be grateful if you could publish more detailed instructions, with perhaps a sketch, in one of your future editions. L-Cpl. R. Flove, R. E."

"Apparently, Corporal," replied the editor, "all you are lacking is the foxhole".[49]

Figure 36 Eldon Phelps in 1981 wearing his WWII uniform. Courtesy Goldie Phelps.

15 Digging In

Besides its literal meaning as the burrow of a fox, "Foxhole" has appeared as a place name in England at least since medieval times. The village of Foxholes in East Riding, Yorkshire is mentioned in the *Domesday Book* in 1086. There is a Foxhole in Cornwall, a Foxholes in Hertfordshire, a Foxhole Heath near Eriswell in Suffolk, and, formerly, a Foxhole Quay in Plymouth. In North America, Fox Hole, also known as Little Bay, is a harbor on the north east side of Popof Island in the Shumagin islands of Alaska. The state of Maryland can claim both a Fox Hole Landing and a Fox Hole Creek. There is a Fox Hole Bay and a Fox Hole Brook in Newfoundland.

As a metaphorical hiding place, the *Oxford English Dictionary* proposes a biblical origin, specifically Matthew 8:20 "And Jesus saith unto him, the foxes have holes, and the birds of the air have nests; but the Son of man hath not where to lay his head", and the earliest examples of its use describe a figurative hole in which a religious opponent may have ensconced themselves and from which they must be plucked out.

Armies have been digging trenches for defense since before the Romans and rifle pits at least since the American Civil War. The term "foxhole" is first used for a defensive fighting position during WWI, but only late and rarely by British and American soldiers. Most of the digging in that war went towards long trenches or large underground shelters. There were smaller holes dug to protect artillerymen and troops on the move, but these were temporary and less formally constructed, simple slit trenches or improved shell craters. To the men they were usually referred to as "dugouts" or "funkholes", a word coined by the British during the Second Boer War, "funk" already an old word, used since the 18th century to signify fear or depression.[1] "Funkhole" originally referred to a niche dug into the side of a trench, but came to signify any hole large enough to shelter in.

The word "foxhole" or *fuchslöcher* to describe a hasty fortification was first used by the Germans. The 1916 manual *Der Spatenkrieg*, or *Spade Warfare*, includes instructions for the "construction of rain and shrapnel proof shelters", very deep, reinforced shelters with two entrances, in case one became blocked. "With suitable ground, earth holes, so-called 'fox-holes' are excavated by mining which often has 3 to 8 meters of undisturbed ground for cover."[2]

The *Modern Language Review* article "German 'War Words'" gives for 'funk-hole' the German words *Kaninchenloch, Löwenhöhle, Fuchsloch,* and *Druckposten,*[3] which translate to rabbit hole, lion's cave, fox hole, and "cushy post".

New German military terms were tracked by the Allies, including those for shelters. The American General Headquarters' *Summary of Information* for November 3, 1918 explained that

> "the term 'fox-hole' is used by the German soldier, as determined from the examination of a large number of prisoners, to describe a hole in the ground sufficient to give shelter from splinters and perhaps from the weather also, to one or two soldiers. In general, there are two types. One is a hole in level or nearly level ground, usually a deepened shell hole, some of them having improvised overhead cover from shell fragments and shelter for protection from the weather. The other is a hole in steeply sloping ground, such as a railroad embankment, the bank of a stream, the deep ditch of a road or the steep slope of a hill. These are often partly closed in with wood or tin, covered with dirt, in order to increase the protection from the weather. Protection from shell fragments is given by the surrounding earth and not by the covering, except in rare instances where a considerable amount of earth has been piled over the covering. The fox-holes in level ground as a rule give best protection against shell fragments, but the fox-holes in steep slopes give better shelter from the weather and are more easily constructed. Consequently the second type is somewhat more frequently found than the first type."[4]

The *Summary* notes that these are temporary fortifications for mobile troops. "In some cases these fox-holes have been so located that they could be linked-up into a defensive line. In most instances there does not appear to have been any such purpose in the siting of the fox-holes. A battalion at rest or in support needs shelter from artillery fire and from the weather, and promptly digs in, preferably where it is protected from observation. Within certain limits the men use their own judgment in choosing the locations of their own shelters. When the battalion moves away a new set of fox-holes is dug. The constant shifting of troops results in great numbers of fox-holes scattered over the front line and support areas. The discovery of fox-holes at any point cannot by itself be taken as indicative of the existence of a line of resistance."

Figure 37 WWI dugouts on the south side of Epinonville Hill, used for observation by the 181st Brigade, 91st Infantry Division, September 26-27, 1918. U.S. Signal Corps photo #53164.

The English-speaking Allies borrowed words from the French during the war, as well as a few from across the lines. Some, like "strafe", which means "punishment", have become part of the English lexicon. *Fuchslöcher* was also borrowed, in a roundabout way, and in its English form.

Figure 38 Individual field fortifications of WWI were usually hastily dug holes or improved mine craters that were not occupied for long. What this soldier has, by comparison, is practically a fortress. Postcard from the author's collection.

Marines today prefer "fighting hole" to "foxhole" but this was not always the case, and at least one source claims "foxhole" was first popularized by a Marine during the June 1918 Battle of Belleau Wood. According to Colonel Robert Heinl, in his *Soldiers of the Sea*: "One abiding by-product of the Belleau Wood action was a new term in the soldier's argot: as the Marines scratched out shallow rifle pits wherever the front lines lay, somebody called them 'foxholes.' The name caught on, a correspondent heard and reported it, and the era of the foxhole arrived."[5]

More likely, if the word spread much among Allied troops at all, it was through military intelligence near the end of the war. Small solid squares represented "dugouts" on most G-2 maps showing enemy positions.[6] By the time the October 25, 1918 G-2 *Enemy Information* map was printed, small solid dots were added, neatly labeled "fox holes".[7]

When the October 31 *Summary of Information* reported that "the entire zone between this switch line and the front line of Michel I is full of small shelters and fox-holes in the open",[8] the term "fox-hole" was well enough understood that the authors felt no need to define it.

Journalists adopted the term and may have been the strongest influence in it spreading. One of the earliest mentions of "fox-holes" as a defensive position in an English language newspaper is from a translation of a German article describing the siege of the Latvian fortress at Dvinsk. Originally printed in *Vossische Zeitung* in November 1915, it was reprinted in the November 12, 1915 *New York Evening World*. "Every rod of land is covered with permanent trenches roofed securely against shrapnel and shell fragments and connected with so-called 'fox-holes', small shelters where the garrisons are secure against the heaviest shells."[9]

"Foxhole" was used periodically over the next few years to describe German positions, often the type of hardened shelter illustrated in *Der Spatenkrieg*. Describing the German defenses at the Russian front, the *New York Tribune* in July 1916 reports that "the whole position is equipped also with 'fox holes', which are proof against the heaviest artillery fire."[10]

By the latter part of 1918 reporters were also using the word for any dugout occupied by American or British soldiers. "The Americans throughout the day kept to their positions in the dripping woods or in their water-soaked fox holes and trenches", reported the *New York Tribune* in September, "while the artillery of both sides sent over shells".[11]

American and British soldiers tended to prefer "funkhole" to "foxhole", at least while the war was still in progress. 1st Lieutenant Arthur McKeogh, in his history of the 77th Division during the Meuse-Argonne Offensive, was firmly on the side of "funkhole", and did his best to settle the issue. "Funkholes are the trenches of open warfare - irregular lines of disconnected nooks in the ground dug by the doughboy individually, or with his 'buddy', and just big enough, accordingly, to hold one or two of them. Everyone has read of 'digging in'. Funkholes are the result of it. And their name has its origin in a favorite British term - funk, or fear. Now, not to side with the polite war correspondents who prefer the word 'foxhole', there's no denying that the average intelligent human being lacks some of the poise of the drawing room when the blithe machine gun bullet, the humming bit of shrapnel or the swift shell fragment is zipping close by. And it is at such times, ordinarily, that funkholes are dug. In common frankness, therefore, it is only right to call a spade - a funkhole; for under stress of heavy fire, a spade plus a few hectic minutes of digging equals a 2x3x3 foot funkhole."[12]

Not everyone was as firm in their conviction as Lieutenant McKeogh. That both "foxhole" and "funkhole" were used interchangeably by at least some Americans is shown in the military glossary of *The 32nd Division in the World War*. A "fox hole" was an "individual shelter, generally a hole in the ground in the side of a hill, ditch or embankment away from the enemy". A "funk hole" was "the same as a fox hole".[13]

Both terms were used for a while in the many novels and histories of the war written after 1918 but "foxhole", more familiar to the reading public, eventually won out. Funkhole only slowly faded and was still occasionally used, mainly by the British, during the Second World War.[14]

There were no detailed plans, no formal instructions for constructing an individual dugout or foxhole during the First World War. Elaborate drawings were provided for trenches, with details of their traces, connections and reinforcement. Individual hasty fortifications were considered ephemeral, improvised as needed, occupied only briefly.

Some of the earliest references to foxholes in American military publications were in ROTC manuals of the early 1920s. The 1921 *Senior Course Manual* instructed that "in a position occupied for immediate defense the first works will be individual rifle pits or fox holes. These may later be connected to form a continuous trench."[15] Foxholes - one word or two - were seen as an intermediary stage to be later "improved" by connecting them to form trenches.

This idea is reinforced in Bond's *Field Engineering* of 1922, which notes that foxholes "would be characteristic of the operations of small and very mobile forces, and would be employed also by a large force in very open warfare, characterized by rapid movement ",[16] but if "occupied for a considerable period and if the position is one of importance and liable to be attacked, the defensive works are gradually extended and elaborated, the fire trenches may be made continuous, communication trenches dug, obstacles placed, shelters constructed etc., until a complete organization results."[17]

The Germans by the 1930s accepted that "fox holes" or individual rifle pits offered better protection to soldiers from artillery fire than trenches, reinforced by their experiences in the Chaco War of 1932-1935.[18]

The Marine's 1936 *Tentative Manual for Defense of Advanced Bases* comes to a similar conclusion in the section describing defense of aircraft on the ground, specifying that "in addition to protecting the airplanes, provision must be made to protect the personnel of the air force. Gas proof dugouts and individual fox holes close to the working areas must be provided for the mechanics".[19]

The 1940 edition of the United States Army *Field Manual FM 5-15* still emphasized WWI style trenches and categorized skirmisher trenches and foxholes as hasty trenches. "The normal inclination of the soldier pinned to the ground by enemy fire is to 'dig in' to hold the ground he has gained. The result of his efforts is a hasty intrenchment or fox hole which he constructs with the entrenching tools carried on the infantry pack. The hasty trenches discussed and illustrated in this section are given as examples of good practice rather than as standards to be followed rigidly. They represent excavations to gain hasty cover and to be developed eventually into forms approximating deliberate trenches."[20]

The foxhole as described in 1940 was a simple affair, a hole three feet wide at the top, illustrated in three forms which were intended to be stages in development. The prone or crouching foxhole, one foot six inches deep, two feet six inches wide at the bottom; kneeling, two feet six inches deep, two feet four inches at the bottom, and the standing, three to three and one-half feet deep, depending on the height of the occupant, and two feet wide at the bottom. All featured a parapet and parados made from the spoil, about a foot from the hole.[21]

By the time the 1944 edition of *FM 5-15* was printed the United States had been in the war long enough to acknowledge that long trenches had no place in modern warfare, and hasty fortifications were elevated to the primary type of entrenchment. Troops occupy their foxholes only when "contact with the enemy is imminent or in progress."[22] This was temporary shelter for rapidly moving troops. The design was now more than a simple hole in the ground and plans for both one-man and two-man versions, "when men must work in pairs or when, for psychological reasons, battlefield comradeship is desired,"[23] were given. They were designed to offer protection against "small-arms fire, artillery shell fragments, airplane fire or bombing, and the crushing action of tanks".[24]

The one-man foxhole was now a rectangle, its long side parallel to the front, four to five feet deep "depending on the height of man",[25] two feet front to back and three and one-half feet wide. The soldier stood on a firestep, two feet square, the rest of the floor sunken an additional one and a half feet. The soldier could sit on the fire step and bend over if a tank passed over, hopefully deep enough to avoid being crushed. A foot from the hole and completely encircling it was a three-foot-wide parapet built up from spoil.

The two-man design was similar, but six feet wide, with two firesteps and a single two by two-foot sunken floor.

"Connecting trenches", it is stressed, "are conspicuous to aerial observers and on aerial photographs, and thus reveal the defensive dispositions. Continuous connecting trenches are not dug as a normal procedure."[26]

The official *Dictionary of United States Army Terms* of 1944 defines a foxhole simply as a "small pit, usually for one or two men, used for cover in the battle area".[27]

The lessons learned during WWII were incorporated into the 1949 edition of *FM 5-15*. "Field fortifications are *defensive* fortifications only. In World War II the infantry learned that to stop and dig in when not actually forced to do so by the enemy was a costly mistake".[28] Foxholes were now "the individual rifleman's basic defensive position".[29] They were to be built "as small as practicable, to present the minimum target to enemy fire", "wide enough for the shoulders of a man sitting on the firing step", and at last three feet wide. The floor below the firing step now sloped ten degrees towards a sump hole, not bigger than eight inches, which travelled downwards at a thirty-degree pitch for eighteen inches. Ideally rain would collect in the hole rather than the floor, and any grenades tossed into the foxhole could be kicked down the hole.[30]

Variations were given for two and three-man foxholes. It was also recommended to add overhead cover, with timbers or "any expedient material at hand".[31] Camouflage was emphasized, and vegetation was replaced over spoil parapets, or else the spoil was carried off somewhere inconspicuous.

During their basic training soldiers were taught to dig in quickly, approximating regulation foxhole dimensions as closely as possible. They were issued entrenching tools for the task. The M-1910, standard issue during WWI, was a fixed blade short shovel, just over 22 inches long, sturdily built and still common at the end of WWII. The M-1943 was issued in the later part of WWII and, with its folding blade, was easier to pack. Whichever the soldier carried, it was considered one of their most valuable pieces of equipment.

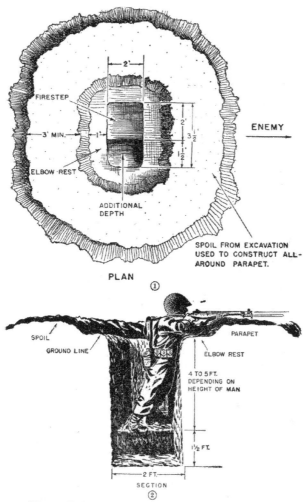

Figure 17. One-man foxhole. (Camouflage omitted.)

Figure 39 A "standard" WWII foxhole. U.S. Army Field Manual FM 5-15 Field Fortifications, 1944.

While troops were encouraged to strive for regulation foxholes during training, those made during combat were not always so meticulous. They were dug quickly, often under fire, sometimes simple holes scooped out of the sand with a helmet, in a forest floor with an entrenching tool, or in a river bank with whatever was available.

Though some soldiers spent more time tidying up their excavations, reinforcing and deepening them, they were usually more simple affairs, rough burrows that were not meant to be occupied for more than a few hours.

Many of the foxholes at Anzio were occupied by the same soldiers for months and were continuously improved for safety and comfort. Logs and wood from ruined buildings were used to reinforce walls that might otherwise collapse. More logs piled with dirt formed a roof that protected from shrapnel and "popcorn bombs", German antipersonnel cluster bombs. Nothing protected from direct artillery hits.

Salvaged doors were used for ceilings to keep the dirt from falling in. Floors were improved, sometimes with straw, sometimes with more salvaged wood. Many foxholes had dry spots for sleeping bags, a shelf or two, a small gallery of pinups and photos from home, a mirror and whatever else could be salvaged from one of the Anzio villas. Some reached epic proportions, and were more like underground parlors than foxholes, wired for lights, with stoves for heat, rugs, and furniture. Ernie Pyle describes one with "a wooden floor, shelves and nails on the wall for every item, a writing desk with table lamp, a washstand with big mirror, porcelain lampshades with little Dutch girls painted on them - and best of all, hidden on a shelf I noticed two fresh eggs."[32]

Pyle wrote about an even more elaborate dugout that was "as big as a living room back home. You can stand up in it." It had a table and chairs, four cots for the tank company officers who occupied it, a wooden floor, "one of those funny Italian stoves, which for some reason are always painted pink",[33] and a radio.

More than a luxury for the fortunate soldier who could find one, a radio was a link to the outside world. The dugout built by Corporal El Joseph Sunyogh of the 3rd Infantry Division in the side of a hill was heavily fortified with logs and soil, cool during the day and warm at night. Out of all the comforts of home he and his buddy managed to add to it, Corporal Sunyogh most valued his simple razor blade radio.[34]

It is a persistent part of the lore of the foxhole radio that they were prohibited and had to be kept hidden. While it is true that troops were not allowed to carry personal radios during an invasion, they were usually overlooked once soldiers were dug in. "They never gave us any kind of a hard time," recalled 45th Division medic Ray McAllister. "I don't even know if they knew that we were doing it, but they had to have because it was a common enough thing. There were probably half a dozen in the company and I'm sure they knew what was going on and I never heard a peep about a problem."[35]

Word of the foxhole radio spread across the beachhead, and the *Stars and Stripes'* Eldon Phelps article took it further. "The military newspaper, The *Stars and Stripes*, published instructions on how to make a crude radio by using the field phone for reception," Saburo Nishime, of the 100th Battalion, 442nd Regimental Combat Team, would later recall. "It involved making up a few wire turns taken from the field communication wire, then taking a razor blade to act as a crystal and moving a single stiff wire around the crystal until contact with a radio station was made. We were able to listen to Axis Sally broadcasting from Rome."[36]

Ray McAllister learned how to make them from another soldier, and while in Nettuno he "got a cardboard carton that oatmeal had been shipped in and I wound my first coil. Of course wire was all over in crashed aircraft and what all, and so I stripped out some wire and stole a pair of earmuffs out of a crashed German plane and earphones and used a razorblade as a crystal and played around with it until I got 'Axis Sally'."

Not one to be content with his first effort, McAllister experimented with foxhole radios for the rest of his time at Anzio. "I used all kinds of different coils, some of them worked, some didn't. Some of them were massive eighth inch copper wire, and I got them out of aircraft and trucks and tanks that had been damaged. Anytime I'd find a coil I'd try it out. Some of them gave me stations and some didn't. You'd move the whisker back and forth over the surface of the crystal until you got something. Sometimes the different coils and transformers I'd find, I'd unwind the wire. And sometimes I would just use them just as I found them. It was not prime listening, I mean, you had to diddle around until you got it and then you'd listen a while, and as I recollect it would fade and you'd have to move the tickler a little bit. It was good enough to kill a lot of dead time, you're otherwise bored out of your everlovin' gourd."[37]

Not every unit had a foxhole radio. Some had one, others had many. They were common enough to be mentioned in unit histories. The

Informal History of the 601st Tank Destroyer Battalion reports that "there were ammunition shortages, 'Paratrooper' scares, 'spy' scares and the funny, ineffective propaganda leaflets. Sally was on the air all day and night with her 'Easy Boys, there's danger ahead!' and the names and addresses of the recently captured. The 'Foxhole radio' came into wide use."[38]

"To help pass the long hours in dugouts", notes the War Department's *Anzio Beachhead*, "men improvised radio sets on which they could listen to the Fifth Army Expeditionary Station and also to Axis propaganda broadcasts".[39]

More foxhole radio stories were being printed in the stateside press. Eldon Phelps' interview appeared in dozens of papers across the country throughout late April and Early May, and in late May the *Boston Daily Globe* printed an anonymous letter from a soldier on the Anzio beachhead to remind readers "how badly the boys out there want radios and perhaps to suggest a solution to ingenious soldiers". The unnamed soldier had some experience making crystal radios as a child. "For the parts that I have, there is nothing to it. So far I can get one station. It comes in nicely. My crystal is an old razor blade. The earphones came out of a tank. They call it the foxhole radio and I sure keep it in one."[40]

New articles continued for months after the breakout from the Anzio beached on May 27, some with more detailed construction descriptions.

Corporal Fred B. Cassel, reported a Biloxi Herald article, built a radio from "nothing more than a flat board, six nails, a razor blade, earphones, and 10 feet of copper wire. The wire is strung from one nail to the other, all of which are partially driven into the board at various intervals. The razor blade serves the purpose of a crystal and the wire is run off the board in two places to act as a ground and an aerial."[41] Other men in his unit, who at first doubted the "contraption" would work, decided they needed their own radio once they heard Cassel's play music. "Nine of them now have sets of their own... and the others are all hustling to get on the bandwagon."

Some articles were not as descriptive as they were hopeful. "Weather here at Anzio is swell. I already have a sun tan", writes Corporal Marvin Peterson. "A buddy of mine is attempting to make a radio from old razor blades and wire. It's just like a crystal set. Hope he makes a good set."[42]

Corporal John Savacool, who edited the Third Division newspaper, provided instructions detailed enough to replicate a working radio. "Attach the aerial to the razor blade. Do the same with one wire from the earphone. The wire from the cat's whisker goes to one end of the coil. One end of the coil and the second wire from the earphone are grounded. The razor blade is tacked to a dry piece of wood or some other piece of insulating material. To tune the radio, move the cat's whisker around the flat surface of the razor blade."[43]

Sergeant Charles Myrick recommended wrapping the coil around a cardboard grenade or bazooka rocket case.[44] He later recalled reading about it "somewhere", possibly in the Stars and Stripes, and that "you had to follow directions exactly, no short cuts".[45]

Very few contemporaneous photographs of field-built foxhole radios are known to exist. A picture taken for *YANK* but apparently never used shows an unidentified soldier sitting in front of a tent, wearing headphones and operating a foxhole set. His radio has a neatly wound coil and what appears to be a simple wire cat whisker used with a razor blade screwed to the board.[46]

One of the many photos Private Waldon H. Johnson of the 34th Infantry Division brought back from Anzio is of the sand bag lined entrance to the foxhole he occupied with his lifelong friend, Bill Dodd, Jr. Seated with them is Milton Fauch, wearing an earphone, his arm resting on a wooden board. On another smaller board is attached, vertically, a wire wrapped tube, the coil of a foxhole radio.[47]

Built by another soldier whose name Johnson since forgot or never knew, the copper wires and headphones were provided by the division's wire crew. It had a pencil for a cat whisker instead of a bare wire or safety pin, and the "copper wire on its original spool"[48] served as the coil. "Axis Sally was the only station we could hear," and it was one of only two razor radios he saw during the war.

Most foxhole radios, or crystal radios, for that matter, have the same basic components. An antenna, which carries alternating electric currents induced by captured radio waves to a coil and, sometimes, a capacitor which form a resonant circuit. A detector demodulates the radio signal, separating audio from the carrier. An earphone or headphones convert the audio signal to sound. A ground serves as a return connection for current. A piece of wood is usually used for a base, and tacks, nails or screws hold everything in place.

Figure 40 Unidentified soldier with a foxhole radio at Anzio. Photograph No. 111-SC-282168; 1944. Records of the Office of the Chief Signal Officer, Record Group 111; National Archives at College Park, College Park, Maryland.

The antenna was made from whatever piece of wire was available, strung between trees or upright boards. More wire was used for the ground, either stuck directly into damp soil or attached to a stake or some other long piece of metal that could be pounded into the earth.

Wire was the easiest thing to find. Any disabled vehicle had more than enough wire to wind a coil and make an antenna. As Fred Sheehan noted, "the miles of copper wire and tubing inside a Messerschmitt or a Focke-Wulf were of much more than souvenir value. With the fine copper wire and an empty K ration box and a razor blade, an imaginative soldier could fashion a workable variation of the old crystal radio set."[49]

Figure 41 A closer look at the "anonymous" Anzio radio.

Figure 42 A foxhole radio at Anzio. Pictured are Waldon H. Johnson, left, William "Bill" Dodd Jr. of Glassboro, New Jersey, inside the dugout, and Milton Fauch of Tennessee, using the razor blade radio. Courtesy Waldon H. Johnson and Ruth Ekberg.

Coils were wound around cardboard tubes that once held ammunition or food, or the wire was left on the tube it was originally shipped with. Some coils were found readymade, some were wrapped around pieces of wood, and at least one was wound around a beer bottle.

Capacitors may have improved tuning but were rarely if ever used in Anzio foxhole radios. One could have been easily built using alternating layers of aluminum foil and paper. Assuming enough foil could have been gathered it would likely not have been worth the effort since tuning was not as critical at Anzio where only one or two stations were broadcasting. If there were several strong stations in an area, however, it would have been possible to hear them all at once.

Some soldiers patrolled at night specifically to find parts for foxhole radios. Warren C. Garman of the Second Battalion, Sixth Armored Infantry Regiment was determined to make his own receiver after listening to one that was made by another battalion. He found most of the parts he needed from a German plane that had been shot down. "This plane, when it went down, it scattered itself all over the place, and I just walked around and found that coil, and I said, dog gone I'm gonna' make me one!"[50]

"The tough part of making our own radios" according to Leroy D. Good "was the fact that you had to use headsets to hear, and they were few and far between.[51] The headphone, mechanically the most complicated part, was the one component that the soldier could not easily make. Those available from crashed aircraft and disabled vehicles were quickly salvaged. Some were borrowed. And some were acquired by other means. Don Welling "used to go out and patrol at night and look for earphones. We didn't give a damn about the krauts, we wanted some earphones. So we'd find a jeep that had a radio on it, and then we would crowd around and we'd talk to the driver and the occupant, just keep them occupied, then we had two guys get right in the back of that jeep and start looking for those earphones. And I'm sure that we had pretty much all of the earphones on the beachhead lined up. I probably made about, well I would guess a dozen sets, and gave them out."[52]

For a cat whisker, Eldon Phelps simply used the end of a copper wire. Others followed suit. The loose wire would have been difficult to adjust and easily knocked out of position. Don Welling and others used safety pins. Found in first aid and sewing kits, they were a common cat whisker substitute before the war and made a firmer contact that was less prone to jarring than a piece of wire.[53] Leroy Good made his cat whisker with a needle stuck through a cork, which insulated the needle from fingers while it was being adjusted. Some, like the one used by Waldon Johnson, used the graphite from a pencil to contact the razor blade.

Although simple to make, the razor blade detector was, in terms of the physics involved, the most complicated part. The soldiers putting them together, without realizing it, were making diodes from scrap. Modeled after crystal detectors, the galena was replaced with the far less sensitive and more difficult razor blade. The substitution is, at first glance, puzzling, but what led to it, besides a spirit of improvisation, was an almost subconscious knowledge of radio lore.

.

16 Short and Neatly Trimmed

A razor blade is a poor substitute for a crystal detector. It is much less sensitive than a galena crystal and much more difficult to adjust. But it does work, and it works the same way, demodulating the radio signal intercepted by an aerial and passing the audio to a pair of headphones.

Many of the soldiers at Anzio would have at some point made or used a crystal radio and at least some would have known what materials made good detectors. A few wrote home to request galena crystals in their care packages, and some remembered that a synthetic galena crystal could be made by melting lead and adding a little powdered sulfur. Knowledge of these more established and reliable detectors would have been at least as likely to spread by word of mouth at Anzio as the exotic razor blade and cat whisker, yet despite the familiarity and availability of other, better detectors, the razor blade was the one that caught on.

There were several things in its favor. For one thing, it worked. As difficult as it was to adjust, hearing music at all, even faintly, would have been astonishing to the soldier who had sat alone in a foxhole for weeks.

And razor blades were common. Not necessarily new, sharp blades, but every soldier had a shaving kit, and most at least had an old dull blade.

The militaries of the world have had a long and complicated relationship with facial hair. Beards and mustaches generally follow the civilian sensibilities of the day, but often whether a man wore a given style of beard or mustache, or, for that matter, hair, depended on his rank, unit or event specialization.

Roman legionaries tended to be clean shaven, while some of the older officers and standard bearers were bearded. Those who shaved used iron blades mounted in bronze handles, or else knapped flint or obsidian.

In Europe beards tended to fall in and out of favor depending on royal fashion. If the king had a beard, then his male subjects, especially those in the upper classes and the military, tended to wear one as well. The ancient Greeks wore beards until Alexander shaved his. Hadrian was the first Roman emperor to grow a beard, and though initially shocking, the men of Rome soon followed.

Beards shrank and grew and disappeared with time, borders, social position and religious edict through the Middle Ages. They were rare in the 15th century except on older men and officials. In 1521 Francis I of France was seriously burned on the face by a piece of burning wood hurled during a Twelfth Night snowball fight that had gotten out of hand. He stopped shaving to conceal the scar, making the beard once again popular in French court. Henry VIII of England, hearing of Francis' beard, had to have one of his own, and the fashion spread to England.

The 17th century saw longer hair and smaller, more stylized beards, and for most of the 18th century the men of Europe and its North American colonies were, for the most part, clean shaven.

Facial hair was a rarity in America and much of Europe for most of the 18th and the first half of the 19th centuries, so much so that some men were persecuted for having beards.[1] Shaving was now done with straight razors, lighter steel blades that held an edge better than the earlier iron blades.

The first manual to outline regulations for the American Army, von Steuben's 1779 *Regulations for the Order and Discipline of the Troops of the United States*, does not mention shaving, though it does discourage unkempt hair.

"The oftener the soldiers are under the inspection of their officers the better; for which reason every morning at troop beating they must inspect into the dress of their men; see that their clothes are whole and put on properly; their hands and faces washed clean; their hair combed; their accoutrements properly fixed, and every article about them in the greatest order."[2]

In the first official American Army order regarding shaving, issued in 1780, General George Washington "expected that the men for daily

Guards will appear upon the Grand and other Parades shaved, combed and powdered and their Cloaths as clean as Circumstances will admit. Although our situation unhappily does not allow us to make as military an appearance as could be wished in the last respect yet it is in the power of the officers to see the first carried into Execution. The officers of the day will pay particular attention to this matter and when any men are found defective as to the above report the Corps to which they belong."[3]

Shaving was specifically mentioned in the *General Regulations* of 1821, the first completely revised army regulations since von Steuben's *Regulations* and its revisions. Non-commissioned officers were responsible for inspecting their men's grooming and hygiene, specifically "that they wash their hands and faces daily - habitually, immediately after the *general fatigue*; that they, at the same time, shave themselves (if necessary,) and brush or comb their heads; that, afterwards, those who are to go on duty, put their arms, accoutrements, dress, &c. in the best order, and that such as have permission to pass the chain of sentinels, are in the dress that may be ordered."[4]

Sideburns had been for some time inching lower and growing ever more robust when the *Regulations for the Uniform and Dress of the Army of the United States* was written in 1839, foreshadowing a renaissance of facial hair. "The hair to be short, or what is generally termed cropped," the *Regulations* specified, "the whiskers not to extend below the lower tip of the ear, and a line thence with the curve of the mouth; mustaches will not be worn by officers or men on any pretense whatever."[5]

Texans should note that the *General Regulations for the Government of the Army of the Republic of Texas* from the same year make no mention of shaving or the cutting or even combing of hair, but, borrowing a page from the 1835 *General Regulations for the Army of the United States*,[6] stress that general cleanliness should be given "the utmost attention" for the "health and comfort of the soldier. Bathing is recommended, and when conveniences for it are to be had, the men should be made to bathe at least once a week. The feet to be washed always at least twice a week."[7]

The mustache took its first tentative steps toward a popular comeback in the 1840s, though the army was not ready to concede when they issued a Circular on May 31, 1843 reminding all commanders and inspectors that they were required to enforce the standing regulations "relative to whiskers, mustaches, and cut of the hair".[8] General Order 35 of July 6, 1848 hinted that the rules might relax. It was essentially the same as the 1839 *Regulation*, except that now "moustaches will not be worn (except by cavalry regiments) by officers or men, on any pretense whatever".[9] The concession for cavalry regiments was served with an admonishment. "The non-observance of the above regulation (tolerated during the war with Mexico) is no longer permitted. It is enjoined upon all officers to observe and enforce the regulation."

Mustaches boldly reappeared on American lips in the 1850s, soon followed by ever more elaborate beards, in what was popularly dubbed "the beard movement", part of an overall trend toward what Victorian men viewed as a more masculine appearance, firmly breaking with the narrow-waisted jackets and other "less manly" folderol of previous decades.

The tide was strong enough that the army, for the first time, permitted beards with *General Order No. 2* of January 6, 1853. "Regulations for the Uniform and Dress of the Army", it instructed, "is amended as follows: The beard is to be worn at the pleasure of the individual, but when worn to be kept short and neatly trimmed."[10] "Short" and "neatly trimmed" would persist in regulations, in one form or another, from clarity or habit, well into the twentieth century.

Beards were never more fashionably acceptable in the United States than in the mid-19th century. Men of all classes were growing and meticulously grooming their facial hair, something that would have been considered an affectation or eccentricity a generation earlier. In 1861 Abraham Lincoln became the first President with facial hair, having grown a beard only months before at the urging of 11-year-old Grace Bedell. Every president from Lincoln through Taft, save two, Andrew Johnson and William McKinley, sported a beard or moustache. None have since.

Both the Union's revised *Regulations* of 1863[11] and the *Regulations for The Army of The Confederate States*[12] of the same year echoed the 1853 *General Order*, requiring "the hair to be short; the beard to be worn at the pleasure of the individual; but, when worn, to be kept short and neatly trimmed." Despite the rule, beards and mustaches reached epic proportions on both sides during the Civil War, especially among older soldiers and officers. There were practical reasons for keeping a short beard, or for shaving altogether, and the Sanitary Commission warned that "the hair and beard should be closely cropped. If vermin make their appearance, apply promptly to the surgeon for means to destroy them."[13] Yet fashion triumphed, and long and elaborate beards persisted despite the threat of lice.

The 1890s saw a decline in beards, though the mustache persisted. The 1895 *Regulations* still permitted beards, more concisely now, specifying simply that "the hair will be kept short and the beard neatly trimmed".[14]

Civilian facial hair was in decline in the early years of the 20th century, hastened by the introduction of King Camp Gillette's safety razor in 1904.

Although most young American men of military age had entered the 20th century beardless, officers and older soldiers often retained their mustaches, and "short and neatly trimmed" remained in the Regulations.[15]

Even mustaches were rare among American troops arriving in France in 1917. Facial hair was more common among European soldiers and British regulations *required* a moustache be worn until the final years of the war.[16] American beards were still allowed in the 1917 *Regulations*,[17] again, as long as they were "short and neatly trimmed".

The navy's rules were similar. The 1913 *Regulations for the Government of the Navy of the United States* simply required that "the hair and beard shall be kept short."[18] The 1918 *Bluejacket's Manual* more thoroughly described a regulation haircut, if not beard style. "The hair and the beard shall be kept short. The hair should be cut close to the back and sides and trimmed naturally down the back of the neck. Hair should be left in sufficient length on the top for brushing, but no 'forelock' will be permitted. Hair should not be cut square across the neck, nor shall the back of the neck be shaved."[19]

The Marines allowed beards, but their 1917 *Uniform Regulations* left it to the commanding officer to determine what was or was not acceptable. "The hair, beard and mustache shall be worn neatly trimmed. The face shall be kept clean shaved, except that a mustache, or beard and mustache, may be worn at discretion. No eccentricities in the manner of wearing the hair, beard, or mustache shall be allowed."[20]

The deployment of chemical weapons in the First World War necessitated the use of gas masks, and rules for their use overrode standard beard regulations. The *Defensive Measures Against Gas Attacks* manual specified that "within 5 miles of the front line a box respirator will always be carried, and every man will be clean-shaven, except that a moustache be worn."[21] It went on to say that "every man should shave at least once a day, as a heavy growth of beard may permit the entrance of sufficient gas to injure a man seriously. For the same reason the hair should be kept short enough to nowhere catch under the edges of the mask."[22]

The First World War did not end the wearing of beards in the United States by young men. That had already happened. It did arguably hasten the decline of mustaches, at least the more elaborate styles. And a well-sealed gas mask required and encouraged soldiers to shave as frequently as possible.

Newly arriving soldiers were often still using straight razors, which required a considerable amount of maintenance to keep properly sharpened. Readily available safety razor blades could simply be replaced when dull, and many formerly loyal straight razor users converted and never looked back.

While working as a salesman for the Crown Cork and Seal Company, King Camp Gillette was inspired by discarded bottle caps to create a new product that would be quickly used by the consumer and replaced. The safety razor had already been invented by the time Gillette hit upon the idea, but available blades were of forged steel, making them more expensive to produce that Gillette's stamped blade.

Production began in 1903, and the following year Gillette sold over 100,000 blades, helped by low cost and successful advertising promising "no stropping, no honing". Sales were already brisk when America entered the war, with 1,094,182 razors and 9,619,030 dozen blades sold in 1917.[23]

In 1918 the army contracted Gillette to distribute the "khaki set" to soldiers, a canvas pouch that carried a Gillette razor, blade and a small mirror. 3,479,472 razors and 3,002,355 dozen extra blades were distributed. Together with a healthy civilian market, Gillette sold 4,580,987 razors and 12,895,618 dozen blades that year.

The Khaki Sets, as well as the "U. S. Service Set", a more ornate version housed in a metal case with an "indestructible" mirror, could be purchased and sent as gifts to soldiers and sailors. The Service Set cost five dollars, the same price as a better civilian set. As a Gillette advertisement said, "every man in khaki ought to have one".

Gillette's contract with the army provided a needed boost in income after overseas sales dwindled during the war, and more importantly it reinforced product recognition and loyalty. In 1920 Gillette sold 2,090,616 razors and 19,051,268 dozen blades.[24] Many returning soldiers were now committed safety razor users, and Gillette blades fit their army issued razors.

Gillette's original razor blade patent expired in 1921, opening the field for dozens of competitors. They responded by dropping the price of their standard razor from five dollars to one dollar. The real money, after all, was in the blades. The gamble paid off, and in 1921 Gillette sold 4,248,069 razors and 19,531,861 sets of blades.[25]

Outside of some religious and cultural circles, beards were still a rarity when America entered World War II. They were still allowed according to Paragraph 7 of AR 40-205 *Military Hygiene and Sanitation* (1942), the army regulation covering hygiene during most of the war. Once again "the hair will be kept short and the beard neatly trimmed".[26]

The navy now borrowed the Marine's regulation of 1917 and specified in the 1943 *Bluejacket's Manual* that no "eccentricities" would be allowed.[27]

Beards were finally prohibited altogether by the United States Army during the Vietnam War, a reaction to the countercultural resurgence of long hair and beards. Mustaches, neatly trimmed, were still allowed.

Razor blades were not rationed during World War II, but the War Production Board limited the amount that could be manufactured, making them less available stateside. The government encouraged civilians to use less metal, including razor blades, and recycle what they could. "It takes 12,000 razor blades to make the tail assembly for one 2,000-pound bomb", the Paramount "Victory Short" *A Letter from Bataan* reminded movie audiences, in hopes that they would conserve if they knew that the blades they save "might make the egg that wrecks the German munitions dump".[28]

Razor blade manufacturers focused much of their efforts during the war on the military market. Contracts were awarded to Gillette, Gem, Star and others to supply blades and shaving kits to post exchanges and ship's stores. Since there were several brands of blades available to servicemen, none necessarily had the significant advantage in brand recognition that had benefitted Gillette during the last war. Instead, manufacturers concentrated on advertising and promotions directly aimed at soldiers and sailors.

The razor blade division of the Marlin Firearms Company, started in 1935 as an extra source of income and to extend the visibility of the Marlin brand, printed a series of humorous cartoon ads directed towards a military audience.

The American Safety Razor Corporation, manufacturer of Gem

razor blades, set up small recording studios in service centers where members of the armed forces could record, free of charge, two-minute messages on light weight "Voices of Victory" phonograph discs to be sent home. Similar services were offered by the Red Cross, Pepsi Cola and the U.S.O.

Gillette, Marlin, and Gem all produced blades in special muted "camouflage" wrappers, ostensibly because they were less visible if discarded than their usual, brightly colored packaging. More to the point, a wrapper specially designed for servicemen had marketing appeal, and the packaging helped to identify any returned stock.

Marlin print ads featured eye catching, humorous single-panel cartoons extolling the advantages of a Marlin blade, or patriotically reminding civilians that "because Marlin Blades are popular in the armed forces - make *yours* last longer!" Promotional matchbooks and snappy radio jingles kept the Marlin name relevant even when blades were scarce.

In May 1944 Marlin received a letter, hand written on three pages of Red Cross stationary, from a twenty-four-year-old Second Lieutenant stationed on the Anzio beachhead. It would be the centerpiece of one of their most successful advertising campaigns and help secure the foxhole radio in the lore of radio enthusiasts and school children for decades.

"May 9, 1944
Anzio Beachhead
Dear Sirs,

Just a few lines to tell you of a way your razor blades are being used that you had not imagined possible. After the blades are used they are usually discarded but that is not the case now. What I am about to explain will probably give you quite a laugh.

Here it is: Your Marlin Double Edge Blade is used to make a fox-hole *radio* for the Yank infantry man on this Beachhead. That's right and believe it or not it works. The materials needed are easily obtained. All that is need is a coil of wire (insulated), a safety pin, a head set & a used Marlin razor blade.

Here is a diagram of how it looks."

The letter included a schematic sketch of the radio, with blade, safety pin, phones, and a coil with 120 turns.

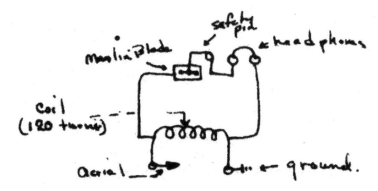

Figure 43 The sketch Maxie Rupert sent to Marlin of his radio. Courtesy Maxie Rupert.

"Here's how it works. The razor blade is tacked down with a wire tapped to it & going on to one side & on to the aerial. The other side of the coil goes to the ground & to one side of the head set. From the other side of the head set a wire goes to the safety pin which is driven into some wood at one end so the pin may be turned. Then the free end of the pin is moved across the unground part of the Marlin blade & in that way you can find your station. Reception is very good & at night we can get several stations including Berlin "Sally" propaganda programs put on in English.

I hope this is as interesting to you as we enjoy having some sort of entertainment.

Sincerely yours,
Lt. M. L. Rupert
Hq. Co. 3rd Bn. 157 Inf."[29]

It was written by 2nd Lieutenant Maxie Rupert, Communications Officer of the 3rd Battalion, 157th Infantry Regiment. Born in Springfield, Missouri, he studied electricity and radio in high school and, upon entering the army in 1942, communications at Fort Benning. The foxhole radio was already established by the time Rupert arrived at Anzio as a replacement, and he was naturally drawn to it. Scrounging the necessary supplies, he built what was by then one of the standard designs of foxhole radio, with a simple razor blade and safety pin detector. For his efforts, like many of the other foxhole radio builders, he was able to listen to German propaganda broadcasts from Rome.[30]

For Baldwin and Mermey, Marlin's public relations firm, whose other clients included Coca Cola and The Hershey Chocolate Company, Rupert's letter was a windfall. It had appeal as a soldier's story and fit well with Marlin's marketing as the GI's preferred blade. To help expand the story, which they planned to distribute to markets across the country, they wrote Rupert's father requesting the younger Rupert's age, marital status, previous interest in radio, and "other information up to 100 words you think would be of interest".[31]

A copy of Rupert's letter was sent to O. B. Hanson, the chief engineer at NBC, who built a working model of the set. It was successfully tested at the NBC Studios and, again for the press, at the Marlin Company office in New York. A photograph taken of the NBC set was widely circulated, becoming a sort of stateside archetype of what a foxhole radio should look like.

Figure 44 Leonard Harrison, advertising manager for Marlin razor blades, with a model of Maxie Rupert's foxhole radio.

Hanson recommended attaching a piece of pencil lead to the safety pin for better reception, an improvement some soldiers at Anzio had already figured out, and a detail that would become part of foxhole radio lore and a standard part of the design in most civilian built sets.

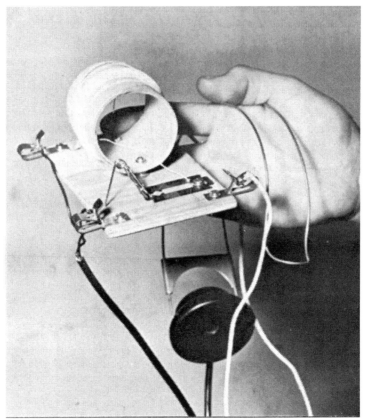

Figure 45 The N.B.C. foxhole radio model. Courtesy Maxie Rupert.

He also stated that the Marlin blade's blued surface was responsible for the rectification, a statement that led to a debate over the rectifying powers of blue versus standard blades that still occasionally flares up among enthusiasts.[32]

Rupert's story was distributed to 1,300 newspapers across the country,[33] most of them printing it sometime between June 12 and June 20. Some of the articles were brief, some were more thorough and included much of the original letter and details from the press release. Papers that included it in their regular radio column tended to add a little flourish of their own.

Jack Gould, radio critic at the *New York Times*, was fascinated with the foxhole radio story and went so far as to build his own set before writing about it. In addition to Rupert's original drawing and letter and Hanson's notes, Gould's article included his own observations. His radio worked with different makes of razor blade, and he recommended finding a "rough" spot, either where the maker's name was stamped on the blade, or else scratched with a nail file. Nails served as binding posts to connect everything, as long as they were not rusty. Gould's model "outdid even the most modern set, in that no tuning was necessary; all the stations came in at once."[34]

The *Times* received several letters in response to Gould's article, including one from Dr. James H. Pittman, Chairman of the English Department of the Newark College of Engineering, who built a set when some of his students doubted that it could be made to work. "Any old radio nut," including, no doubt, himself, "can see that it ought to work if the signal is strong enough." The set worked well and gave him "a nostalgic thrill relearning how to listen to subaudible signals after all these years", though he preferred the radio programming of his youth to "the tripe the razor blade brought in today".[35]

Fourteen years later Gould would again write about the foxhole radio in a book that would reinforce its place in amateur radio lore.

At 1 P. M. on June 18 the foxhole radio story was broadcast during "Your Radio Reporter" over WEAF in New York and simultaneously on 99 NBC Red Network affiliate stations. It was read by Ed Herlihy, whose voice was well known on radio and Universal Newsreels, and who in later years appeared in several movies, notably as Mr. Buxton in *Pee-wee's Big Adventure*.

"... And now, as they say, here's one for the book ... What do you do with your old razor blades? That's been a familiar quip for many a year. But leave it to those GI's over in the Anzio foxholes to find the answer. They've discovered a clever use for the discarded wafers of steel. Yes, believe it or not, they make radio sets out of them. Fantastic as it may seem, here is the story.

A New York business firm received a letter from a Lieutenant who said that his soldiers had found a way to listen to radio programs while crouched in their slit trenches and foxholes. Their radio sets, he said, consisted of a Marlin blued steel razor blade, a safety pin, a few turns of wire wound on a wooden form or around the pasteboard carton of a K ration, and a telephone receiver borrowed from the communications squad. Sounds almost like a Rube Goldberg contraption, doesn't it, but it actually works.

When the lieutenant's letter was shown to O. B. Hanson, vice-president and chief engineer of the National Broadcasting Company, he turned it over to one of his staff. In a matter of minutes, the complete receiving set, only a few inches square, was working perfectly, bringing in a local station with volume to spare. Here is the way Hanson explains the workings of the little gadget: the secret, he says, lies in the blued surface of the blade. The sharp point of the safety pin, pressing down on the blue coating acts exactly like the old time crystal detector. No batteries are needed but the antenna must be a wire of good length unless the station is close by and very powerful.

But Hanson sends a helpful suggestion to the doughboys. Use a short piece of pencil lead in place of the safety pin, he says, and the little wonder receiver will work even better. The Anzio Lieutenant added in his letter that with the improvised razor blade and safety pin radio, his men had no trouble in picking up 'Berlin Sally', the Nazi propagandist who sandwiches her silly remarks about America and Americans between selections of popular music. The soldiers, the Lieutenant added, don't take her remarks seriously but they do love the music she plays for them ..." [36]

Several magazines also printed Rupert's story. *Broadcasting* ran it in their June 19 issue and mentioned both Rupert's letter and Hanson's involvement, including a picture of the NBC set. [37]

Parts of Rupert's letter were printed in the radio section of the July 17 issue of *TIME*, this time with a new drawing by James Cutter, chart maker for *TIME* and, later, the mapmaker for *Newsweek*. Cutter's stylized illustration, featuring a razor blade and safety pin mounted on a block of wood, headphones, and a schematic of the coil, antenna and ground, would be reprinted several times and become one of the "standard" foxhole radio drawings. [38]

TIME printed several responses to the article from soldiers and civilians who had built their own foxhole radio, some less successfully. Private Thomas Rees, while giving a lecture to his company, was met with skepticism when he made a sketch of the foxhole radio. "I promised that one would be made to see if the idea was practicable. One was made. It didn't work." [39]

Figure 46 Lt. Maxie Rupert. Courtesy Maxie Rupert.

Another frustrated builder was more succinct. "To date we have tried several gauges of coil wire - the article gave no particular gauge - with no success. Should we dig a foxhole?"

Charles Rinde did produce a functional radio, recommending the addition of a variable capacitor for better selectivity, and he cautioned that it took "tops in patience, skill & headphone sensitivity, plus excellent ears."

The NBC photograph was printed again in the August 1944 issue of the industry magazine *Electronics* along with a brief description but little in the way of construction details.[40] Eldon Phelps' set was also briefly mentioned the following month in *Electronics*.[41]

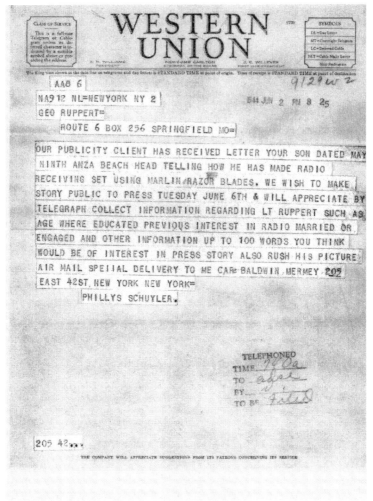

Figure 47 The telegram sent by Baldwin and Mermey to Maxie Rupert's father. Courtesy Maxie Rupert.

The first foxhole radio magazine article with any workable detail likely to be read by amateurs, and one of the first printed outside of an American publication, was in the September 1944 issue of the

British magazine *Wireless World*. It is a wry retelling of Jack Gould's *New York Times* article, including Rupert's drawing and Gould's recommendation for using a rough spot on the blade. "It goes without saying", concedes the author, "that results are excellent since neither you nor I have ever read a wireless construction article in which this claim was not made, except, of course, in *Wireless World*".[42]

Popular Mechanics included Hanson's photo of the NBC set and succinct directions for building one in their October 1944 issue, but made no mention of Rupert, Marlin or Hanson.[43] More historical detail, albeit brief, was included as a side note in the October *Popular Science* article "Radio Detectors and How They Work".[44] An assembly diagram is shown, and, once again, a photograph of the NBC set. Rupert and Hanson, but not Marlin, are mentioned. The author compares the razor blade detector to a "plate-and-needle detector", alluding to Branly's 1902 tripod self-restoring coherer, which also, unlike filings coherers, worked as a rectifier.

These two articles were the first to reach a wide American amateur audience, although many amateurs were likely already aware of the foxhole radio. As early as August 1944 classified advertisements were printed in *Popular Science* and other magazines offering plans to make a "tubeless radio with razor blades" for thirty-five cents.[45]

Marlin continued their foxhole radio marketing for several months. A large board for use in store window displays was printed with a photograph of a helmeted soldier working a foxhole radio while standing in a foxhole at night. Rupert's letter was printed in the foreground, with text announcing the "strange use of a Marlin blade - soldier builds radio set using Marlin blade as 'crystal' - it works!" Some stores also received replicas of the radio to use with their displays.

An issue of Marlin's *Illustrated Current News*, a photo news poster sold by subscription to retailers by a separate Marlin division, was dedicated to the foxhole radio.[46] It featured a photograph of Lieutenant Rupert, James Cutter's illustration from *TIME*, and the ubiquitous photograph of the NBC set. A laminated copy of this edition of the *Illustrated Current News* has hung in the American Forces Network Broadcast Center (formerly AFRS) in California since it was received in 1944.[47]

Maxie Rupert was not trying to create marketing for Marlin or notoriety for himself when he wrote his letter. He only wanted a better radio and hoped Marlin would send him one.[48] Instead, they offered him a lifetime supply of Marlin razor blades, an offer he outlived by several decades.[49]

He made a career of the army, receiving three Bronze Stars for valor, a Purple Heart and Combat Infantryman Badges for both WWII and Korea. He retired with the rank of major from the Defense Property Disposal Service in 1982.

Rupert's radio was one of the later sets built at Anzio, but for a while it was the most famous. Its basic design would be revived by authors for decades, even after most had forgotten who built it or the Marlin campaign. It was the iconic foxhole radio, a simple circuit with a coil of 120 turns, safety pin, and, after O. B. Hanson reviewed it, a pencil and blue razor blade.

But there were other designs, less publicized, that offered clues as to why a razor blade would have been used as a crystal. As novel as a razor blade radio detector may have seemed, it had a long and complicated ancestry.

Figure 48 Promotional material provided by the Marlin Razor Blade Division to their dealers. Reprinted in Marlin Firearms by William S. Brophy, published by Rowman & Littlefield. Used with permission of Rowman & Littlefield.

178

17 How the Darn Thing Worked I'll Never Know

"Have just read your article about a razor-blade radio" wrote Private Ralph E. Evans, in response to the *Stars and Stripes* article about Eldon Phelps and his foxhole radio, "I have an idea which is more simple and useful to front-line boys."

The letter, printed June 1, 1944 in the Mediterranean Naples edition of *Stars and Stripes*, included an illustration of a radio that still used a razor blade, but in a very different way. "Affix two carbon sticks (taken from flash-light batteries) to a dry board. Attach an aerial to one stick and your ground wire to the other. Then attach one of the earphone wires to each of the carbon sticks. Use a razor blade for a dial by sliding it back and forth on the carbon sticks. It works."[1] The coil was simply a wire turned several times around the upright carbon sticks. There was no cat whisker, the blade simply rested on top of the carbons.

A slightly different version of the set was submitted by Lieutenant William H. Rosee, formerly of the press department at NBC's Chicago office, to the *Field Artillery Journal*. "The 'Razor Blade' radio pulls in from two to four stations - and sometimes all four at one time!" The coil was "about 75 feet of copper wire (combat wire will do) wound around a grenade container. Ear phones? - ask GI where he picks em up!"[2] The diagram shows two carbon sticks straddled by a razor blade with a flashlight battery added for bias.

Rather than the blade-as-crystal style detector used in other sets, this was a microphone detector, similar to those used by David Edward

Hughes in his 1870s experiments and by Greenleaf Whittier Pickard that led to his development of the cat whisker and mineral detector.

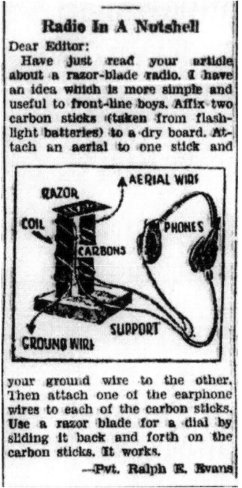

Radio In A Nutshell

Dear Editor:

Have just read your article about a razor-blade radio. I have an idea which is more simple and useful to front-line boys. Affix two carbon sticks (taken from flashlight batteries) to a dry board. Attach an aerial to one stick and

your ground wire to the other. Then attach one of the earphone wires to each of the carbon sticks. Use a razor blade for a dial by sliding it back and forth on the carbon sticks. It works.

—Pvt. Ralph R. Evans

Figure 49 An unusual foxhole radio design from the June 1, 1944 Naples edition of Stars and Stripes.

Rosee's detector was also similar to the Massie style microphone detector, two sharpened carbon blocks straddled by a steel needle, developed by Walter Wentworth Massie in 1904. What made it different was the razor blade. Massie detectors used a needle or straight pin, which soldiers would have had in their sewing kits. Razor blades seem like a strange substitute for needles in Massie detectors, but there were other types of microphone detectors that did use them.

Not
in the BOOK

MUSIC (?) FOR YOUR DUGOUT

There's no limit to a GI's ingenuity. One battery on the Anzio beachhead has a "Razor Blade" crystal radio set for every dugout! Each antenna is about 70 yds. of wire—any kind. The coil is about 75 ft. of copper wire (combat wire will do) wound around a grenade container. Ear phones?—ask GI where he picks them up! The carbon sticks act as a crystal, the razor blades as the "tickler."

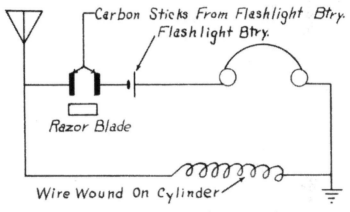

This "Razor Blade" radio pulls in from two to four stations—and sometimes all four at one time!

Lt. William H. Rosee, FA

Figure 50 A "microphone" style foxhole radio. Field Artillery Journal, July 1944.

In their heyday there were several types of microphone detector, some using carbon blocks and needles, some with a needle set on two pencil leads mounted parallel in binding posts.[3] The Shoemaker detector, a sort of reverse of Massie's detector, used carbon rods straddling upturned knife edges. Already considered out of date by Alfred Powell Morgan when he wrote about it in 1909,[4] it shows up only rarely in popular books, but when it does, as in *Modern Electrics*

1909 "Novel Detector"[5] and the *St. Nicholas* 1917 wireless station article,[6] the knife edges were usually replaced with razor blades.

The microphone detector would have already been a rarity when many WWII era soldiers were children, a relic replaced by crystals and vacuum tubes. However, it did still occasionally appear in popular radio books and magazines, and some soldiers would have encountered one in their youth, from books or older radio amateurs. The Massie and the Shoemaker versions merged, and the razor, instead of being the upright Shoemaker knife edge, became the Massie needle. The resulting razor-on-carbon configuration was the preferred microphone detector at Anzio, the result of the conflation of two subtly different, nearly forgotten devices.

As word spread that a radio had been made using a razor blade, somewhere along the line a soldier more familiar with crystal sets than microphone detectors assumed the razor was a substitute for the crystal. It worked, it was simple, and the new design took off.

Confusion of designs sometimes led to strange hybrids of microphones with cat whiskers. Leroy Good "wrapped copper wire around a spool, used carbon out of a flashlight battery, put a needle in a cork above with a razor blade between the carbon and the needle. How the darn thing worked I'll never know."[7] Douglas Bailey had a similar parts list, with "a little piece of flat wood for a base, a double edge razor blade, a piece of copper wire, the carbon out of a flashlight battery, a piece of lead out of a pencil. You would have to move the lead around the blade to pick up a radio station."[8]

The crystal radio was the standard point of reference for most of the foxhole radio builders at Anzio. Many, like George Avery of the 84th Mortar Battalion, had fond memories of building crystal sets in their youth. "Radio was new and of extreme interest to any young boy. Our church young boy's club provided plans and instructions required for assembly. So in 1930 in the midst of the depression years I produced my first set. In those times - in my depressed neighborhood - any toy that could be made without cost was a cherished asset, the only cash requirement was the purchase of the crystal at 10 cents. Obtaining the 10 cents for such frivolity was a barrier (don't laugh, my brothers worked for $1.00 a day). All other required items were easily obtainable, a thin wire wrapped around a cylinder cardboard oatmeal box, a bright safety pin to find the sensitive spot on the crystal, and, hardest of all, an earphone, in my case scrounged from a trash pile after much searching."[9]

Because crystal sets were more familiar, microphone detectors were often described as if they were crystal detectors. Even Lieutenant Rosee, who remembered the microphone detector down to the pre-Pickard battery bias, referred to it using more familiar crystal radio terms. "The carbon sticks act as a crystal, the razor blades as the 'tickler'." Harry Evans, in a letter he wrote to *QST*, describes a "source of crystal action" using the flat surface of a razor blade held against a carbon rod from a battery.[10]

The microphone style foxhole radio was not as well publicized as the crystal type, but it may have been just as common. Warren Garman, who saw several foxhole radios at Anzio, did not recall any of them looking like crystal sets. "Way I remember it, we had two carbons out of flashlight batteries. It was just two round carbons, just laid them on there and fastened them some way and put a razor blade across these two. And then slide the razor blade across both of them 'til we got the station. And that's the way you tuned it."[11]

Stuart B. Hunt skipped the carbon and "employed 3 low quality double edged razor blades. Two blades stuck parallel into a block of wood and the third (via a kitchen match prop) was moved across the other edges as a 'slider'... when a shell landed (frequently) you should have heard the QRN!" With his steel-on-steel detector he was able to pick up German propaganda from Rome, Armed Forces Radio in Naples, 100 miles away, and occasionally the American station in Tunisia, 200 miles away.[12]

Sergeant Dale Stonehouse of the 5th Company, 2nd Battalion, 2nd Regiment had a similar setup, with two blades stuck side by side in a piece of wood, with tank earphones wired to each. A third blade, its sharp edge covered by a piece of cardboard, was placed on top.[13]

Sometimes microphone detectors act like their namesake, as Private Aubrey Thomas of the 6638th Engineer Mine Clearing Company found out when he built his own copy of the receiver Ralph Evans had described in *Stars and Stripes*. "We Got the *Stars and Stripes* quite regularly. I saw an article in there on how to build a radio out of a couple of the carbon cores from regular flashlight batteries and a razor blade."[14]

Several men from his outfit followed suit, and Thomas found that "these radios took so much antenna I thought maybe we should put them all together. Our dugouts were about 50 yards apart so all together we should get better reception yet. One problem was we could hear when someone was scratching around looking for a station. One day I heard voices when I was relaxing on my bunk. It wasn't a radio station. I went to a dugout where there was a card game going on. I told them to talk into the earphone when I got back to my dugout. Sure enough we had our own private telephone line. So we could find out where the game was without leaving our dugout."[15] The razor blade and carbon microphone, rather than the headphone, was more likely to have picked up the soldier's voices.

There were other foxhole radios with Massie style detectors near Warren Garman's dugout. He used a telephone handset for a headphone, and a wire strung between trees as an antenna. "I remember that another squad hooked up to it and we could talk to one another from hole to hole."[16] Stuart Hunt made a similar discovery. "The company phone lines acted as the antenna and you couldn't pick up a phone anywhere without hearing music."[17]

Other accounts of foxhole radios, though not as detailed, hint at microphone rather than crystal style detectors. Douglas M. Bailey of the 463rd Parachute Field Artillery, saw a radio made from a "phone handset, razor blade, carbon out of a battery, lead pencil, and wire".[18] And Thomas Daniel Murphy, in his history of the 100th Infantry Battalion, wrote that "receiving sets, made with the help of the battalion communication section, consisted of two or three double-edged safety razor blades, a few pieces of wire, and a dry battery. Small enough to fit nicely into a mess kit, they could pick up 'Axis Sally,' who was broadcasting nightly from Rome."[19]

Taken all together, foxhole radios were a patchwork of radio history, a bits-and-pieces timeline of detectors, from Hughes' microphone of nails and carbon, to autocoherers and microphones, the battery biased needle detector that led to crystals and cat whiskers, and found object components cobbled together over decades by resourceful amateurs, folk detectors that used safety pins, oatmeal box coil forms, and tin foil capacitors.

They were semiconductors, field made, from scrap, born of the collective knowledge of every soldier who built one, each with their own piece of the lore, each in turn adding to it, half remembering their father's or grandfather's detector and recasting it into something more familiar. That the detectors were confused and recombined is a testament to the memory and improvisation of the soldiers that built them, and to the ability of lore to hold on to even the most obscure and antiquated details.

The soldiers who built these radios were not necessarily interested in the historical significance of their detectors. They simply wanted a working radio, some entertainment to distract them for a moment, some connection to the outside world. And if they were going to go through the effort of gathering supplies and building them, there had to be something to listen to.

18 Be Kind to Your Sets, Boys

"When we left Oran, Algeria for the invasion of Italy, she came on the LST radio and told us 1st. Armored Division soldiers we'll never reach Italy," Sergeant Warren Lee Nicely of the 69th Armored Regiment recalled about the German propaganda broadcaster known to most as "Axis Sally". "The first night at sea, the Germans bombed us and we lost two ships."[1]

There were two "Sallys". Mildred Elizabeth Gillars, who had worked in Berlin since 1935 as an English teacher, was hired in 1940 as a radio announcer by the *Reichs-Rundfunk-Gesellschaft,* the by-then nationalized German broadcasting network. Her broadcasts became more propagandistic after 1941, with tales of faithless wives and certain defeat aimed at Allied soldiers in Europe and North Africa, all interspersed with enough jazz and swing music to keep the troops listening. Though she never directly referred to herself as "Sally" on the air, she was aware the Allies had given her the nickname.

Rita Luisa Zucca, the daughter of a New York restauranteur, moved to Italy in 1938, renouncing her American citizenship to protect her family's property interests. In 1943 she was hired as an announcer by the Italian radio network for a show modeled on the propaganda broadcasts of Mildred Gillars. *Jerry's Front,* broadcast to Allies in the Mediterranean theater, followed the same basic format as Gillars' *Midge at the Mike* and *Home Sweet Home* programs, mostly clichéd propaganda interspersed with popular music. Since it was already a well-established nickname, Zucca did refer to herself as "Sally", and because of that and their similar voices and styles, Zucca and Gillars were often assumed to have been the same person, a fact that incensed Gillars.

This was not always the case, however, and the June 18, 1945 issue of *Stars and Stripes* notes the arrest of "Axis Sally" in Italy, while "Berlin Bessie", another less common name for Gillars, had not yet been located.[2]

Because it was transmitted from a strong station in Rome, *Jerry's Front* was the most likely program to be heard on radios at Anzio. "Went over to hear a radio program called 'Jerry's Front', put on by the Germans for propaganda purposes," wrote Sergeant Bill Oden of the 1st Special Service Force. "Dance records for half an hour, with bits of news. Of course this is all in English for the benefit of the American soldier. Then for the second half hour a German orchestra murdering American popular tunes, and two commentators, Sally and George, discuss the different fronts, heckle Churchill and Roosevelt. We all get a kick out of it. They read names and addresses of American P.O.W.'s too."[3]

"George" was Carl Gödel, a German broadcaster who had created the Jerry's Front program, and the band that "murdered" American tunes was "Charlie and His Orchestra", also known as "Bruno and his Swinging Tigers", a swing band that replaced some of the lyrics of popular songs with Nazi propaganda intended to discourage Allied listeners.

Jazz music was considered degenerate by the Nazis and was for the most part prohibited, though an underground jazz culture continued for some time. Propaganda Minister Joseph Goebbels despised it but saw it as a useful tool to broadcast propaganda to the Allies.

Jerry's Front opened with a band playing "It's a Long Way to Tipperary" then Zucca cooing "hello, boys. This is Jerry's front calling". "Yankee Doodle" played next, and Zucca added "this program is especially dedicated to Uncle Sam's boys" before giving the time and frequency of the next broadcast, something that was also advertised with leaflets.

Propaganda leaflets were dropped on the beachhead often, usually printed with images and messages meant to demoralize or encourage surrender. For the most part they were ineffectual, gathered as souvenirs by allied troops. One of the most collected flyers depicted a map of the coastline superimposed with a skull, with Anzio and Nettuno in the eye sockets, the water below filled with sinking ships and downed airplanes, emblazoned with the words "Beach-Head

Death's Head". Rather than having the demoralizing effect the Germans intended, the Allies made the image their own, and would later use the design for the flag of the Anzio Beachhead Veterans Association.

Figure 51 German leaflet dropped on American soldiers at Anzio advertising "Jerry's Front". Author's collection.

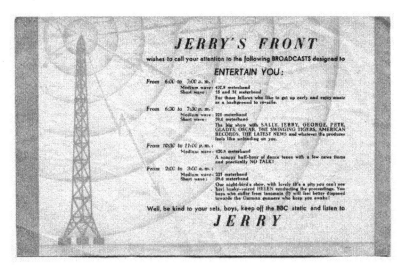

Figure 52 "Jerry's Front" leaflet, reverse.

Several leaflets advertised *Jerry's Front*, complete with broadcast times and frequencies printed over a picture of a microphone or radio tower. Rather than conceal the propagandistic nature of the broadcasts, the leaflets made light of it, even jokingly discouraging Allied soldiers from listening, at the same time criticizing the BBC. "You American doughboys are duly warned that such broadcasts are only designed to mislead and trick you under the cover of entertainment. Don't listen to Sally, Jerry, George, Pete, Gladys, Oscar, the Swinging Tigers, Helen and the rest, but stick to the British Bunking Corporation."[4] The Germans knew that the Allies were already listening. "Well, be kind to your sets, boys, keep off the BBC static and listen to JERRY."

Some programming was specifically intended for British soldiers, some for the Americans, and some was even more narrowly targeted. "We were entertained by Axis Sally's music and propaganda and thought it amusing," recalled Sergeant Hidenobu Hiyane of the 100th Infantry Battalion. "Sometimes Hawaiian songs & music to try to convince us Hawaiian boys to quit fighting and go home to loved ones."[5]

The propaganda was considered stale and laughable and usually had little effect on the Allies. "Sally" was such a part of beachhead routine and her propaganda so inane that she became something akin to a mascot, partly because the soldiers enjoyed her music, and partly because it helped to diffuse any negative affects her broadcasts may have had. One LST crew went so far as to create an Axis Sally of their own, installing an Italian statue of a bather toppled by German shell fire on the deck of their boat, giving it a helmet and naming it after the broadcaster.[6]

Lieutenant John Zappitello of the 2nd Engineer Battalion, 36th Engineer Brigade, "listened to the news (propaganda) from Axis Sally early every day, plus enjoyed the beautiful band music of the time. She actually helped the front line boys even though she attempted to send messages about home, loneliness, and fidelity regarding our wives and girlfriends."[7]

The transition from music to propaganda was sometimes intentionally jarring. Sergeant Ed Butwell of the 3rd Infantry Division recalled that "a nice song would be playing then all of a sudden machine gunfire could be heard. It would interrupt the station. Then the propaganda would be announced."[8]

Jerry's Front often broadcast information from German Intelligence in Rome specific to activities on the beachhead. "Axis Sally a lot of times would come on late in the day and give us the password for the night," recalled Ray McAllister. "If it was 'eagle sweat' you were supposed to say 'eagle' and the guy that you were challenging would say 'sweat' or you fired. It was kind of disconcerting to have 'Axis Sally' tell us 'your password for the night is eagle sweat' and then it would come down from headquarters that the password for today is 'eagle sweat'. I figure it didn't do us a whole lot of good if Axis Sally knew it and broadcast it."[9]

Sometimes the intelligence gathered was more personal. Russel Weiskircher of 157th Infantry Regiment, 45th Infantry Division, heard "Sally" read his intercepted mail, part of a truckload of mail captured by the Germans.[10]

Names of captured American and British soldiers were read along with exaggerated descriptions of how well they were being treated as POWs. "Every evening that we could we would listen to Sally and George", recalled Vere "Tarzan" Williams of the 157th Infantry Regiment. "I don't remember how long they would be on the radio but they had the popular songs from the States. Then they would give the names and serial numbers of the GIs who were captured then tell us we should go over on their side as we were fighting a losing battle anyway."[11]

The station would also from time to time announce airstrikes or artillery barrages directed towards the beachhead. Intended to be demoralizing, the announcements were usually far enough in advance that they gave troops some time to prepare. Lee Palmer of the 45th Infantry Division knew that if Sally "told us that Jerry was coming over to see us tonight (she knew exactly where we were), we knew that we would be bombed and strafed. And, of course, there was all kinds of propaganda about our wives and girlfriends running around with draft dodgers."[12]

"'Sally of the Axis' on her propaganda program, that we listened to whenever she broadcast, would state when this gun was going to fire," wrote Edmund Ball in *Staff Officer with the Fifth Army*, "and she was pretty accurate because, if she said it would fire at 10:10, we could expect to feel that dreaded thud at exactly that time."[13]

Other stations were available to soldiers with long enough antennae, stronger radios, or shortwave sets. Some heard the other "Sally's" broadcasts from Berlin, or at least assumed they were. "While I am writing you this letter we have our short-wave radio going and getting some good music from Berlin," wrote Private Joe Nemec, 1st Battalion, 7th Infantry Regiment, to his parents. "We are waiting for 'Sally' to come on soon. She is called the Berlin Bi__h and the program is for the fighting yanks and to lower our morale, but I think it raises it and has some real good music on. See it pays to be in the radio section and have a radio in your tent."[14] A few, like Stuart B. Hunt, heard American broadcasts from as far away North Africa.[15] BBC broadcasts could be heard with the right receiver, and *Jerry's Front* was not the only station broadcasting from Rome. "We made a crystal set out of razor blades and wire", wrote Lieutenant Thomas Welch of the 601st Tank Destroyer Battalion to his mother. "With the earphones from our tank radio we picked up High Mass from St. Peter's in Rome. It was really quite amazing."[16]

But by far, most of the men at Anzio were hearing "Sally". And though they dismissed the propaganda, General Eisenhower knew that the cumulative effects could be detrimental. His men needed their own station as an alternative to *Jerry's Front*, and they needed the freedom to run it themselves.

19 In the Field with the Fifth Army

Though wire still played a dominant tactical role for land forces, radio was indispensable during World War II on ships, aircraft, and land-based vehicles, and between units of fast moving troops, whose demands hastened the development of smaller, more dependable and rugged transmitters and receivers.

Signal Corps equipment grew increasingly specialized and sophisticated during the war. Their equipment catalogue, which listed 2,500 separate items during World War I, increased to over 100,000 by the end of World War II.[1] Anzio saw the first combat use of the SCR-300 "walkie talkie", a backpack mounted set that was the first truly portable FM transceiver. The five-pound SCR-536 "handie talkie", a self-contained hand held two-way radio, was the smallest transceiver developed by the Signal Corps during the war and was a favorite for front line use.

Radar improved significantly during the war through cooperation of the army and navy and through the research of civilian scientists at the Radiation Laboratory at MIT. The Rad Lab, as it was commonly referred to, worked closely with British scientists, whose development of the resonant cavity magnetron, a vacuum tube device for producing high power microwaves, allowed for the design of radar systems capable of detecting smaller objects at greater distances.

Radio surveillance took a larger role, and consequently encryption became more sophisticated. And radio was essential for resistance fighters, both to communicate between cells and to coordinate operations with Allied forces.

World War II also saw the first widespread use of radio propaganda. On the home front it was used to reinforce ideology, significantly with the state-controlled broadcasts of Nazi Germany. In the United States it was used to rally a less than enthusiastic population around what many saw as yet another European war. Propaganda broadcasts to the enemy, if used properly, could convince them they were fighting for a lost cause.

To counter enemy propaganda, the United States military would build a broadcast system of their own, to entertain, inform, and instruct. But before that was in place, some servicemen stationed in isolated outposts, using what resources were at hand, on their own initiative, built their own radio stations.

Though these stations operated independently, both from the War Department and from each other, their formats were similar. Popular music and entertainment, both recorded and live, was interspersed with news and announcements.

One of the first uses of radio to counter propaganda had its beginnings in 1939 when General Electric set up a shortwave transmitter and station as part of their exhibit at the Golden Gate International Exhibition in San Francisco. Station KGEI, using some of the newest and most sophisticated broadcast equipment of its day, could transmit to Asia or Latin America. With no firm editorial direction before the war, KGEI was at times a platform for isolationist rhetoric, a fact the government found especially problematic since the broadcasts reached well beyond national borders. Though still a private station during the war, their broadcasts took a decidedly more pro Allied and anti-Axis tone after some roundabout intervention by President Roosevelt.

KGEI was heard and rebroadcast by American forces across the Pacific, on ships and submarines, in the Philippines, New Caledonia and the Solomon Islands before other stations could be established in the Pacific and beyond.

In early 1940 the United States Army's Panama Coast Artillery Command put into place a defense network to protect the Panama Canal. The fortified artillery positions, scattered across the country in remote locations, maintained communication with headquarters through small radio sets. Because many of the emplacements were not monitoring their radios consistently, Sergeant Wayne Woods, editor of the *Panama Coast Artillery News*, was tasked with finding a way to make sure radios would be kept on and monitored. He consulted Technical

Sergeant Joseph Whitehead, who ran the transmitter, and Master Sergeant Paul Doster, the command Public Relations NCO, and the three decided that the best solution was to add recorded music to the broadcasts to keep the artillerymen listening.[2]

The plan worked and led to the establishment of station PCAC, broadcasting news, music and information on a semiregular schedule. To provide fresher material for a growing audience, Doster and Woods wrote to stateside singers and film stars hoping some would send recordings. Jack benny sent the first material, an autographed transcription disk, the first of many he would provide. More performers followed and were happy to contribute.

The station remained on the air until December 7, 1941, shut down due to concerns that attacking Japanese aircraft may use the signal to navigate by.

Several unofficial stations were built by servicemen in Alaska who had been sent there in early 1941 to defend against potential Japanese invasion. The only entertainment available to soldiers stationed on remote Alaskan islands, apart from broadcasts from Japanese propaganda stations, were a few worn out records. To fight the tedium, six men stationed at Fort Ray in Sitka - Walter Welch, Charles Gilliam, Boyd Wood, Earle Greer, Fred Wiethucter and Frank Kasala - built a small radio station with $400 of their own money.[3] Using local talent and whatever recordings they could find, station KRB gained a following among both soldiers and civilians almost from their first broadcast in October 1941. The station was unlicensed and unauthorized, facts that base officers chose to overlook. Operating at different times as KRB, GAB and, briefly, GIN, the station was ordered shut down in early 1942 by the FCC for failure to secure a license.[4] Undaunted, Private Charles Gilliam, who had been a radio technician in civilian life, along with ham radio operators Charles Green and Chet Iverson, vowed to return to the air.

Around the time the Sitka station was being built, Captain William Adams, the base finance officer at Fort Greely, Kodiak and a former radio station employee in San Francisco, announced a meeting in the base newspaper for anyone interested in starting a radio station. The twelve men who responded were assigned to develop programming, find talent, and set up an experimental station which, rather than transmitting over radio, was wired to a speaker mounted to the mess hall. The first "broadcast", a fifteen-minute variety show featuring a live band and comedy sketches, went out on October 8, 1941.[5]

Civilian contractors who were building military installations in the area took notice, and under the direction of their superintendent J. C. Henry they held three raffles to raise money for a 15-watt transmitter, turntable, microphones, and other equipment needed to run a station.

The station set up in the base's ordinance building for their first experimental broadcasts. Henry and his group, realizing the value of a permanent local radio station to morale, built a studio, control room, and auditorium that could seat a hundred people.[6] Station staff named the studio in J.C. Henry's honor.

Station KODK made its first official broadcast on January 1, 1942 programming music, locally produced shows, and news picked up from the shortwave.[7] In July 1942 the FCC granted the station a license, but since KODK had already been requested for a nearby, as yet to be built commercial station, they were given the sign WVCQ, making "the Voice of Fort Greely" the first FCC registered army broadcast station.[8] The transition to the new call sign was gradual, and the station was often referred to as KODK through 1944. Popular with both the military and civilian population, the local Rotarians raised $1,825 for a twelve-month radio transcription service for the station.[9] WVCQ broadcast from its original building almost until Fort Greely was placed in caretaker status at the end of 1944.

Meanwhile in Sitka, Charles Gilliam and his crew went to work to get back on the air, this time following FCC rules. The citizens of Sitka were pleased to be getting a local station and took a sense of pride and ownership in it, donating what money, records and talent they could. The Sitka Hotel supplied equipment, and the Sitka Rotary Club donated $1000 toward the station, which went back on the air as KRAY on August 16, 1942.[10] It was licensed by the FCC as WVCX, "Your Station North of the Nation", on November 19, 1942.[11] Though it was an army station, it was very much part of the greater community, broadcasting locally produced news, variety shows, live country music performances and church services with military and local talent.[12]

These unofficial stations were unknown to the War Department when they took their first steps toward creating a broadcast network for all armed services.

In late spring 1941 the Radio Division of the War Department's Bureau of Public Relations, responding to soldier requests, began broadcasting sports by shortwave to American forces stationed overseas. The program was expanded to include music, and initial plans included a disc jockey playing records requested by service men. Entertainers were eager to contribute their talents after December 7, and the proposed format changed to a live broadcast of troop requested performances. The new program, "Command Performance", first aired from the CBS Theater in New York on March 1, 1942. A month later it moved to a more permanent home in Los Angeles to accommodate performances by Hollywood talent. Many of the biggest film and recording stars of the day contributed. The show was popular but could only be heard by personnel with shortwave receivers, and where it could be heard the quality was affected by static and signal fading.

By May 1942 plans were underway to establish a more extensive radio system under the Special Services Division to educate, entertain and inform servicemen. General George Marshall, the Army Chief of Staff, believed that providing accurate information for troops was vital to the war effort. Soldiers, he felt, should know why they were being asked to fight; an informed serviceman is a better citizen and therefore a better serviceman.[13] To that end, Special Services would use radio, film, and print. Radio, if done right, could be the most accessible for servicemen, and certainly the most immediate.

In May 1942 Thomas H. A. Lewis, a radio executive known for his work in advertising and audience research, was commissioned by the army's Special Services Branch to build a worldwide radio network that would serve all service members, not just those who had access to a shortwave receiver.

Under Lewis' direction the Radio Section, Information and Education Branch, Morale Services Division, later renamed the Armed Forces Radio Service, was established on May 26, 1942.

Rather than relying on shortwave, the AFRS would borrow time from local broadcast stations and provide radio transcription discs, reserving shortwave for up-to-date news and sports coverage. With assistance from the Research Branch of the Special Services Division,[14] Lewis surveyed thousands of enlisted men regarding their radio listening habits to help build better programming.[15]

Lewis now needed to find the best way to get radio receivers to servicemen, and to plan how their stations would be set up and operated.

While the AFRS was planning, station KODK in Alaska was running out of programming. There was still plenty of live talent and news, but their limited record library was wearing thin. On their own initiative, station staff wrote to several radio and recording stars, hoping some would send recordings of their performances. The stars were eager to help, but by now wartime restrictions against mailing recordings outside of the continental United States were in place. Not wanting to disappoint the station, they wrote letters requesting clearance, which came as a surprise to the War Department, who until then were not aware of any military broadcast stations in Alaska.

As a result, Lewis was invited by playwright Murray Brophy, Chief of the Coordinator of Information's Overseas Facilities Bureau, to tour the stations in Alaska and to see firsthand what servicemen lacked in recreation, education and information.[16] A conversation with a driver there who had no real understanding of why he had been assigned to Alaska further convinced Lewis that soldiers would need to understand why they were fighting if they were expected to win.

Lewis was impressed with the stations in Alaska. He found them to be professionally run, providing the right balance of information and entertainment, without any real intervention or assistance from the War Department, and saw in them his model for all future AFRS stations, operating locally and more or less independently, by soldiers, for soldiers.

Once they had a budget, AFRS expanded service in Alaska and the Aleutians, absorbing the stations already there and building new ones, producing their own shows and securing agreements to rebroadcast commercial shows recorded on transcription disks.

The first AFRS stations rented time from local broadcast stations, but that proved to make scheduling difficult, and so they built their own stations.

By late 1943 AFRS controlled most overseas broadcasting for troops. A few stations still operated independently. On October 1, 1942 the First Broadcast Operating Detachment was activated and attached to the 3rd Infantry Division, tasked with taking over and operating stations in Rabat and Casablanca after the Allied invasion of North Africa on November 8. The French beat them to the Rabat station, and since there was no Casablanca station the detachment commander Lieutenant Andre Baruch asked General Patton, in charge of the Task Force at Casablanca, for permission to build one. In good spirits that day, Patton granted Baruch's request, and the detachment borrowed a 45-watt transmitter from the French and the rest of the equipment from wherever they could find it. On December 15 they made their first broadcast as "The Army Broadcasting Service - The

Voice of an American Soldier and Sailor".[17] The station, though only broadcasting a few hours a day, was an immediate success. Over time they increased their schedule, playing records, reading news, and writing their own skits. Visiting actors often lent their talents, like Humphry Bogart and Frederic March, who performed a radio play written by Baruch.

In January 1943 the Special Services Division, unaware of Baruch's Casablanca station, sent 250-watt and 1,000-watt transmitters to set up an AFRS station there. Tom Lewis selected Major Charles Vanda to run it. The equipment arrived late, and while Vanda tracked it down, orders were received transferring the men of the Broadcast Operations Detachments to the Psychological Warfare Branch.

Figure 53 The Army Broadcasting Service station in Casablanca, 1943. From left to right: Sergeant Barney Weadock, Corporal Milton Wolfe, Sergeant Frank Douthit, Lieutenant Andre Baruch and Sergeant Howard Ailberg. U.S. Army photo, author's collection.

Lieutenant Martin Work of the AFRS arrived shortly after to investigate the situation. Impressed with the Casablanca station, he transferred Baruch and his unit to Special Services to keep them in North Africa. Vanda eventually found his missing equipment and transferred the 1000-watt transmitter to Baruch for the Casablanca station. The 250-watt transmitter was sent to General Mark Clark in Oujda, Morocco to set up a station for his Fifth Army.

The Casablanca station remained independent of AFRS, and by March was broadcasting as "An Army Expeditionary Station - An American Station for the Soldier and Sailor".[18] General Eisenhower ordered additional AES stations set up wherever practical to entertain the troops and, more importantly, to counter the propaganda broadcasts emanating from German stations. Baruch was placed over the AES in North Africa, and a second 1000-watt transmitter was ordered to establish a station in Algiers. To run it, Lieutenant Work selected Sergeant Vernon N. Carstensen, a radio professional stationed at an army air field in Tunisia.[19]

Vern Carstensen, born May 24, 1914 on Clinton, Iowa, took his first broadcasting role as a college student in 1936. An advertising major, one of his professors suggested he interview for an open position at station WSUI, a public radio station operating on campus.[20] After working there for a year, he took an announcing job at WOC in Davenport, Iowa, then worked for a year at WBBM in Chicago before returning to Clinton to open and serve as program director for KROS, the city's first commercial radio station.[21]

After Pearl Harbor, Vern Carstensen was placed in the Army Air Corps because, according to him, he could type. He participated in the invasion of North Africa in November 1942 and the organization of airfields in Tunisia after the Axis forces surrendered there. It was in Tunisia that Lieutenant Martin Work found him.

Arriving in Algiers before the transmitter and other equipment arrived, Carstensen arranged with the local Moroccan radio station to broadcast for two hours a day, one in the morning and one at night. Records were "promoted" from navy ships for a DJ style show, and news was edited and read locally. Once the transmitter arrived the station moved to the Shell Oil Company building and expanded their broadcast schedule to a full day.[22]

As part of the planning for the Allied invasion of Italy, General Mark Clark authorized a radio station be set up that could be broken down and reassembled as the Allies advanced. Vern Carstensen requested to be part of the effort. He was commissioned as a First Lieutenant and assigned to design and build the station. On October 5, 1943 the new Fifth Army Broadcasting Station, built mostly with equipment borrowed from other AES stations, signed on for the first time in Naples.[23]

Figure 54 Vern Carstensen. Courtesy Jim Carstensen.

The original plan was to disassemble, move and reassemble the station as the Allies moved up the boot of Italy and out of the range of the Naples station. It was a slow process, and by the time a new, suitable location was found and the station was broken down and set up, it may have been out of range again. Carstensen needed a more agile solution.

Major Francis McAloon, the Fifth Army Assistant Special Service Officer, suggested setting up a station in a truck that could be moved quickly and easily with minimal setup. Ideally, only the antenna would need to be raised. He and Carstensen presented the plan to General Clark, who liked the idea. His signal officer, however, concerned that the equipment would be damaged as the trucks traveled down war torn roads, needed more convincing.

To prove the concept, Carstensen made drawings of a station built snugly into two trucks. One would carry the transmitter and control room, with two turntables and a control console in a rear corner, opposite shelving holding records and radio transcriptions. Nearer the cab of the truck would be the transmitter itself. The second truck would carry a sound proofed studio, complete with chairs, tables, a piano, and microphones. Windows placed in opposite sides of both trucks faced each other, providing a view of the studio from the control room. Blackout material covered the gap between the trucks, blocking any stray light.[24] The drawings convinced the skeptical signal officer, and the mobile station was approved with Carstensen in charge.

Two GMC CCKW 2½-ton trucks were refitted to carry the studio and control room, which were soundproofed and lined with plywood captured from the Germans. The transmitter, turntables and microphones were supplied by the army. Everything else had to be scrounged or improvised. Tables, easy chairs and rugs were found for the studio. Powdered egg cans were converted into light fixtures, and the "on air" sign was a Spam can. Though small, the studio was efficiently designed and comfortable, and so impressed Irving Berlin when he visited that he felt "this is the first time I've been in New York since I left New York."[25]

Sections of Italian artillery field observation towers were pieced together to form an antenna. And from the nearby *Mostra d'Oltremare*, a fairground built in 1937 originally to showcase the economic progress of Fascist Italy, Carstensen found a small upright piano that fit neatly at one end of the studio. On the side of the trucks was painted "The Fifth Army Mobile American Expeditionary Station" and a white-on-olive rendition of the station's insignia, an announcer's microphone, tilted, on a blue background, below it a winged truck wheel, and above, the insignia of the Fifth Army. The station was a model of efficiency, both in use of space and operation, and could be broken down, moved and ready to broadcast again within two hours.

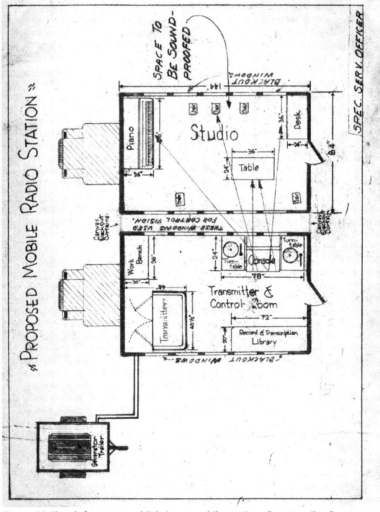

Figure 55 Sketch for proposed 5th Army mobile station. Courtesy Jim Carstensen.

Figure 56 One of the trucks and trailers of the Fifth Army Mobile Station. Photograph 111-SC-282148, 1944. Records of the Office of the Chief Signal Officer, Record Group 111. National Archives at College Park, College Park, Maryland.

Carstensen selected his own staff, many of them with some experience in radio.[26] Though they each had their specific duty, each was able to fill in where needed outside of their departments, including a turn at cooking.

"This is the American Expeditionary Station - in the field with the Fifth Army. A radio service for American fighting men and their allies" began their first broadcast as a mobile station on 15 February 1944 from Caserta, Italy at 196 meters with a five-kilowatt transmitter, eventually boosted to fifteen kilowatts.[27]

They were highly regarded by men in the field and were sent fresh bread and baked goods from nearby units in appreciation. One ordnance outfit built an office and living quarters for them from a captured Italian trailer, and an engineering unit converted a German trailer into living quarters for the men who had been living in tents.[28]

The station broadcast entertainment and news sixteen hours a day every day. They carried a library of frequently replenished AFRS transcriptions as well as a collection of popular records. Radio plays were written and performed by local talent from nearby units, and the Fifth Army Dance Band was broadcast as they performed before a live audience.

The station tended to not follow the strict AES programming format. Carstensen "wanted to bring the troops a radio broadcast just like they were at home, commercials included. I wanted them to feel as if they really were home".[29] AES headquarters was not altogether happy with their non-standard broadcasts, but after General Clark interceded the station was allowed to continue operating independently.

News and sports were programmed, and the station was able to rebroadcast much of the 1944 World Series.[30] Most popular were music programs, and the request show "The Old Oaken Bucket" issued a membership card to every soldier who mailed in a request as well as to visiting performers. It was essential to Carstensen that his listeners, the soldiers in the field, feel as if they were listening to radio back home and that they be provided with dependable news and a better understanding of the war.

Live shows by touring performers were a highlight of the Fifth Army Mobile Station's programming. There was a standing rule that any visiting USO performer had to first be interviewed by the station when they arrived. Bob Hope, Irving Berlin, Marlene Dietrich, and Jimmy Durante were among the many stars who visited. An outdoor studio with a camouflage netting roof was set up for performances. Shows were performed live for nearby frontline and were broadcast for everyone else.[31]

From Caserta the station on wheels moved to Sparanese on March 26, then to Mondragone on April 30. After hearing that soldiers in the field hospital there could only receive Axis Sally broadcasts, the station moved to Anzio on June 5, the same day Rome fell to the Allies. Because the beachhead was still being shelled, engineers dug a trench large enough for the station's trucks and trailers to park in. "Sure, we could feel the vibrations from the bombings" recalled Carstensen, but they didn't affect our radio operations, and we kept on broadcasting."[32]

Five days after arriving at Anzio the Fifth Army Mobile Station packed up and moved to Rome.

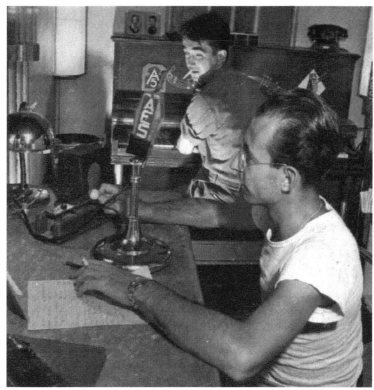

Figure 57 Studio, 5th Army Mobile Station. Courtesy Jim Carstensen.

The Germans monitored the station, and "Jerry's Front" would occasionally exchange barbs with the Fifth Army broadcasters. Carstensen and his crew were aware that they were a tempting target for the Germans, a fact that "Sally" would often remind them of. "Sally" threatened during a broadcast that they were on their way to take out the Fifth Army station's transmitter, and the Germans made good on their promise. Chief engineer Sergeant Walter Kirk, while sitting outside of the transmitter truck, heard a distinctive whistling that he recognized as an airplane coasting. A German pilot had followed their signal in. Switching off the transmitter just in time, the plane still dropped its bombs but, having lost its target, it missed by a few hundred feet.[33]

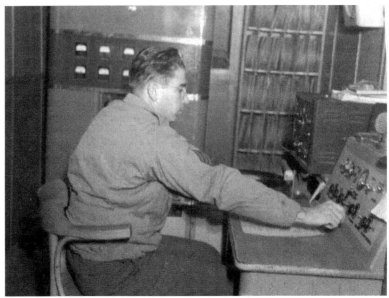

Figure 58 Control room, 5th Army Mobile Station. Courtesy Jim Carstensen.

From Rome the station continued up Italy, logging 685 miles with twelve stops in sixteen months. Their final broadcast was June 15, 1945 at Brescia in northern Italy.

The Fifth Army Mobile Expeditionary Station was awarded the Fifth Army Plaque and Clasp of Meritorious Service for their efforts, and Vern Carstensen was awarded the Bronze Star Medal for his "meritorious achievement in support of combat operations".[34]

Carstensen wrote a *Guide to Operation Practices Polices*[35] for operating future mobile radio stations, with details on production, personnel, administration and moving the station. He began with a list of broadcast objectives. Similar stations should provide the finest in radio programs that tried "to make the listener, regardless of his surroundings, think that he is listening to the radio back home". It needed to stay close to the fighting troops, especially those in forward areas, moving as necessary. The soldiers should be kept informed, with accurate and timely news broadcasts and programs that give him a better understanding of the war and his role in it. And the station needs to build and maintain morale. "It must be realized", wrote Carstensen, "that high morale is a powerful weapon and makes all other weapons more effective."

Finally, the station should give the soldier a voice, encouraging him to "display his talent and to offer suggestions. This will not only be an aid to the individual morale but will also provide good program material inasmuch as the army contains considerable entertainment talent of excellent quality".[36]

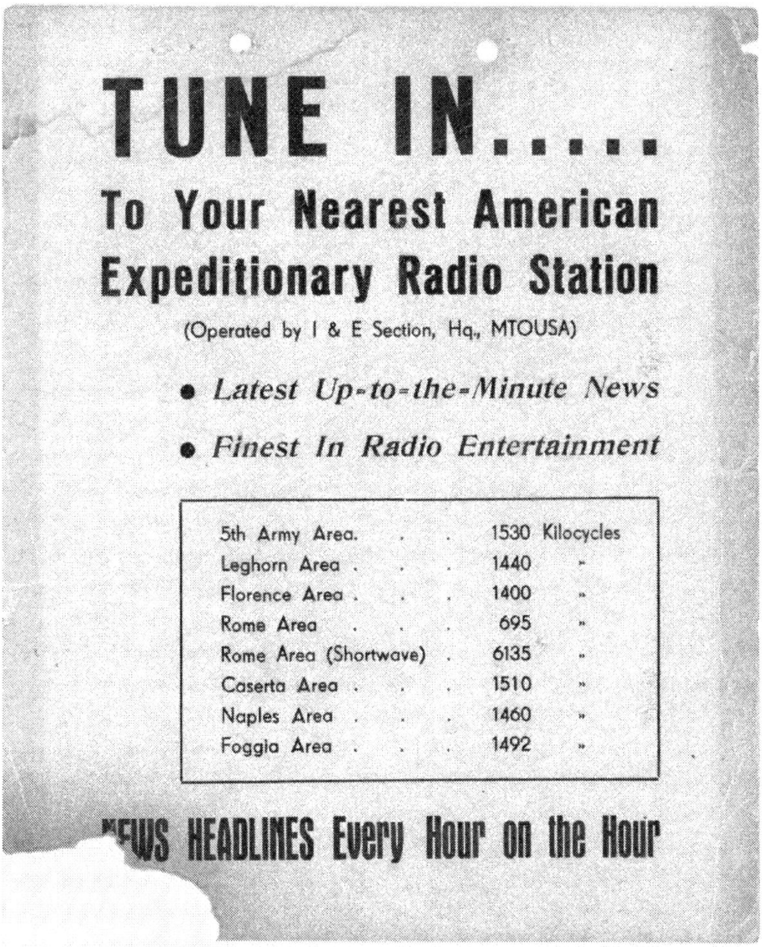

TUNE IN......

To Your Nearest American Expeditionary Radio Station

(Operated by I & E Section, Hq., MTOUSA)

● *Latest Up-to-the-Minute News*

● *Finest In Radio Entertainment*

5th Army Area.	1530	Kilocycles
Leghorn Area .	1440	"
Florence Area .	1400	"
Rome Area	695	"
Rome Area (Shortwave) .	6135	"
Caserta Area .	1510	"
Naples Area	1460	"
Foggia Area .	1492	"

NEWS HEADLINES Every Hour on the Hour

Figure 59 A flyer for U. S. Army radio stations operating in the Mediterranean Theater of Operations. Printed before June 15, 1945, the final broadcast of the Fifth Army Mobile Station.

The guide also covered topics like censorship, supply, equipment, and air raids. With their encounter with a German bomber in mind, Carstensen included in the instructions for emergency precautions that "before going off the air, after being informed of approaching enemy planes, the program will be faded and the following announcement made; 'Hold your hats kids--here they come.'"[37]

Based on the successful design and operations of the Fifth Army Mobile Station, 1000-watt stations were assembled to follow the 1st, 7th and 9th Armies. Carstensen was transferred to AFRS headquarters in Los Angeles and placed in charge of developing similar mobile stations for what then seemed the inevitable invasion of Japan. After the war he continued to serve as a reservist with the AFRS, retiring with the rank of Lt. Colonel on November 27, 1961.

Most soldiers who heard the Fifth Army Mobile Station at Anzio before the breakout were not hearing it on foxhole radios. Because there was no tuning, a foxhole radio would most likely pick up the strongest available station, and before the breakout that was *Jerry's Front*. There were exceptions. "We had a local radio station of our own", recalled Bryan Compton, "and then we had news coming from England, and also Germany. Germany had a girl over there that would tell us what the password was."[38] Compton, understandably, assumed the Jerry's Front broadcasts originated from Berlin rather than Rome.

There were other radios here and there, "real" radios, commercial sets with vacuum tubes that could be tuned to the BBC or the Fifth Army Station. But for most soldiers on the beachhead, if they were going to have a radio, they would have to build one. And those radios were evolving, moving beyond the beachhead to other Allied servicemen, with subtle refinements and design variations added along the way. And not all of them used razor blades.

Figure 60 The patch of the Fifth Army Mobile Radio Station. Courtesy Jim Carstensen.

20 It Was Surprising

Whether or not a soldier ever encountered a foxhole radio at Anzio depended at least somewhat on his location. Infantry units at the front line were less likely to see one. Many never saw any kind of broadcast radio. For Isaac Franklin Caudle of the 157th Regimental Combat Team the only thing to listen to at Anzio was the sound of "exploding shells".[1] Warren L. Nicely of the 69th Armored Regiment wondered "how anybody had time to build a radio. Shells were coming in day and night for 4 1/2 months."[2]

Some, like Russel Weiskircher of the 157th Infantry Regiment, heard radio occasionally because there happened to be a nearby tanker's radio, but never considered building his own receiver as there was "no room for a radio in a bed roll or a full field pack".[3]

Some infantrymen saw foxhole radios only in rear areas. Derk Doombos of the 3rd Infantry Division "saw a few of these radios, but not in foxholes. We didn't have the tools or materials to make them". More likely, according to Doombos, they would have been made by "ordnance, quartermaster, artillery, engineers and medics".[4]

Some, Like Howard Waugh of the 39th Engineer Battalion, heard about them but never had the chance to use one. "One location I was in, a buddy and I were dug in. Holes were everywhere, some 100 yards away were two fellows. One came over to our hole one day and told us his buddy had made a radio with a razor blade and some wire and safety pin. Said they listened to Axis Sally. After he left we just laughed it off... I did hear that some had been made, I never did see one".[5]

In some areas they were more common. According to Ray McAllister, Company C, 3rd Battalion, 180th Infantry Regiment had at least a half dozen foxhole radios, and some units had more.

"There were a lot of them on the beachhead", recalled Don Welling. "You could tell it because there was an awful scarcity of headsets."[6] Some men, like Welling, were especially good at making foxhole radios and built them for other soldiers in the area. "If that beachhead had lasted another month, I probably could have retired off that."

"It was surprising how many men had the little crystal radio set", wrote Vere "Tarzan" Williams. "With a couple of flashlight batteries, some wire and an old razor blade they could get a signal - it wasn't loud, but you could hear it".[7]

Other than the earphones, the materials for making a foxhole radio could usually be found somewhere on the beachhead, wire from wrecked equipment, a grenade container for a coil form, a safety pin for a cat whisker. Substitutes were found when there were no razor blades available. Corporal John Savacool, who edited the Third Division news sheet, found that other bits of metal could be used. "If razor blades aren't available, a piece of shrapnel will do, and there's plenty of that."[8]

Some soldiers, like Phil Amico, used galena crystals, shipped in care packages from home, to build "proper" crystal radios. Amico, who was given his crystal by another soldier, kept it, the first specimen in what turned into a post-war passion for rock collecting.[9]

Harry Evans remembered that synthetic galena crystals could be made by melting lead and adding a little powdered sulfur, a potentially hazardous bit of radio lore that requires some finesse, but that nevertheless will produce a workable crystal if done right. He melted lead from a broken storage battery in a steel nut and sprinkled in sulfur powder from the medics. More popular in his unit than razor blades, he reported that there were at least a hundred being used.[10]

A few more sophisticated radios were built, usually by radio men with the spare parts and knowledge to cobble them together. T/5 Hidenobu Hiyane, part of the 100th Infantry Battalion's Radio Section, spent evenings on night patrols and most daylight hours under cover. "I had lots of time to think and since I had some scrounged radio parts an idea came to build a simple radio. A member of my radio comm. team came up with a two tube circuit. I needed a chassis to build it on and the mess kit cover came in handy. When not in use, the cover and the other half was put together and useable for mess. And the rest is history." Besides the American mess kit and tubes, Hiyane used Italian condensers and German resistors and phones.[11] Because the radio could be tuned, he was able to hear Jerry's Front as well as the Fifth Army Mobile Station.

Four photographs were taken by a *YANK* photographer for an article on the Fifth Army Mobile Station but were never published. One, mentioned previously, shows an anonymous soldier sitting in front of a tent with a razor blade radio, one of the only contemporaneous photographs depicting a foxhole radio.[12] Two show Corporal Hiyane and his radio, the first in a jeep, the radio closed and connected to a Signal Corps battery.[13] The other shows him seated on the ground, his M-1942 mess kit open to display the radio components neatly installed into the lid, vacuum tubes mounted sideways, all arranged to conserve space and avoid shorting on the metal base.[14] The fourth photo is of Private James Kubokowa, also of the 100th Infantry Battalion, reading a copy of *Stars and Stripes* while listening to a radio built in an Italian mess kit.[15]

Most foxhole radios however used razor blades, and Americans were not the only ones building them. Corporal Dennis Spencer, of the British 5th Infantry Division, remembered "sitting in the dug-out on the 6th June and hearing the news, on a razor-blade radio (similar to a crystal set) that the Allies had landed in Normandy".[16]

There is a surviving British foxhole radio in the collections of the Imperial War Museum in London, significant not only because it is British but because it is one of only a few surviving foxhole radios. A coil of copper wire is wound around a brown beer bottle, which in turn is lashed to a board with twine. One wire runs from the bottle coil to a raised nail in the board, labeled "earth" in pencil, and continues to form a cat whisker resting on a razor blade attached to two smaller stacked scraps of wood. The other wire from the coil runs to more nails marked "aerial" and "headphones", and on to the attachment point for the razor blade. Though the maker is unknown, the Museum's description confirms that this is a "wireless set made by men of the 5th Divisional Signals in the Anzio beachhead to relieve the monotony for troops deployed in exposed positions".[17]

Figure 61 A British foxhole radio, its coil wrapped around a beer bottle. Wireless Receiver Made by 5th Divisional Signals, 1944. Catalogue Number COM 993, Imperial War Museum, London.

The British *Eighth Army News* printed a letter in their March 3, 1945 issue from Bombardier H. W. Clarke, R. A. requesting details about foxhole radios he had seen at Anzio. "At the time of the Anzio bridgehead a number of the fellows there constructed simple wireless sets on the lines of a crystal set and using razor blades to make one of the components. Could you possibly discover from among your readers the details of this type of set and how one could be made? I should very much like to know."[18]

A follow up to Bombardier Clarke's request was printed on March 15 after "a number of readers responded quickly to his appeal, supplying diagrams in most cases".[19] Three of the diagrams were reprinted, labeled with the soldiers' names who sent them. Two were the same basic style built by Eldon Phelps, Maxie Rupert and others, a wire or safety pin in contact with a razor blade. Corporal Percy's set was a reprint of James Cutter's diagram from the July 17, 1944 issue of *Time* based on Maxie Rupert's set.

Sapper Shelton's set was also a basic Phelps / Rupert design but with some subtle differences that would have improved reception. Instead of using the free end of the coil wire, a finer gauge wire was attached to it and used as a cat whisker, and the blade itself was covered with "graphite writing" to make a carbon and metal detector.

Gunner Poxon's set used an unusual detector and more sophisticated configuration. The antenna circuit is inductively coupled

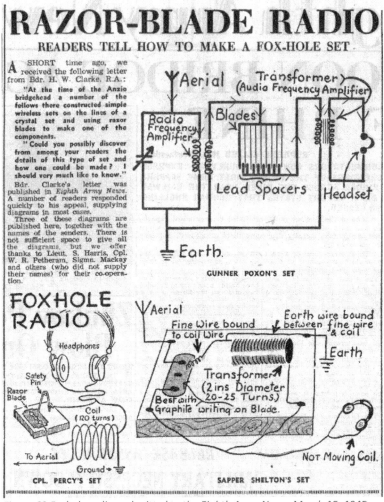

RAZOR-BLADE RADIO

READERS TELL HOW TO MAKE A FOX-HOLE SET

A SHORT time ago, we received the following letter from Bdr. H. W. Clarke, R.A.:

"At the time of the Anzio bridgehead a number of the fellows there constructed simple wireless sets on the lines of a crystal set and using razor blades to make one of the components.

"Could you possibly discover from among your readers the details of this type of set and how one could be made? I should very much like to know."

Bdr. Clarke's letter was published in *Eighth Army News*. A number of readers responded quickly to his appeal, supplying diagrams in most cases.

Three of these diagrams are published here, together with the names of the senders. There is not sufficient space to give all the diagrams, but we offer thanks to Lieut. S. Harris, Cpl. W. R. Petheram, Sigmn. Mackay and others (who did not supply their names) for their co-operation.

Figure 62 Foxhole radios submitted to the Eighth Army News, March 15, 1945.

to the detector circuit to amplify the radio signal, and the headphone is connected through a transformer to amplify the audio. The detector is a row of razor blades, attached at one end and separated by lead spacers. How it worked is unclear and there may be a part, such as a carbon rod straddling the blades, missing from the drawing. Regardless, the *Eighth Army News* sets show an evolution of design, both in subtle improvements and major reconfigurations, as the foxhole radio progressed across Italy.

American soldiers at Anzio were building foxhole radios until the May 23rd breakout and beyond. In a V-mail letter to his father written on May 13, Private William Ahrens describes a razorblade radio he and his buddy made. "Last night and tonight Walter and I spent making a radio, now that we have the place all fixed we're starting on luxuries. It's a very simple crystal set."[20] The letter includes a diagram, elegantly simple, of a basic razor blade set with a "carbon point" cat whisker, nearly a month before O. B. Hanson added a pencil lead to Maxie Rupert's set. "Yep dad it plays. Strange as it seems, only a half hour to make. We still have the other radio. Now there is a race on to see who can get the most stations. We are going to add a battery tomorrow. Who was this guy 'Marconi'?"

By newspaper and word of mouth, the foxhole radio continued to spread across Italy and the rest of Europe. Air Gunner Wilbur Wannenburg of the 34 Squadron South African Air Force built a foxhole radio while stationed at the Celone Airfield near Foggia. A photograph dated April 1945 shows WOII Wannenburg and WOII Alf Klein standing in front of their tent, a tall pole carrying an aerial beyond the top of the photo to pick up the American Expeditionary Station in Foggia. "We found out that it was possible to build a crystal radio set using a razor blade and understood that a good aerial was necessary. We did not believe in half measures - note the aerial reaching for the sky. To listen to the Yank radio station in Foggia we used our flying helmets - one lead to the tip of the male plug, another to the back. Don't ask me how the thing worked!"[21]

It seems likely that Allies from other nations serving in Italy built improvised radios in their foxholes, and a more extensive search in local archives may yet uncover a letter, journal, or article describing one of these sets.

Lieutenant Bob Reichard of the 456th Bomb Group (H) saw a foxhole radio at Cergnolia near Foggia that resembles Wilbur Wannenburg's setup. "There was an Armed Forces Radio Station (AFRS) at Foggia, but radios were few and far between. A select few had recovered some from crashes and put them on line. One tent had a novel setup. They had the ingenuity to stick a wire antenna out the top of their tent and this they connected to a combination of earphone, wire coil, and a razor blade. The result was an unpowered crystal radio which brought in the AFRS Radio Station. The end of the coiled wire had been bent to touch the razor blade and that acted like a crystal."[22]

While in England in April 1944 Vic Politi, a radio operator with the 286th Joint Assault Signal Company, was assigned to pick up radio and telephone equipment gear from several signal depots in preparation for the invasion of France. He met a fellow ham at one of the depots who gave him a "mimeograph schematic of a razor blade radio, which all the guys at the depot were using. I bummed some wire from him and when I got back to my station I put together the parts I had scrounged up and lo and behold it worked as the strong BBC signal just saturated the area we were in."[23]

He packed the radio in his duffel bag, retrieving it after D-Day and using it whenever he had the opportunity. "The BBC came through like gangbusters as they were running megawatts of power from their new location up in the Lake Country of the UK. I even made a SW model by taking turns off the coil and was able to copy the BBC on the 49 meter band." He brought the original radio home with him after the war, one of the few know to have returned.

Though it was forbidden for troops to carry radios on D-Day, at Normandy "radios were playing from foxholes on D plus one",[24] reported Captain William R. Denslow of the 745th Tank Battalion and a former writer for Chicago's WGN radio. Some radios were distributed by Special Services, and some had been purchased or captured from the enemy earlier and arrived after the invasion. "Lots of men make their own radios", adds Captain Denslow. "Two radio technicians in my section have made half a dozen sets using an oil can for a case and miscellaneous parts they can get their hands on. The fact is the American soldier is very ingenious". Most radios were in the rear areas, and news there was passed down "until the individual man with the rifle right out in front gets it. And he gets it in good time".

It is a testament to the comfort American fighting men found in the simplest mementos of home life that they made it a priority to find or build radio sets only one day after the Normandy landings.

First Lieutenant Bill Bastian of the 203rd Engineer Combat Battalion, 6th Engineer Special Brigade, built a razor blade foxhole radio while at Omaha Beach after reading about one in Stars and Stripes. "I found the proper blade, maybe a Marlin blue blade, and having 900 companions and being an Officer I soon had headphones and wire. I used a toilet paper roll for coil winding and no slider or tuner. BBC was so close and powerful that their signal strength trod over any competition."[25] He never heard an American station and was too far from Berlin or Rome to hear either "Sally".

The foxhole radio was a luxury and Lieutenant Bastian's only communication with the outside world for months. "I had no radio or field phone during Normandy June - October. I went 150 days without seeing running water, basin, tub, toilet or shower. My best friend and accessory was my steel helmet (all round plumbing fixture). All this time there was no entertainment other than two shows and a couple of field movies."[26]

Some foxhole radios were carried through France all the way to Germany. Communication Sergeant Victor V. Kubilius, with Company E of the 18th Regimental Combat Team, 1st Infantry Division, built a foxhole radio during a brief rest period in the battle of Aachen. "In one of the homes in Aachen, Germany I made a crystal set with a razor blade detector and sound power earphones. The antenna was the dormant house wiring and the ground was a steam radiator. It worked. From a station in Germany I heard 'Lord Haw-Haw' explaining how the German army was going to wipe out the 1st Infantry Division. That didn't happen."[27]

Lord Haw-Haw was a nickname given by the Allies to several German propaganda broadcasters, most famously William Joyce, an American born fascist who broadcast for the Nazis with an affected English accent. After nearly three weeks of intense fighting with heavy casualties on both sides, Aachen was the first city on German soil to be captured by the Allies.

The foxhole radio was well known by the time Victor Kubilius built his and was a popular subject for the civilian press. The amateur radio magazine *QST* first wrote about it in their July 1944 issue, reporting on a letter received from Pfc. Toivo J. "Jack" Kujanpaa, a licensed ham and radio operator on the Anzio beachhead. There was little description of the radio other than it was a "field version of a 'crystal' set using a razor as a detector", and that it received "jive" programs and propaganda from Rome.[28] A larger audience learned of the foxhole radio when *Time* reported on Maxie Rupert's set in their July 17th issue, including James Cutter's diagram.[29]

Also in July the Queensland *Northern Miner*[30] described Eldon Phelps' set, making it one of the first descriptions of a foxhole radio in civilian media outside of the United States.

In August a follow up letter from an anonymous correspondent in Italy was printed in *QST* with more detail about the razor blade radio. Tuning was achieved by "moving the point of the safety pin, anchored at the other end, over the opposite end of the blade from where it is connected to the coil and antenna. The 'phones are inserted between the pin and the grounded side of the coil".[31] Reception was reported as "very good". *Electronics* magazine covered Maxie Rupert's set the same month, along with the picture of O.B. Hanson's NBC set.

A classified advertisement ran in the August 1944 issue of *Popular Science* offering plans for a "tubeless radio made with razor blades! Complete plans 35 cents." It was the first of many ads that would run in popular magazines for decades capitalizing on the foxhole radio's fame.

More articles followed, in September's *Wireless World*, and again in *Electronics*, this time mentioning Eldon Phelps and his receiver.[32] *Popular Science*[33] and *Popular Mechanics*[34] both covered the foxhole radio in October, both using the photo of Hanson's NBC receiver.

QST printed a letter from Justin Garton in their October issue along with a new diagram by the author.[35] It is a standard foxhole receiver, with coil, razor, safety pin and headphones. A two-inch coil form was specified, with 120 turns of wire, though the gauge of wire is not mentioned. Garton claims that a ham from New York invented the razor blade radio, though his name remains a mystery.

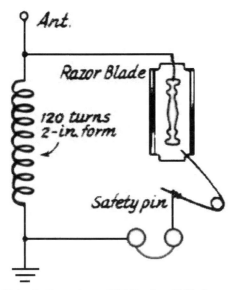

Figure 63 Justin Garton's set, QST, October 1944. Courtesy QST.

The January 1945 *QST*, reporting on the activities of the Tucson Short Wave Association, mentions that one of that club's members picked up Phoenix from 100 miles on a razor blade receiver based on Justin Garton's diagram.[36]

In the September 1944 issue of *Radio Craft*, Hugo Gernsback applied some historical perspective to the foxhole radio. "If you have read the newspapers and magazines lately, you will have observed that there has been a regular rash of emergency radios which ingenious GI's have constructed at the front and in foxholes".[37] He traced their history starting with Lieutenant Rosee's set in the *Field Artillery Journal*, through Jack Gould's description of Maxie Rupert's set in the *New York Times*, to James Cutter's drawing in *Time*.

Gernsback saw little new in the foxhole radio, "because all these nice 'discoveries' of 1944 are just too ancient for words. Indeed, the original 'Razor Blade Radio Detector' was published by your schoolmaster in his magazine *Modern Electrics* in the January 1909 issue, page 352, just thirty-five years ago!" He is referring to Clark Pettingill's "Novel Detector", the simple microphone made up of two upturned razor blades and a pencil lead.

Gernsback takes it back further, to a not-previously-published detector made from a nickel and a coiled cat whisker, and to a carbon auto coherer sold by his Electro Importing Company in 1906, a glass tube filled with carbon granules and small brass rods inserted at each end.

In Gernsback's opinion, these were all imperfect contact detectors, direct descendants of David Edward Hughes' microphone. He never mentions demodulation, or any relationship to crystal detectors, but he does establish part of a family tree leading to Hughes and writes at least part of the history of a detector that would have seemed at the time an artifact specific to the Italian beachhead, a local phenomenon born of necessity.

The foxhole radio was difficult, worked only moderately well, and there would have seemed little reason for it to move beyond Anzio. However, military personnel and civilian amateurs would continue making them for years, partly to recreate a clever bit of GI improvisation, partly to prove to themselves that this strange and troublesome detector actually worked.

Figure 64 Hidenobu Hiyane of the 100th Infantry and his mess kit radio set.
Photograph 111-SC-282167, 1944. Records of the Office of the Chief Signal Officer,
Record Group 111. National Archives at College Park, College Park, Maryland.

Figure 65 Hidenobu Hiyane. Photograph 111-SC-282165, 1944. Records of the Office of the Chief Signal Officer, Record Group 111. National Archives at College Park, Maryland.

Figure 66 Private James Kubokawa listens to a radio built into an Italian mess kit while reading the Stars and Stripes, Anzio. Photograph 111-SC-282166, 1944. Records of the Office of the Chief Signal Officer, Record Group 111. National Archives at College Park, Maryland.

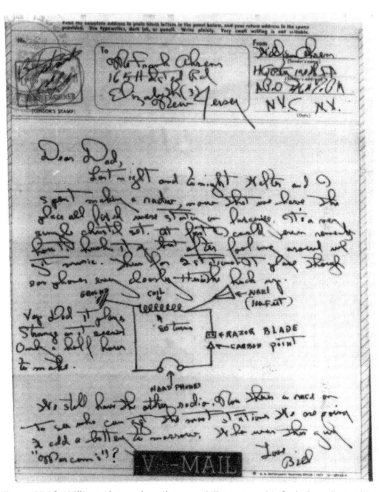

Figure 67 Pfc William Ahrens describes - and illustrates - his foxhole radio in this V-Mail from May 13, 1944.

Figure 68 WOII Wilbur Wannenburg (left) and WOII Alf Klein (right) Celone Foggia, Italy April. Their razor blade radio antenna is visible in the background. Used with permission from Tinus le Roux.

21 A Cockeyed Invention

"Men, do you still struggle with the old-fashioned type of foxhole - the type without music, funny cracks and Raymond Gram Swing?" asked *Leatherneck* magazine. "Do you lie awake listening to the patter of rain on your shelter-half? Are you lonely, tired, board? Then, Jack, this message is for you."[1]

Radios for servicemen were scarce on Guam in 1945. AFRS station WXLI had been broadcasting there since October 1944, and Special Services distributed tropicalized commercial receivers across the Pacific. Most of these went to recreation facilities, leaving few if any for the field. Undaunted, Ships Cook 3/c Edward E. Bourgault, 13th Special Naval Construction Battalion, a radio hobbyist since his youth, decided to make his own. "I remembered that a double edge razor blade would give rectifying action for signal detection without the aid of crystals or tubes. After a few nights of tinkering I got together this 'foxhole companion' which consists solely of a safety pin, a loop of wire, a wood base and the used razor blade. It not only picks up standard wave lengths but also pilot jabber from nearby airfields. I've been trying for 'Tokyo Rose' but no luck as yet."[2]

"The blade - preferably blue steel type - is tacked to the base and a wire taped from one side of it to one side of the coil. The coil's other side is grounded and a lead attached to one side of the headphones. Then another wire is taped from the safety pin to the other side of the headphones. The safety pin is tacked to the board so the point can be moved across the unground part of the blade. This is how you select your stations."[3] According to Bourgault, the receiver gave "sharp"

225

reception.[4]

A navy photograph shows Bourgault, seated on a cot in his tent, his socks laid out and drying above him. His radio, resting on a wooden chair, is built on a scrap of plywood, its coil wrapped somewhat haphazardly, the razor blade fastened to the board with black tape. The safety pin, without a pencil lead, rests on the edge of what appears to be a Gillette Blue Blade. Drawn in pencil near the blade is a schematic sketch of the radio with symbols for the ground, antenna, detector and phones.[5]

Whether Bourgault knew of earlier foxhole radios or figured it out on his own, his receiver looks like those at Anzio. It also looks like many simple pre-war crystal receivers, and, as someone versed in the lore of amateur radio, he was as likely as any soldier at Anzio to conflate the crystal and what he remembered of the razor blade microphone detector. It is possible that there were multiple independent inventors of the foxhole radio, even in Italy, considering the diversity of detectors appearing in a relatively short period of time.

Several versions of Bourgault's story were syndicated and printed in stateside papers. Shorter articles usually included the navy photograph. "Using ingenuity plus an old razor blade, bent pin and wire, ship's cook 3/c Edward E. Bourgault, Newton Center, Mass., devised fine radio set. He says it works like any other, bringing in considerable static.[6]

A longer version provided more construction detail. "The Navy's fabulous Seabees have come up with many a cockeyed invention during the war. Their latest is the 'Foxhole Companion', a radio built from a discarded razor blade, a safety pin, a loop, of wire and headphones. Ship's Cook Edward E. Bourgault, Newton Center, Mass., started the radio craze when his outfit landed in the Marianas. 'There was little one could do for amusement after working hours' he explained. 'So I decided to experiment. After a few nights of tinkering I got together the Foxhole Companion. It not only picks up standard wave lengths but also pilot Jabber from near-by airfields.'

The blade - preferably the blue Type - is tacked to the base and a wire tapped from one side of it to one side of the coil. The coil's other side is grounded and a lead is attached to one side of the headphones. Then another wire is tapped from the safety pin to the other side of the headphones. The safety pin is tacked to the board so the point can be moved across the unground part of the blade."[7]

The articles made Bourgault something of a celebrity. "Seldom a mail call goes by without a letter for Edward E. Bourgault, SC3c, of Newton Center, Mass." reported *All Hands: The Bureau of Naval Personnel Information Bulletin.*

"'The kids has broke our good radio and there ain't no way to get it fixed. Please mail directions on how to make a 'Foxhole Radio' like the paper said you built. Pa is handy with tools and we like music at mealtimes.'

'We read in the paper where you build a 'Foxhole Radio' out of scraps and old razor blades. We thought you might want some more blades so you could make radios for your buddies. So here's all the razors that have been used in this hotel in the past week.'

'… So when you come home on leave, Eddie, please stop in at our place at International Falls, Minn. We'll show you how fine your radio works on hunting trips.'

It started when Bourgault, a member of a special Seabee stevedore battalion, constructed an ingenious receiving set from a few short wires and a razor blade. Word of his accomplishment went around and the story was published in papers in the States. Since then he has been swamped by letters from newspaper readers, all over America. Requests for detail directions, says Bourgault, are the major part of his mail, 'though now and then I run across a 'hot' one' like one from a junior miss who claimed 'deep and enduring love' after seeing Bourgault's picture in the paper."[8]

By the time news of Ed Bourgault's receiver made the rounds, the foxhole radios built in Italy were well enough known that Private Frank F. DeAngelo wrote to *Leatherneck* to set the record straight. "Sirs: In your July issue I read that Seabee Edward E. Bourgault and a Marine had got together and invented the so-called foxhole radio. To my knowledge, the foxhole radio was first invented by a lieutenant in the Fifth Army on the beachhead at Anzio in the early part of 1944, and I think credit should be given."[9]

Whether or not Ed Bourgault built the first foxhole radio in the Pacific Theater, his design was widely copied. Marine Sergeant Phil Edwards, the announcer for the popular WXLI talk show *Bivouac Banter*, described the receiver on one of his morning broadcasts. "Letters began pouring in requesting a diagram showing how to make such a set", reported *Leatherneck* magazine. "Edwards conferred with

Seabee Bourgault, who drew the diagram of his invention. The diagram and instructions were mimeographed, thousands of copies made and these were distributed free as a courtesy of 'Bivouac Banter.' Now radios, which a few months ago were as scarce as hod-carriers at a debutante's ball, are as plentiful as coconuts in the Marianas. You, too, can have one - and you don't even have to clip a coupon and mail it."[10]

Figure 69 Edward Bourgault and his Pacific built radio. Photograph 80-G-49100, 1945. National Archives at College Park, College Park, Maryland.

Foxhole radios were built on Guadalcanal, Saipan, Guam, and likely any Pacific island taken by the Allies that was anywhere near a radio station, though, other than two notable exceptions, they never received the same attention from the press as the Anzio radios.

Private Alio J. Benedetti, of the 3rd Battalion, 6th Marines and the 1st Provisional Marine Brigade, listened to American stations on tanker's radios when they were nearby, and, when nothing else was available, to "Tokyo Rose", the name given by Allied soldiers to several female broadcasters of Japanese propaganda. As with Axis Sally in Europe, many Allied troops enjoyed the popular American music the broadcasters played, and for the most part dismissed what they considered hokey propaganda.

Figure 70 A closer look at Ed Bourgault's radio.

There were no nearby tank radios while Benedetti was in training on Guadalcanal, so to hear local AFRS station WVUQ he "made a little radio out of a razor blade for the detector",[11] wrapping the coil around an oatmeal box given to him by a navy cook. Making the foxhole radio inspired him to become an amateur radio operator, and he was granted license W8NPH, remaining an active ham for the rest of his life.

In September 1945 *QST* printed one of the most detailed descriptions of a foxhole radio to date.[12] Sent in by Lieutenant Paul M. Cornell, a Signal Corps aircraft communications officer serving in the Pacific, it would become the best known of the Pacific made foxhole radios, its design reprinted several times over the next few decades.

Included in the article are a schematic, a labeled drawing, and a parts list giving specific construction details. The wooden base is 4 inches square, 1/4-inch-thick, the connections for the headphones are made

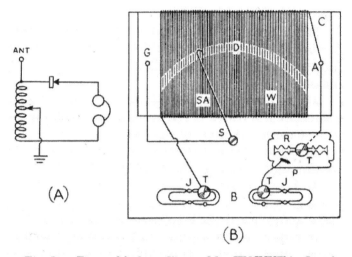

Fig. 5 — Razor-blade radio used by W8EFW in South Pacific. A pictorial layout is shown at (B). The schematic diagram is shown at (A).

A — Antenna connection. This nail also fastens the coil form to the baseboard.

B — Baseboard. 4 inches square, ¼ inch thick.

C — Coil form. Wood block, 3¾ inches long, 2 inches wide and ¼ inch thick.

D — Area of coil scraped clean along arc of switch arm.

G — Ground connection. This nail also fastens coil form to baseboard.

J — Jacks for 'phones. Paper clips held down by tacks.

P — Detector. Pencil lead wrapped with copper wire and resting lightly on razor blade. Some adjustment of the location and pressure of the lead on the blade may be required.

R — Razor blade held down and connected to wire by tack.

S — Screw or nail for pivot of switch arm.

SA — Switch arm made from paper clip.

T — Thumb — or any kind of tack.

W — Coil winding, approximately 175 t. No. 26 insulated wire.

Figure 71 Paul Cornell's radio as seen in QST, September 1945. Courtesy QST.

from paper clips and the detector is a razor blade and pencil lead. The coil, not the usual cylinder, is a wood block 3 3/4 inches long by 2 inches wide and 1/4-inch-thick, with a winding of approximately 175 turns of no. 26 insulated wire.

It is similar to the radios built by Phelps and Rupert, with a coil, detector, headphones, ground and antenna, but there is one significant difference. Instead of the ground connecting to one end of the coil, it is attached to a straightened paper clip, held to the base at one end by a screw so that it could pivot, the other end free to rest along an arc across the top of the coil. The enamel insulation is removed from the coil with sandpaper where it contacts the paperclip slider, just enough to make electric contact but not enough to short adjacent wires. The slider effectively shortens and lengthens the coil, allowing for some tuning of the radio.

Cornell was well versed in radio from an early age, having received his amateur's license and call letters W8EFW at 15. As his QSL card said, he had been "pounding brass since April 1930". Before the war he worked for a while as an air traffic controller in Oklahoma, and for the FCC's office in Michigan. During the war he was assigned to the Signal Corps where he served as a control tower officer in the Pacific.

He built several foxhole radios while on Saipan, based on a circuit his father had taught him, but using what parts were available locally, wood from packing crates, nails, and paper clips. "I usually pulled in some abandoned telephone wire from nearby fields to use for antennas" recalled Cornell. "For a ground, we drove a long nail into the ground."[13]

There were two broadcast radio stations on Saipan. KSAI, the Voice of America station which broadcast programming to Asia and specifically to Japan, shared a collection of Quonset huts with WXLD, the local American Expeditionary Station. WXLD was part of the Pacific Ocean Network, a string of independently operating stations operating on Guam, Tarawa, Makin, Kwajalein, Eniwetok, Iwo Jima and several other islands, the "network" growing as islands were captured. The Jungle Network centered on New Guinea and the Philippines, while those in a string from Auckland to New Caledonia were collectively known as the Mosquito Network.

Prior to the AES, the shortwave station KGEI, broadcasting news from San Francisco, was available to anyone in the Pacific Theater, provided they had access to a shortwave receiver. "Nothing else, neither good news nor bad, neither programs of jive nor of classical music", reported the New York Time, "stirs the soldiers, sailors and marines on duty in the far Pacific as does the simple, straightforward introductory sentence to KGEI programs, 'This is the United States of America'.[14]

During the Japanese invasion of the Philippines General Douglas MacArthur wrote to KGEI requesting they broadcast information specifically for his troops and the Philippine civilian population. A 1,000-watt transmitter was set up to rebroadcast transmissions from KGEI, making it the main source of news, information, counterpropaganda and entertainment for MacArthur's troops. In January 1942 the transmitter moved to Corregidor with MacArthur, who dubbed it "The Voice of Freedom".[15] In New Caledonia a string of amplifiers was set up so that Americans there could hear the station, which came in clearly despite Japanese attempts to jam it from the captured Manila station KZBQ.

Figure 72 WXLD, the Pacific Ocean Network station on Saipan. U. S. Marine Corps photo, author's collection.

By July 1942 radio stations in New Zealand were broadcasting transcriptions of American radio shows for Allied personnel in the Pacific. Portable public address equipment and small transmitters were sent to the Allies as they moved through the Pacific islands, and several independently operated stations sprung up where equipment was available. A small transmitter in Noumea, New Caledonia, broadcast news and entertainment for the nearby airfield. Operated by United States service personnel, it was eventually taken over by the Information and Education Branch and assigned the call sign WVUS.

The Noumea station was the first of the "Mosquito Network" of AES installations, an affiliated group of stations located on several Pacific islands including Guadalcanal, Bougainville, New Georgia, Tutuila, and Espiritu Santo. The stations broadcast frequent reminders for service personnel to take their anti-malarial pills, and to reinforce this they adopted the ever-present mosquito as their mascot.

Because it was in an area where troops trained and was widely covered in stateside press, WVUQ on Guadalcanal was one of the best known of the Mosquito Network stations. The control room and studio, dubbed Radio City by those who worked there, was set up in a Dallas hut nestled in a grove of coconut palms.

Harry James' recording of "Flight of the Bumble Bee" announced "The Atabrine Cocktail Hour", broadcasting at 5:30 each evening from a different fictitious cocktail lounge. The fifteen-minute show provided music and subtly reminding listeners to take their antimalarial Atabrine. From the "Fungus Festooned Fern Room" or "The Starlight Roof high above Hotel DeGink in downtown Guadalcanal"[16] the message was often understated and always humorous. "Going out tonight, dogface? Then be sure to wear your Chanel Number Five. Make yourself Alluring. Be Repellant".[17]

Besides news, music, and time signals announced on coconut shell "chimes", listeners were occasionally treated to local talent.

Smaller independent stations continued to operate in the Pacific after the AES stations were established. "Rock Radio" was operated by three Marines in a repair shop on American Samoa. Radio Technician First Class Kenneth D. McCoy, Radioman First Class Stanley T. Dixon, and Radioman Third Class Charles H. Wilson took turns running the makeshift station during their off duty hours.[18]

Though most of the AES stations were only strong enough to be heard on the island where they were located, KSAI, the Voice of America station on Saipan, had a 50 kW transmitter that could be heard in Japan and beyond, strong enough "so that B-29 bomber crews could listen to the music on the 7 - 8 hour flight back to Saipan, Tinian, and Guam".[19]

Paul Cornell gave away most of the foxhole radios he built while on Saipan, but he saved two for himself to bring home. He was discharged from the army in 1946 and served in the Air Force Reserve until retiring as a First Lieutenant in 1951. He continued to work in radio and was an active ham for the rest of his life. The foxhole radios went with him to any ham related events, and still worked even decades later.

One still has its razor blade, an original double-edged Marlin, held down by a thumbtack, the cat whisker simply a piece of mechanical pencil lead wrapped with bare copper wire. It is neatly laid out. The coil of red enameled wire is wrapped around a rectangular scrap of wood as wide as the base, with nail contacts for the wires clearly labeled "G" for "ground" and "A" for "antenna" in pencil. The slider is held to the base with a brass screw, and two paper clips, terminals for headphones, are attached with small brass bolts and washers. Cornell wrote on the bottom, in pen, "built on Saipan Apr. '45 by: W8EFW".

Figure 73 A QSL card from Paul Cornell. Author's collection.

Figure 74 Radio City, WVUQ, Guadalcanal, "situated in a muddy coconut grove", part of the Mosquito Network. U. S. Marine Corps photo, taken by Sergeant James Mundell, author's collection.

Figure 75 "Mosquito Network" banner on Guadalcanal, 1944. Author's collection.

Figure 76 Paul Cornell. Courtesy Ann Cornell McNea.

Figure 77 One of Paul Cornell's foxhole radios, built on Saipan in April 1945. Courtesy Ann Cornell McNea.

The bottom of Paul Cornell's foxhole radio.

Military personnel stationed stateside tried their hand at the foxhole radio as well. B-25 crewmen Pfc. Elias Vivero and Pfc. Huel Butler built a simple foxhole radio while stationed at Brooks Field in San Antonio. The receiver, with a safety pin and blade but no coil, was built so they could "play the radio while the fellow in the next bunk is asleep".[20]

Figure 78 Pfc. Elias Vivero and Pfc. Huel Butler with their "scrap pile radio". San Antonio Express, December 21, 1944.

William Lloyd Wiley was drafted into the navy in May 1944, a few months after returning from a two-year stint in England setting up electrical installations at military airfields. Because of his electrical experience, both in England and before the war in his father's electric repair business in San Antonio, he was assigned to an electric shop at the Amphibious Training Base on Coronado Island, California.

"We'd take our lunch out on the side of the building and sit down there in the sunshine and eat our lunch, you know", recalled Wiley. "And this radio operator - our shop was right next to the radio shack - one day he said 'you know, it's a shame that those boys over there in those foxholes couldn't have a radio.' I said they could. He said 'oh no, you can't get crystals and you'd have to have a crystal'. I said they can make a radio without a crystal. Well, I had access to everything I needed in the electrical shop, so I went and got me a roll of wire and wound it around a talcum powder can and closed it in".[21]

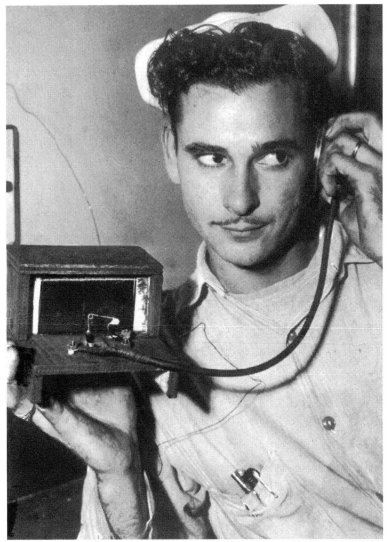

Figure 79 William Lloyd Wiley and his razor blade set. Courtesy William Lloyd Wiley.

The radio was solidly built on a stained plywood base with components held in place by brass nuts and bolts. A double edge razor blade and safety pin without a pencil lead served as the detector, and the coil was tucked away in a plywood frame.

Wiley made his radio without knowing about the foxhole radios already built at Anzio and elsewhere. As a child he built crystal sets at his house near Gonzales, Texas, often falling to sleep at night while listening to stations broadcasting from San Antonio, waking with the earphones still on his head.

He remembered the basic crystal radio circuit years later when he built his set at Coronado, but he also remembered that, somehow, a razor blade could be used as a detector. Well versed in the lore of radio and electricity, he may have been, like some of the soldiers at Anzio, recalling the microphone detectors of his father's generation.

"So I called that radio operator to come in there and showed it to him. I said 'put those earphones on and see what you think about it'. And he looked at that thing and said, 'ain't no way that things gonna' work'. And he stuck those earphones on and he said 'oh my gosh, it's so loud I don't need to put 'em on my ears'.[22]

Word of the radio soon spread. "The captain called me in and said 'I understand you made a radio'. And I thought, well, this is sea duty now. And I said 'yes sir'. He said go 'get it'. So I went and got it and hooked it up to a hot water connection on the wall and threw the antenna out across the floor. He stuck those earphones on his ears and he said 'oh my gosh this thing is loud!' And he said 'well, has anybody called the paper here on the base about it?' I said they took some pictures but I haven't seen them in the paper. But I got home that night and my wife said 'the milkman told me that your picture was in the paper'. We went and got a paper and, sure enough, it was in the paper."[23]

The story was printed in papers across the country. "Gonzalez, Tex. 2/C William L. Wiley, formerly here, is credited from Coronado, Cal., with building a radio receiving set from an old razor blade, a safety pin and some wire. The bluejacket built the novel radio just to show his mates it could be done."[24]

The *San Antonio Light*, not far from Wiley's hometown of Gonzales, printed a more detailed account. "One of America's oldest and most harassing household problems was solved recently when Seaman Second Class William L. Wiley at the Amphibious Training Base, Coronado, Calif., did not discard his old razor blade."[25] The article included a photograph taken of Wiley with his radio by the Photographic Section of the Landing Craft School, Amphibious Training Base, the components of the radio clearly displayed, Wiley wearing his white service uniform and sporting a Clark Gable mustache. "Converting inaudible high frequency radio broadcast waves to low audio frequency vibrations that become voice and music in the earphone is a function of the derided, unsung, discarded razor blade that Mr. Gillette in his wildest dreams undoubtedly never thought of. He designed his double-edged blade for man's comfort, but Bluejacket Wiley has redesigned its use for man's entertainment."[26]

Figure 80 A closer look at William Lloyd Wiley's radio.

To monitor the progress of the war and improve morale, allied POWs would often construct carefully hidden radio receivers from whatever materials could be improvised, smuggled in or bartered for. The positive effect on morale of hearing news from the outside world outweighed, for some, the risk of punishment or, in the Japanese camps at least, execution if caught with a radio receiver. Many of these POW radios survive in museums, and many more in photographs and the accounts of those who built and operated them.

The simplicity of the foxhole radio's design would seem to make it a good candidate for a POW radio, but most of the surviving receivers were more sophisticated crystal sets or contraptions with vacuum tube detectors. Prison camps, for the most part, were far from Allied broadcast transmitters and so more sensitive and selective receivers were needed to hear distant stations.

The sets, usually built by those prisoners with a good working knowledge of radio, were not only skillfully engineered, considering the resources available, they were also well enough disguised that most were never found during inspections.

A receiver built by Captain Ernest Shackleton, Royal Corps of Signals, while a prisoner at Oflag IX A/Z, Rotenburg, used vacuum tubes and other parts taken from a broken movie projector, coils wrapped on toilet paper tubes, and condensers with blades cut from a cocoa tin.[27] It was hidden under the floorboards and tuned with knitting needles. So important to Captain Shackleton was the radio that he officially requested to return to the prison camp after being liberated to retrieve it, specifically to donate it to the Imperial War Museum in London where it still resides.

Sergeant John Hardy Owen of the 131st Battalion, along with several of his fellow POWs, managed to scrounge enough parts over a period of months to build a radio while working on the Burma Railway. Despite horrific conditions and certain execution if the Japanese located it, the radio, operated by a British sergeant, was finished in time to hear news of the first atomic bomb and the earliest hints of Japanese surrender.[28]

Radioman 1C J. Harold Harveston built a radio to monitor the progress of the war while at the prison camp at Cabanatuan in the Philippines. He used swiped tubes, bottles for batteries, tin cans, mess kit parts and scrap wire.[29] Lt. W. D. Gibson, who had been the technical engineer with MacArthur's "Voice of Freedom" station, built a one tube radio while at Cabanatuan. He and Lt. Frank Burgess used whatever scraps could be made to work, including a tooth paste tube packed with acid for batteries. They were able to hear news of the outside world which they passed around the camp. The radio was still operating when the camp was liberated on January 30, 1945.[30]

A receiver built at Changi Prison in Singapore and brought out after liberation by Russell Francis Wright of the 8th Australian Division, Australian Army, 2nd Australian Imperial Force was built to be hidden in a broom head.[31] Made of "liberated" tubes and improvised parts, it was tuned with screwdrivers.

Another radio from Changi was built by Flying Officer Jeffrey Skinner into a beam that was part of his bunk.[32] Using parts that were scrounged or traded for with civilians, the radio was adjusted with screwdrivers inserted through holes in the beam, which were disguised by nail heads when not in use.

At the Sham Shui Po POW camp in Hong Kong Lt. Herb Dixon gradually built a receiver from old car parts, foil from cigarette packs for capacitors, pencil leads for resistors, and vacuum tubes obtained from the camp hospital by a POW willing to fake appendicitis to swipe them. The finished receiver was hidden in an old kerosene can with a false bottom.[33]

An American civilian POW at Batavia, now Jakarta, named Gaylord Alexander Buchanan built a set which he concealed in his own wooden leg.[34] Buchanan, who lost his leg during his third year at Annapolis, was an engineer for the Sperry Gyroscope Company before being captured. The set, using two small tubes, parts from another broken radio and other scrounged parts, was built into an aluminum cup that Buchanan fitted into a hollowed-out section of the leg.[35]

There were many more POW sets, and volumes could be written about them and the brave men who built and operated them. Though most of the documented sets used vacuum tubes, there were a few with crystal detectors. Galena crystals could be bartered for with willing guards, or otherwise smuggled into camp. Radio components were disguised and sent in relief packages by the British MI-9 and the American MIS-X along with compasses, maps and other escape aids and may have included galena crystals. MIS-X was able to get complete crystal receivers into some camps disguised as cribbage boards.

A receiver at the Imperial War Museum built by N. Norris at Stalag III-D in Berlin used a galena crystal that he traded for a pack of cigarettes with a German sentry. It was built into a metal water bottle with a hidden bottom that could be filled without damaging the radio.[36]

The National Prisoner of War Museum at Andersonville displays two POW made crystal sets, one built by Sgt. Lonnie B. Rutledge, 8th Air Force, 100th Bomb Group, while at Stalag 17-B, and another built by Sgt. Phileas Boase, 97th Bomb Group. A third set is pictured with its builder, John L. Anderson of the 95th Bomber Group. All appear to use galena crystals and have coils that can be tuned.

There may well have been WWII era POW radios with razor blade detectors, but none are documented. There are however hints of non-standard, improvised crystals. The Reverend George C. Dobbs G3RJV, in his contribution to the classic British *Ladybird* book series *Making a Transistor Radio*, describes an experimental POW radio with a crystal made from a piece of coke, a fuel made by heating coal until mostly carbon remains.[37]

Though Reverend Dobbs' coke detector is theoretical, Private John Dale Chew of the Royal Army Service Corp did recall that while at Stalag XXI-A "the more resourceful Signal Corps camp members found that among the coal supply to the cookhouse there were small particles of minerals" that would work as radio detectors.[38]

There is a documented POW built "foxhole" radio from the Vietnam War. Captain Charlie Plumb, at some point during his six-year captivity, remembered a fifteen-cent set of foxhole radio plans he mailed away for as a child and determined to build his own. The antenna, coil and ground lead were made of wire found during occasional visits outside, and the detector, a microphone type, was a piece of pencil lead balanced on two razor blades. The difficult part, as usual, was the earphone, which he made from a wire wrapped nail, a porcelain insulator that had been attached years earlier to a wall, and another razor blade for a diaphragm.[39] He never could get the phones to work, but, as he later recalled, "it kept me occupied for months!"[40]

The foxhole radio continued to appear from time to time in the field after WWII. Paul C. Wilson of the 41st Infantry Division, early in the Allied occupation of Japan, built a razor blade set with a variable capacitor, one of several extracurricular radio projects he took on while attending an army communications course.[41]

Vic Politi, who took his razor blade radio with him to Normandy, still had it in 1948 when his brother Dan was stationed in Germany with no batteries for his portable radio. "He kept bugging me to send him batteries so as a joke I sent him the razor blade radio as I knew he was stationed next to one of the AFN stations. He used it successfully for two years and brought it home when he was discharged. In the 1950s I replaced the razor blade with a WE Co. radar diode and used it to listen to WCBS in NYC."[42]

Pfc. J. L. Warren Linn of San Saba, Texas began making foxhole radios during WWII so that he and his buddies could hear Axis Sally. His detector was the microphone type, a razor blade straddling two carbon sticks "placed parallel on a block of wood. Wire connects one stick to an antenna and grounds the other. Earphones are connected to the carbon sticks, and the razor blade is then slid up and down the sticks for tuning." He was still making them in Korea, where they were copied by the men of the Tank Company of the 38th Regiment.

Though not as well documented, foxhole radios were popular

among American soldiers in Korea, both during and after the war. They were well enough established in the lore by the 1950s that they were used as a demonstration for a 4th Division radio course. "Over 30 men in the 40th Div.'s 625th FA Bn. have enrolled in a beginners' radio course", reported Stars and Stripes in 1954. "Plans call for the demonstration of simple radio construction including a 'razor blade radio' that can be built from a razor blade and scrap wire".[43]

American soldiers were still making radios from razor blades in Vietnam. Karl Kolbus recalls that their "crystal radios were much the same as the foxhole radios of the WWII, in that we used razor blades for the detector, AND for the headset".[44] The phone was made from a small ration can that previously contained jelly, a razor blade held in place by candle wax, and wire wrapped around a nail driven through a piece of bamboo.

Long before Karl Kolbus and his contemporaries built their sets in Vietnam, while news of the original Anzio receivers were still being printed in newspapers, foxhole radios were becoming part of the popular lore of the civilian amateur.

Figure 81 Helen and William Lloyd Wiley, 2007. Author photo.

22 Midnight Requisitioning

The foxhole radio was especially appealing for children, who were the de facto guardians of home science, craft and archaic radio lore. Here was a project that was simple and could be built from common household objects. There was a weirdness to it, the sort of thing that had to be made to be believed. And that it was built by soldiers in the field made it even more intriguing.

In late 1945 Popular Science Press released the *Boy's Fun Book of Things to Make and Do*, a selection of 216 projects mostly based on articles from *Popular Science*. Model airplanes, rope tricks, wood working, science stunts, and camping were all covered, along with several radio construction projects, starting with the simplest, the razor blade and safety pin radio. "Unbelievably simple set actually works well for local stations", the one-page article begins. "One of the war's wonderful gadgets undoubtedly was the 'foxhole radio receiver' designed by Lieut. M. L. Rupert while he was attached to an infantry outfit serving on the Anzio beachhead in Italy. If you want to make a set that is so simple as to be unbelievable, and that costs virtually nothing beyond the price of a set of earphones, here's your dish."[1]

It was the first detailed description of a foxhole radio printed in a popular book, and the first of many foxhole radio projects intended for a younger audience. It included much of the text from Maxie Rupert's letter to Marlin, and was illustrated with the photo of O. B. Hanson's NBC radio, as well as the diagram used in the October 1944 *Popular Science* article "Radio Detectors and How They Work".[2] A blue razor blade was recommended as well as Hanson's addition of a pencil lead because it would give a "decided increase in volume", reinforcing the blue blade and pencil lead combination as part of the standard design.

Newspapers were still reporting foxhole radios late in and after the war, both in the United States and abroad. It is likely that at least some Australian and New Zealander troops would have built foxhole radios, though they received very little if any newspaper coverage. The *Auckland Weekly News*[3] did reprint the *Eighth Army News*[4] article of March 15, 1945 describing sets submitted by readers. The Eldon Phelps story was also printed in several Australian newspapers.[5]

In 1947 the *Sydney Morning Herald* published an article on foxhole radios intended for children in their "Playtime" section along with an elegantly simple illustration. It is a standard, simple crystal type set, though the mounting of the safety pin is unique. The head "is cut off and that end of the pin is hammered into the board" The pointed end is bent midway at a forty-five-degree angle, the point contacting the blade as usual. "Positive results are not always obtained", the article warns. "If this happens try another blade. It is also possible to get several stations at once in some positions. This depends on the particular blade-and-pin's peculiarities."[6] Thin, cotton covered wire was specified for the coil, 120 turns of it around a two-inch non-conductive form.

One of the most influential foxhole radio articles, in terms of readership, was printed in 1950 by DC Comics in *Superboy #6*. Drawn by Albert Borth "Al" Wenzel, "Superboy's Workshop" was a filler page in several 1950s issues of *Superboy* featuring crafts and projects for readers to make. Pinhole cameras, periscopes, secret code machines, even cloud chambers were described, and in the February 1950 *Superboy #6* Wenzel took on the foxhole radio.

"Hey, fellers and girls! Here is something you can make!" a screwdriver-brandishing Superboy tells us.[7] The set has a two-inch coil wound with 120 turns of 28 or 30-gauge cloth-covered wire. The razor blade is blue, and the head of the safety pin is removed, its sharp end stuck into the base, a pencil lead attached to the other end. The phone is connected this time using Fahnestock clips, a type of spring clip for electric wires, set at the edge of the board like Hanson's NBC set. The drawing looks very much like the Hanson set photo, with the same arrangement of coil, pin and blade. Even the headphone is depicted in a similar position.

The page was titled "Razor Blade Radio" rather than "Foxhole Radio" and no mention was made of its military origins, though many readers by then would have been familiar with the story. It was reprinted several times, first in Great Britain in the *Superboy Annual* for 1954, followed by *Superboy # 68* in October 1958, and the *Four-Star Spectacular #4* in October 1976, establishing the foxhole radio's place in childhood lore for at least two generations.

Starting in 1946 General Electric produced a series of educational comic books covering subjects such as jet power, atomic energy, engineering and electricity that were distributed, free of charge, to middle schools. In 1950 the School Service Division of Westinghouse distributed their own comic, *How Does It Work?* that explained the basic concepts of flight, atomic energy, and other inventions. Each section included a simple project, and on the radio page was a nutshell diagram of a foxhole radio titled simply "make your own radio". There were no instructions, but the illustration was clearly labeled with safety pin, razor blade, headphones, long antenna, ground and "coil 120 turns on 2 1/2" diameter cardboard tube".[8]

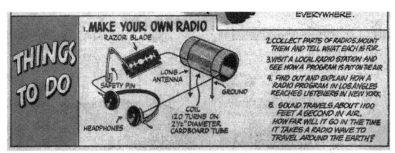

Figure 82 The foxhole radio from How Does It Work? Westinghouse Electric Corporation, 1950.

The Boy Scouts of America, almost from its beginning in in 1910, has been something of a repository for radio lore. Many scouts over the years have been radio enthusiasts and amateur operators. In the early years some troops set up small stations, and in 1951 K2BFW, the first official BSA station, went on the air. *Jamboree on the Air*, an annual international Scouting radio event, began in 1957 in conjunction with the ARRL and continues to this day.

The first edition of the Scout's *Handbook for Boys* included detailed directions for construction of a spark gap wireless transmitter and a matching galena crystal receiver, prepared by the Boy Scout Wireless

Club of Newark.[9] One of the original requirements for the Electricity merit badge was to "construct a machine to make static electricity or a wireless apparatus".[10] Wireless became a separate merit badge in 1919, renamed Radio in 1923.

1920s editions of the *Handbook* included plans for a crystal receiver and were a standard feature in Cub Scout manuals starting in the 1930s, with diagrams in several editions of the Wolf, Bear and Lion manuals.

The Boy Scout magazine *Boys' Life* ran its first wireless article in its February 1912 issue. "With wireless telegraphy being used for the tracking of criminals and saving passengers from sinking liners, it is not surprising that many boys are taking it up as a hobby".[11] What is somewhat surprising is the article's instruction requiring the reader to construct a coherer, considering much simpler mineral detectors were cheap and easy to get in 1912.

By 1920 *Boys' Life* ran radio articles in most issues, both on construction and ham radio activities. They tackled the foxhole radio in February 1951 with the "Bantam Radio", a razor blade radio that looked very much like Paul Cornell's receiver, complete with a flat, tunable coil.[12] As with the *Superboy* article, there is no mention of the "crystal-less" crystal set having originally been built during the war.

The "Razor Blade Radio" depicted in the November 1959 issue[13] is so minimal that it seems unlikely to work. A razor blade is attached to a piece of wood with a screw, the ground wire and one of the headphone leads running to the same screw. To a second screw is attached the other earphone wire, the antenna, and a piece of stiff wire wrapped around a pencil lead, which acts as a cat whisker. And that is all of it. No coil, no capacitor, only a detector, antenna, ground and phones. It is the barest minimum that will function as an AM receiver. It will work, if there is a strong enough station nearby, but the sound will be faint, even with a good antenna and ground. There is a similar war era foxhole radio, the no-coil "scrap pile radio" built by Pfc. Elias Vivero and Pfc. Huel Butler at Brooks Field in San Antonio.[14]

The design worked well enough that it was covered again in the 1963 issue of *Elementary Electronics*.[15] Art Trauffer, a frequent contributor of electronics articles to *Popular Science*, *Popular Mechanics* and *Popular Electronics*, presented it as "a more rugged version" of the two razor blade and pencil lead microphonic detectors he believed were the more common type of set in foxholes. Like the 1959 *Boys' Life* set, a razor blade is fastened to a block of wood with a

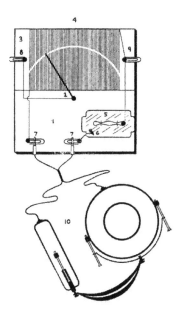

Figure 83 The Bantam radio, Boys' Life February 1951.

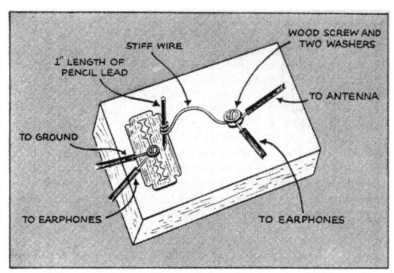

Figure 84 The minimalist razor blade radio from the November 1959 issue of Boys' Life.

screw. A pencil lead held by a wire serves as the cat whisker. He recommended blue blades, and, although his drawing is strikingly similar to the *Boys' Life* receiver, he instructs the builder to "use with a conventional circuit and a good antenna and ground", likely intending the detector to be wired with a coil and capacitor to form a resonant circuit.

In the 1950s and 60s public fascination with atomic energy, the transistor, and the space race fueled a golden age of home science and science themed projects. This was the era of volcano models, charcoal crystal gardens, and homemade cloud chambers. The first school science fairs were held in the 1940s and grew in popularity throughout the 50s. Don Herbert brought science to generations of children through television with the popular *Watch Mr. Wizard*. Authors like Herbert S. Zim, Mae and Ira Freeman, Nelson Beeler, Franklyn Branley, and Isaac Asimov wrote books on science and science experiments that would remain school library standards for decades.

Crystal radios, still a childhood staple, found a wider audience through a resurgence of popular radio books. The introduction of Sylvania's 1N34 and later improved 1N34A germanium diodes made the prospect of building a crystal radio more appealing, leaving the hobbyist free to concentrate on design rather than continuous readjustment of the detector.

Alfred P. Morgan, who in 1909 sent a letter to *Modern Electrics* comparing Clark Pettingill's "novel detector" to the microphone detector of Harry Shoemaker, wrote *The Boys' First* through *Fourth Book of Radio and Electronics* between 1954 and 1969, the standard resources for younger mid-century radio enthusiasts. The Raytheon CK722, the first low cost transistor available to the public, was released in 1953 and cost only a dollar, less than most vacuum tubes. *The Boy's Second Book* was published in 1957 and several projects took advantage of the readily available CK722. *The Boys' First Book*, however, was first printed in 1954, when the CK722 was still new and relatively expensive, and so is still rooted in vacuum tubes and crystals. Though foxhole radios are not mentioned, the book does give an overview of spark, coherers, and carbon steel microphonic detectors.

In 1953 Random House published *All About Radio and Television*,[16] the second book in their popular *All About* series of science related books. It was written by Jack Gould, the *New York Times* radio and television critic who had written an extensive article on Maxie Rupert's foxhole radio in 1944.[17] The book, written with younger readers in mind, gives a clear, detailed overview of the principals behind radio and television broadcasting and reception. At its heart are instructions for building a foxhole radio which, though written for children, are the clearest and most thorough description of razor blade radio construction to date. Gould devotes a full eleven pages to the foxhole radio, explaining in detail how to shape the safety pin, and how far to push in the thumbtack that holds the razor blade in place, all of it thoroughly illustrated by children's author Bette J. Davis.

Figure 85 Jack Gould.

According to his son Lewis, Jack Gould was happiest when repairing electronics, and would bring vacuum tubes with him on business trips to repair hotel television sets. He had a special fondness for the foxhole radio, teaching it to his sons who in turn built their own for school projects.[18]

All About Radio and Television, which Gould wrote to help fund his three boys' college careers, was translated into several languages, several hundred thousand printed in English alone. It was a favorite in grade school libraries for decades, inspiring generations of science fair projects and influencing many to pursue radio and electricity as a career or avocation. As *Superboy #6* had introduced a generation to the foxhole radio, *All About Radio and Television* kept it going for several more.[19]

The *Rick Brant* series, published between 1947 and 1968, with a 24th volume released in 1990, followed the adventures of the titular character and crew as they solve mysteries with science. In book 15 of the series, *The Blue Ghost Mystery*,[20] released in 1960, Rick found himself in need of a radio during a power outage. Remembering a description of a foxhole radio from one of his father's colleagues, he gathered together the components and, to the astonishment of his companions, built one.

Though the narrative provides enough detail to build a working foxhole radio, *Rick Brant's Science Projects*, a collection of longer versions of the science projects from the novels, expands on the original and throws in a good dose of radio theory. A diagram is provided of a basic razor and pencil lead set, along with a more traditional crystal set complete with capacitor, 1N34 diode and tunable coil. The soldiers and Marines who built these sets, the book tells us, could find wire on the battlefield to wrap coils, razors and pencils for the detector, earphones from wrecked equipment, and "a bayonet stuck in the ground is as good as a water pipe for a ground".[21]

With a wealth of literature in school libraries, the foxhole radio became a popular subject for school projects and science fairs. In 1947 the Brooklyn Children's Museum exhibited a "radio built of razor blades" and other projects built by members of their Science Club.[22] Foxhole radios were used for classroom projects as early as 1950 when instructor Don Oakes of Hayward High School, California, assigned the construction of a razor blade receiver to every student in his classroom.[23] As a science fair project they were most popular in the late 1950s through the early 60s and continued to make appearances well after. A foxhole radio was exhibited as recently as 2004 Southern Colorado Regional Science Fair with illustrations from *All About Radio and Television*.[24] While copies of the *Rick Brant* and *All About* books are still available in a few middle school and public libraries, 21st century students are more likely to find foxhole radio plans among the thousands of web pages featuring them.

The foxhole radio occasionally made some unexpected appearances not always directly related to radio. A detailed orthographic drawing of a Cornell style foxhole radio was printed in the 1954 textbook *Drawing Sketching and Blueprint Reading* as an exercise in the interpretation of blueprints.[25] Although it is a Cornell type receiver, it bears some resemblance to the *Superboy* set, specifically the angle of the drawing and the Fahnestock clips overlapping the front edge.

The 1960 textbook *You and Science* recommends the student build a simple radio for further study, either the foxhole radio from *All About Radio and Television*, or, for "much better results", a set with a diode and tuning capacitor.[26] 1964's *Modern General Science* also includes a plan for a crystal radio. "You can substitute a blue razor blade and a safety pin for the diode", instructs the text. "It will not work as well as a diode, but if you are near a very strong station, you should be able to hear it."[27] And the 1961 edition of *Casebook for Technical Writers* includes a foxhole radio as a beginning exercise in technical writing, including a simple diagram of a razor blade and safety pin type set.[28]

In April 1960 the foxhole radio was mentioned in a letter written to the popular *Ask Ann Landers* syndicated advice column after a concerned reader asked for advice regarding her husband's aunt who, despite being well educated and in good standing with the community, claimed during a dinner party to have intercepted "radio messages between Red China and the Russians through her bridgework".[29] Eppie Lederer, who had written the column under the Landers pseudonym since 1955, was incredulous. "Urge her to see a doctor. She may have been a community leader in her day but she is sick now and needs professional help. If you are unable to prevent her from going to the F.B.I. I assure you they will recognize her condition and you'll be hearing from them."

Many of Landers' readers took issue with her response and felt compelled to cite examples of the phenomenon. "This is what my mail has been like for the past three days. You can draw your own conclusions."[30] A letter from Yonkers claimed "there is an established case of a carborundum worker who retained enough of the dust so that it acted as a detector in his mouth. He had a great deal of gold work, plus a sensitive jaw bone. This man did bring in Station WOR in New Jersey."

Debates still flare up about whether radio can be heard through dental work. Proponents usually suggest that it is caused by dissimilar metal fillings acting as a semiconductor, though most evidence is anecdotal. "I'm a ham and hold a second-class radio-telephone license", reads a reply from Little Rock. "I've known people who have received radio signals through the fillings in their teeth — particularly when they have two different types of metals in the mouth. The teeth carry the vibrations to the brain by bone conduction, as in a crystal-tuned circuit."[31]

In 1974 Lucille Ball described her own experience with the phenomenon to Dick Cavett, claiming to have heard in 1942 not only a strong local station via her temporary fillings, but the Morse transmissions of a secret Japanese radio transmitter.[32] Lucy originally told the story to Ethel Merman, and from her it made its way into the script of Cole Porter's 1943 musical *Something for the Boys*.

Some readers of the Ann Landers column were less convinced. "One question, please", read a letter from Stamford, Connecticut. "Did that woman who said she was receiving secret radio messages between Red China and Russia understand Chinese or Russian? Surely the messages were not being transmitted in English."

To at least one veteran, the story of two dissimilar metals acting as a radio detector made sense. "During the war we had lots of fun listening to radio messages by attaching a safety pin to a rusty razor blade and a little piece of copper wire. We actually got Tokyo Rose."[33]

In 2003 the Discovery Channel's *Mythbusters* attempted to settle the issue by recreating a dental radio using combinations of several different metals.[34] To demonstrate the theory behind the myth, program host Adam Savage built a foxhole radio, which, to his apparent surprise, worked. Also in 2003 R. Lee Ermey, host of the History Channel's *Mail Call*, demonstrated several viewer-built foxhole sets sent in to the program.[35]

The foxhole radio has been the subject of several works of art. In 2008 Norwegian artist Catherine Kramer exhibited a disassembled, sculptural foxhole radio at the *Works in Progress Show*, Royal College of Art. Artist, composer and educator Paul DeMarinis created *Four Foxhole Radios* in 2000 as part of a decade-long series of pieces examining electromagnetic communication.

Razor blade radios have made appearances in radio history books, hobby manuals and communications textbooks. Historian Erik Barnouw refers to them in *The Golden Web*, volume two of his monumental history of American broadcasting, as part of a broader discussion of radio use by American soldiers during WWII.[36]

Byron G. Wels describes his building of a foxhole radio during WWII in the introduction to his 1968 *Transistor Circuit Guidebook*. "I suppose my first experience with solid-state devices marks me (along with many other World War II GIs) as somewhat of a pioneer in the field. We were using solid-state receivers before the transistor was known. Unlike today's experimenter, with a choice of sealed, encapsulated, and very exotic devices with which to experiment, we had to construct our own semiconductors!"[37]

Although he never mentions where he was at the time, Wels does recall hearing Tokyo Rose, so likely he was somewhere in the Pacific. "After you swiped a pair of earphones from the nearest plane, jeep or tank," the wire from one half of the phones was wrapped around an empty toilet paper tube to form a coil. The catch was removed from a safety pin, which was stuck into a piece of wood so that the point contacted the razor blade, "none of the fancy plastic-coated, ribbons-of-steel, but a blued blade — quenched-blued, mind you, not lacquer blued". He suggests a "bayonet stuck hilt-deep in the ground" to serve as a ground, something also described in *Rick Brant's Science Projects* and other sources. It would seem an unlikely use for something as valuable as a bayonet if it were not a veteran describing it.

Wels had already written about the foxhole radio in more detail, from the perspective of the soldier building it, in the 1958 edition of *Electronic Projects You Can Make*. "You can emulate with ease what many G.I.'s built under severe battle conditions. The requirements, of course, are simple. You need a piece of wood (any ol' piece of wood), and the cardboard core of a toilet paper roll. You will also need a blued razor blade -not lacquer blued, but blued by heat quenching which puts a film of oxide on the blade. You'll also need a safety pin. Now for the hard part. You need a pair of earphones, and the approved method for obtaining these is to wander casually over to either a parked tank or an unguarded airplane, and very quickly and deftly unplug the nearest pair of earphones and shove them under your shirt. After this bit of 'midnight requisitioning,' high-tail it away from there."[38]

After obtaining wire, either from one half of your newly acquired headphones or from another source, some it is used as an antenna, "one hundred feet will be just about right, and the higher you can get it the better reception will be". The rest is used to wind the coil and to wire between components. "Drive your bayonet into the soft earth wall of your foxhole" to attach the ground wire. "Another small length is connected to the razor blade, but first remove the bluing from a small portion of one end with some fine sandpaper, and, if tools are available, solder the wire to this cleaned part of the blade. Now connect the razor blade to the antenna side of the coil, and the safety pin to the open side of the earphones… You must probe round the blued surface of the blade with the 'cat's whisker' safety pin, until you hit a sensitive spot. You'll know when you find this spot, as you'll hear the local radio broadcast."

Razor blade radios were written about in magazine and newspaper articles long after World War II, many of the sets closely resembling those built during the war. A set described in the October 1962 *Popular Mechanics* looks like Paul Cornell's design, down to the coil wrapped around a piece of wood and the paper clip slider.[39] Joe Tartas, the author of the article, was himself a radio operator during WWII serving in the Pacific and may have seen similar sets first hand.

The Cornell style receiver shows up again in the July 1964 issue of *S9*, a magazine for citizen's band radio enthusiasts.[40] The author, who also built razor blade sets during the war, advocates the foxhole radio for those readers who want a first project to learn the basics of electronics.

Nearly twenty years later the Cornell set returned in the March 1983 issue of *Popular Communications* with a diagram and a mention of Korean War era sets,[41] and then again in the August 1985 *73 for Radio Amateurs*,[42] this time giving credit to W8EFW Paul Cornell and his 1945 *QST* article. The author also adds a tuning capacitor and battery bias for a "high performance" version.

The foxhole radio is discussed in a series of letters printed in the December 1986, April and July 1987 issues of *Radio-Electronics*. What type of razor blade should be used - the editor preferred a "quench-type, not lacquered"[43] blade - and the *Illustrated Current News* featuring Maxie Rupert's receiver that hung on the wall at the AFRTS "as long as anyone can remember"[44] were discussed.

The set featured in the January 1988 issue of *Hands-On Electronics* was a standard Rupert style configuration with the addition of a tuning capacitor. The author stressed the historical significance of the foxhole radio and the "list of parts as nostalgic as the era it came from".[45] Walkman style headsets, which would not work for the set, were more readily available by now than high impedance headphones, and the author thoughtfully includes a circuit using an LM386 amplifier for use with modern phones.

In 1994 The *Minneapolis Star Tribune* printed plans, including illustrations from *All About Radio and Television*, in response to a letter from a WWII veteran who was trying to remember how he hooked up the receiver he built at Anzio.[46]

In 1997 the Xtal Set Society, dedicated to the art of crystal radio construction and lore, printed an article on foxhole radio theory, a frequent topic of discussion among their members. It included an ingenious pencil and blade detector made from a piece of two by four lumber. A slit is cut into the wood to hold the blade, and a hole is drilled, just large enough for a pencil to fit snugly, all the way through to where the blade will be inserted. The pencil is inserted into the hole until it meets the blade, forming a carbon and blade connection that will resist jarring.[47]

CQ magazine ran a two-part article on crystal radios in their October and November 1999 issues. Written by columnist Dave Ingram, K4TWJ, the articles are a fond tribute to crystal radios and a summary of their current state among radio and electronics enthusiasts. They prompted several letters from readers and two follow-ups in August 2000 and July 2001, the latter of which includes a "stripped-down Foxhole Radio" which, like the 1959 *Boys' Life* set, lacked a coil. The author remembered building one similar as a child "and actually hearing two different stations at different pencil-point settings on the single-edge, blue blade razor".[48]

One of the more charming razor blade radio articles was printed in the June 2005 issue of *Popular Communications*.[49] Author Shannon Huniwell recounts the story of an eleven-year-old boy and his friends who are taught how to build a foxhole radio in 1962 by a radio station owner. The article includes a sketch and construction tips drawn by the station owner on the back of a radio survey card.

The Reverend George Dobbs, author of the Ladybird book *Making a Transistor Radio*, wrote an article on making "radios from odds and ends" for his regular "Carrying On the Practical Way" column in the British magazine *Practical Wireless*.[50] Iron pyrites, razor blades, and rusty hobby knives are all discussed as alternative detectors in hopes of encouraging readers to try making a radio from junk. Some of his best results, he reports, came from the rusty blade with an ordinary safety pin. He also revisits the "coke" detector of his Ladybird book but, unwilling to purchase a large sack of coal for the experiment, used a small piece of barbecue charcoal, which he found to be "fiddly but when set at the 'sweet spot' it was quite effective".

In 2011 the *Ex-POW Bulletin*, the magazine of the American Ex-Prisoners of War, described the foxhole radio, including a drawing from Jack Gould's *All About* book as an example.[51]

The prehistory of the foxhole radio and the development of radio detectors leading to the razor blade and safety pin are explored in "Build a World War II Foxhole Radio" in volume XVII of the *Electronics Handbook*.[52] Detailed and well-illustrated directions are given for construction of a set similar to Cornell's but with a round coil, as well as a "Deluxe Set" with tuning capacitor and battery bias. The article sparked a resurgence of interest in foxhole radios among enthusiasts.

Responding to reader demand generated by his *Electronics Handbook* article, author WB5REX Lance Borden started the Borden Radio Company, selling radio parts and kits, including a "Cornell WWII Foxhole Radio".[53] Kits such as these, along with the sharing of radio lore on the internet, have helped keep the hobby of home electronics alive for a new generation.

Yeary Communications, who marketed radio kits in the 1980's, also offered a foxhole radio kit, and before that several companies ran classified ads in *Popular Mechanics*, *Popular Science* and other magazines and newspapers selling razor blade radio plans, from 1944 well into the 1970s. "Look, Boys!" announced a 1953 newspaper advertisement. "Make a razor blade radio. Fun to make, simple to build, costs almost nothing," other than forty cents for the plans.[54] "Amazing serviceman's pastime", according to a 1945 ad in Popular Mechanics. "Batteryless, tubeless, schoolboy thrill."[55] "Famous Razor blade radio! Illustrated plans."[56] Some ads offered supplies as well as plans. "Razor blade radio. Make one. We supply headphones" for $1.75, or twenty-five cents for just the plans.[57] By 1970 printing costs had risen, and the reader would need to shell out $1.00 to make a "fantastic razor blade radio. Household parts and our plans let you build it easily."[58]

The foxhole radio, for decades part of the lore of devoted radio hobbyists, local radio clubs and amateur radio groups such as the Crystal Set Society,[59] has found a larger audience through the internet and through the DIY spirit of the maker movement. Though maker culture will eagerly adopt new technologies, simpler and older devices that can be reworked and repurposed into novel forms are also sought out. Foxhole radios are appealing because of their history and because they can be built and modified relatively easily.

Figure 86 WB5REX Lance Borden displaying some of his radio kits at the Belton, Texas Hamfest in 2017. Mr. Borden's magazine articles and kits have helped renew interest in foxhole radios and homemade radios in general.
http://www.xtalman.com

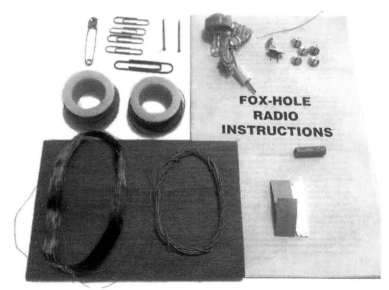

Figure 87 A vintage Yeary Communications foxhole radio kit.

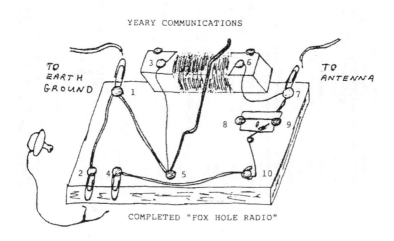

Figure 88 Yeary's illustration of the completed foxhole radio.

It is possible to build a sophisticated and selective crystal receiver. Many sets built by crystal radio aficionados are highly refined, with excellent fidelity and precise tuning. Razor blade sets are a different matter.

Foxhole radios, though simple to build, are notoriously difficult to adjust properly, not very selective, and usually provide only faint audio. They were born of a lack of better components and boredom. People still build them, mostly because of their history. Recreating a functional artifact built by soldiers during wartime is appealing. And this type of point contact detector occupies a significant position on the evolutionary path between the coherer and the integrated circuit.

Vacuum tubes overtook crystal radios after the First World War, relegating the old galena detectors to hobbyists and, for a while, to those unable to purchase or operate a tube receiver. But tubes are power hungry, quickly depleting batteries which had to be frequently recharged. They are hot, fragile, and their large size limited miniaturization. And many radio enthusiasts, even in the heyday of tubes, felt crystals provided greater fidelity, and longed for a new "cold" detector.

Progress was finally made in that direction, not in commercial radio, but in radar. Early systems used relatively low frequency radio waves that could be detected by vacuum tube detectors. In the early 1940s radar operating in microwave frequencies was developed, allowing for the detection of smaller objects and, as the antenna was smaller, the installation of radar in aircraft. Vacuum tubes are not very good microwave detectors, but crystals can be, and so silicon point contact detectors, essentially the same arrangement as a cat whisker and mineral radio detector, were tried and later replaced by sealed, fixed crystal diodes.

In 1939 Russell Ohl, while investigating purely refined silicon for use as point contact rectifiers, noticed that one of his samples had areas that were more electrically resistant than others. The sample had two regions with different impurities, one with a slight excess of electrons, the other with a slight deficiency. Ohl dubbed the regions "n" and "p" and the barrier where they met became known as the P-N junction. He found that purifying silicon or germanium as much as possible before doping it with impurities would allow for the creation of consistently similar diodes.

Knowledge gained through wartime semiconductor research for use in radar systems led to the development of the point-contact transistor by William Shockley, John Bardeen and Walter Brattain at Bell labs in 1947. Commercial versions were produced and were soon replaced by more rugged bipolar junction transistors.

Greenleaf Whittier Pickard, while recounting the history of the solid rectifier in 1948, appreciated how revolutionary the transistor would be. "A recent Bell Laboratory development, of which no technical details are yet available, indicates that a solid amplifier has been produced. This should make the prospect brighter for the advent of a supplantive device for the vacuum tube. It is interesting to speculate on the simplification of radio receiver design which might result from such developments. Such amplifier units would be smaller than vacuum tubes, and would require no heater or filament supply. They would require no warming-up interval before coming into action. Also, hearing aids could be reduced to a lighter and more compact unit. It is, however, unlikely that power tubes, such as are used for transmitting, will be similarly supplanted."[60]

The pursuit of a single semiconductor "chip" containing multiple electronic components and circuits began almost as soon as news of the transistor was announced. Work by Jack Kilby, Robert Noyce, Kurt Lehovic and others in the late 1950s and early 1960s led to practical, commercially available integrated circuits.

The availability of inexpensive specialized chips has both drawn hobbyists to design complex projects that would be impossible without them and to rediscover older, lower tech devices, in some part as a response to a perception that integrated circuits are less "hands on".

As a tool for learning basic principles, a crystal radio with a diode detector is a much more predictable and less frustrating first project than a cantankerous razor blade and pin foxhole radio. And yet, for many radio enthusiasts, their history and place in the lore make the foxhole radio irresistible. Debates have flared over the type of pencil lead used,[61] when and where they were built, even if soldiers ever built them at all.[62] But no element of the foxhole radio elicits more discussion among radio enthusiasts that the nature of the razor blade.

23 Tops in Patience

What type of razor blade should be used has been debated among radio enthusiasts almost since the foxhole radio was invented. Post-war articles often specify "blue" blades which, according to foxhole radio lore, were used in the original sets. Many companies made blue colored blades in the 1940s, but only a few of the World War Two era servicemen who built foxhole radios ever specified what type of blade they used. Maxie Rupert famously used a Marlin blade, and NBC engineer O. B. Hanson declared that the blade worked as a rectifier because it was blue. Hanson never mentioned why the blue blade worked better, only "that the blued steel surface on the double-edged Marlin razor blade used provides the rectifying action necessary for the detection of strong signals".[1] Regardless, it was now cemented in the lore.

Ed Bourgault recommended a blue blade[2] and one of Paul Cornell's radios has a blue Marlin double edge blade. Both sets were built nearly a year after Rupert's, plenty of time for the blue blade requirement to make the rounds. *The Boy's Fun Book*,[3] *Superboy #6* and several other post-war sources reinforced the need for a blue blade.

Some authors came to different conclusions. *Rick Brant's Science Projects* tells us a blade "either of white steel or blue"[4] will work as well. Jack Gould, who built several foxhole radios, says in his *All About Radio and Television* that "a plain white-looking blade often works better than 'blue' blades".[5] The Reverend George Dobbs had better results with rusty blades,[6] and some, like Corporal John Savacool, sometimes skipped the blade altogether and instead used a piece of steel shell fragment.[7] But it was the blue blade that persisted, and many articles, books and radio amateurs suggest that one is necessary to build a functional or authentic foxhole radio.[8]

What makes a blue blade blue is also debated among enthusiasts. One persistent theory is that it is from a "cold" chemical bluing, like the type used to touch up the finish on firearms, and that the bluing solution contains selenium which acts as a rectifier.[9] Some cold bluing processes do use selenous acid and copper nitrate, forming a thin layer of copper selenide, which is a semiconductor. However, this would be a costly and laborious process for hundreds of thousands of razor blades, and manufacturers would likely use a cheaper method.

Heat treating was the usual process, forming a thin layer of iron oxide, typically magnetite (Fe_3O_4), on the surface. The layer is thin enough that some light passes through, allowing for thin-film interference, like that seen in a soap bubble, which produces blue and other colors on the surface. Two different WWII era blue Marlin blades analyzed using energy-dispersive X-ray spectroscopy have a surface layer of approximately 42-46% oxygen by weight, 51-56% iron and a few trace elements, but no selenium.

Magnetite is a semiconductor, and blue blades with more of it on their surface should theoretically be more efficient radio wave detectors. Of the two blades analyzed, a Marlin military issue "camouflage wrapper" and a civilian "blue wrapper" blade, the blued surface of the civilian blade had a higher oxygen content (46.48% by weight) compared to the military blade (42.03%) and therefore more oxidation. It was also 40% more effective as a detector when used with a safety pin cat whisker, and 60% more efficient when used with a pencil lead.

Because the amount of surface oxidation varies, some blue blades work better as detectors than others, not only from different manufacturers, but between individual blades of the same make.

Some blue blades were lacquered to add an extra defense against rust. They will not work well or at all as detectors unless some of the insulating layer of lacquer is scraped off, which may explain why Jack Gould recommended scratching an area of the razor blade with a nail file[10] and why several articles warn to avoid lacquered blades and recommend "quenched" or heat treated blades.[11] Some blades were both heat treated and lacquered, sometimes with a blue lacquer, prompting the author of the "Razor Blade Radio" article in the

November 1959 issue of *Boys' Life* to suggest that not only the lacquer but the bluing itself may need to be scraped off.

Likely the first and certainly the best known "blue" blade of its day was sold by Gillette. In 1931, after several years of overstated earnings, inferior blade production and declining sales, Gillette's reputation was suffering. To turn the company around, the board selected Gerard B. Lambert, who had made a name for himself with his marketing campaign for Listerine. Lambert ordered new equipment installed to produce improved blades, which he asked his engineers to color blue to set them apart from Gillette's older blades.

In June 1932 Lambert placed an advertisement in newspapers across the country that was as much an apology as it was an announcement of the new blades. "A frank confession", the ad began in large capital letters. It went on to explain why quality had declined and promised that the new Blue Blades were "the sharpest ever produced". The advertisement worked, the blades were actually better, and Gillette's sales climbed.

Gillette still safeguards the original process[12] but there are some clues. When Gerard Lambert asked for a blue blade, his engineer replied that he "would just put on a blue lacquer. I made it clear that I did not want a blade to look like blue steel, I just wanted a different color, something other than the plain steel."[13]

A process outlined in a patent filed in 1932 by A. R. Stargardter of Gillette[14] describes a method of heat treating blades to produce a blue color. Steel is usually tempered to decrease its hardness. There are several methods, but generally the hotter it gets, the softer it will be. The color of the iron oxide layer that forms when steel is heated, from light yellow through brown, purple, blue and grey, is an indicator of the temperature reached. Heating to 300° C or so will give the desired blue color but will make the blades too soft to keep a sharp edge. By carefully controlling the oxidizing and reducing gasses used in the tempering furnace and then cooling the steel on chilled plates, Stargardter was able to give the steel a blue surface at a lower temperature, "independently of hardness or temper."[15]

A patent infringement suit filed by Gillette against the Triangle Mechanical Laboratories Corporation[16] sheds more light on the process. Gillette engineers showed that their process of bluing using controlled amounts of oxidizing and reducing gasses produced a coating of ferrous oxide (FeO) and not the usual magnetite. The blades were then labeled with acid-dipped stamps and given a coat of lacquer to prevent corrosion.

Gillette successfully proved that their process was unique and their patent was valid, however an earlier case allowed companies to produce blue colored blades so long as they did not attempt to pass them off as substitutes for Gillette Blue Blades.[17] By the 1940s dozens of razor blade manufacturers were making one type or another of "blue" blade, presumably using processes different from Gillette's.

Marlin Firearms began selling razor blades in late 1935,[18] many of them made in the factories of other razor blade companies, a common practice at the time. By the 1940s they sold blades with at least five different center slot patterns, all from different factories.

The design of the center slot in a razor blade, used to fix the blade in place in a razor, is generally unique to a specific company. The first Gillette blades had three round holes which seated onto three pins in the head of Gillette razors. Gillette's original patent expired in 1921, opening the field for dozens of companies waiting to make blades that would fit Gillette razors. Probak, a division of the AutoStrop Safety Razor company, made blades in the late 20s with a long center slot overlapped by one central and two end patterns corresponding to the original three-hole pattern on Gillette blades. Instead of being simply round, the holes in the Probak blades were combinations of diamonds, crosses, or narrow oval shapes. Probak blades would fit in AutoStrop razors, which had matching shaped pins, as well as in Gillette razors, but Gillette blades would not fit in AutoStrop razors.

Gillette developed a slotted blade design at around the same time that resembled one of Probak's previously patented designs, resulting in a patent battle and eventual purchase of AutoStrop by Gillette in 1930. Most double-edged blades afterwards had a central slot spanning roughly 80% of the width of the blade overlapped by one central and two end holes corresponding to the original three-hole pattern on Gillette blades. The Gillette blade of 1933 and onward, for example, had two narrow slots with rounded ends on either side of a small diamond at each end and a round hole in the center. Other manufacturers designed new patterns that would not infringe on Gillette's design but still fit Gillette razors.

Marlin blades, even those with the same wrapper design, came with several different slot designs. Two of them, one with a large shaped center hole and one with a rectangle that spanned most of the center of the slot, closely resembled blades sold by Blue Strike and Durex.[19] There were at least two versions of the Marlin military issue "camouflage" blade, both with plain tan wrappers with "Marlin" written in script at an angle. One blade had a small diamond shaped center hole and was stamped "Perfect Edge", and the other had a wider central diamond that reached the outer holes and was stamped "Perfect Edge" and "Made in U.S.A." The civilian version of the "camouflage" blade, with a blue wrapper, had a long narrow rectangular central hole, again running the length of the middle of the slot, and was also stamped "Perfect Edge" and "Made in U.S.A." Other civilian versions of the Marlin blade had wider center rectangles or ovals. Undoubtedly there were others.

Testing Razor Blades

To understand how well some of these blades worked as detectors, several were tested in the same radio using both a plain safety pin cat whisker and a pencil lead. The radio used was like the ones used by Eldon Phelps, Maxie Rupert and others, the "standard" receiver with an untuned coil, detector and phones. The coil was wound with 120 turns of 26-gauge enameled wire around a two-inch cardboard form. Voltage was measured across the headphone connections to determine relative signal strength using different detectors.

At first a local radio station was used as the signal source using a 100-foot antenna and a copper rod for a ground, but results were so sporadic that this was soon abandoned, and an ancient Heathkit radio frequency generator operating at 1190 kHz was used instead. The strongest signal that could be found and held for more than a few seconds was measured, and where possible more than one of the same model of blade was tested and the results averaged. Sixteen WWII era blades as well as a 1920s steel Gillette, a 1960's Gillette "Super Blue", a modern stainless blade, a galena crystal, a 1N34A diode, a nail and a metal spoon were compared.

This test was not meant to be definitive; rather, it was intended to provide a comparison of a specific group of razor blades under a specific and controlled set of criteria. Detection can vary widely between different blades of the same model, and between different spots on the same blade. Most of the blades tested, though still wrapped, were at least seventy-three years old and were likely affected by oxidation or other chemical or mechanical changes, making them better or worse detectors over time. Results in the field may have been very different.

Using a safety pin with any of these blades produced at best a faint signal in the headphones. It is astonishing that anyone at Anzio was able to hear a radio station thirty miles away using only a razor and safety pin. Only a few spots on each blade worked at all and the signal faded or was lost altogether after a few minutes or when the set was lightly jarred or even breathed on. As Charles Rinde said in his letter to *Time* in 1944, it takes "tops in patience" to tune and hear a station.[20]

With a Safety Pin	mV
Gem "Micromatic" single edge	2
Durex	1.5
Gillette "camouflage", scratched	1.4
Gillette "Thin", scratched	1.4
Blu Strike	1.3
Modern stainless blade	1.3
Gillette "Super Blue", scratched	1.2
Gillette "Blue Blade", scratched	1
Marlin "Perfect Edge" blue version of camo wrapper	0.8
Gillette 1920s blade	0.5
Gilt Edge	0.5
Marlin High Speed large rectangle and "1122" in corners	0.5
Marlin "Perfect Edge" camo wrapper, large diamond	0.5
Pal	0.5
Marlin High Speed with large rectangle	0.4
a nail	0.3
Club blue, scratched	0.3
a spoon	0.2
Marlin "Perfect Edge" camo wrapper, small diamond	0.2
Star, scratched	0.2
Marlin with oval center hole	0

Figure 89 WWII civilian razor blades and their military issue equivalents. Gem produced a special "Armed Forces" box of five blades but the blade and wrapper were the same available in the civilian market. The Marlin on the top left (civilian) is deep blue, the one on the right (military) is a coppery brown. Likewise, the bottom left Gillette blade wrapper is red, and the one on the right is tan. All of the blades on this and the following four pages can be seen in color at https://foxholeradio.blogspot.com/2019/06/wwii-era-razor-blades.html

Figure 90 WWII era Marlin razor blades. Two versions of the "camouflage" military issue blade, made by different manufacturers, top, and a civilian "Perfect Edge" blade sold in the blue version of the same packaging, second row left. The rest are "High Speed" blades made for Marlin by different manufacturers. Bottom left is the same model blade found in Paul Cornell's radio. "Blu Strike", "Durex" and a few other blades had the same slot shapes and all may have been made by Club.

Figure 91 WWII era Gillette blades, top to bottom the camouflage military issue blade, the civilian "Thin Blade", and the Blue Blade. All of these had a varnish coating. The camouflage blade is from 1944. This particular "Thin" blade is from 1935 and the Blue is from 1942 but both models were still in limited production throughout the War.

Figure 92 Blades tested as detectors. From top left: WWII era Blu-Strike, Club, and Durex; a military issue Gem single edge plain steel blade; a Gillette "Blue" blade; a military issued Gillette blade in camouflage wrapper; an early 1920s Gillette blade; an early 1960s Gillette "Super Blue" blade; a WWII era Gillette "Thin" blade.

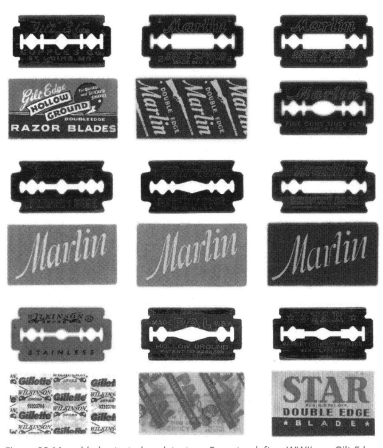

Figure 93 More blades tested as detectors. From top left: a WWII era Gilt Edge; a Marlin "High Speed" with 1s and 2s in the corners, similar to the one used in Paul Cornell's radio; a civilian "High Speed" blade (note that the Marlin "High Speed" blades have the same center slot design as the Blue Strike and Durex blades in the previous photograph and likely were made by the same manufacturer); Marlin blade with an oval slot design; two versions of the Marlin "Perfect Edge" military issue blade in camouflage wrappers; the civilian version of the Marlin "Perfect Edge" blade with yet another slot design; a contemporary stainless Gillette Wilkinson blade; WWII era Pal and Star blades.

At the top of the list was a military issue Gem single edge plain steel blade with two millivolts detected at the headphone connections. Keep in mind that this was the *best* signal with a blade and safety pin. By comparison, 55 mV was measured using a galena crystal, and 114 mV with a 1N34A diode.

Next was a Durex blue blade at 1.5 mV, followed by Gillette "camouflage" and "Thin" blades at 1.4 mV. The two Gillette blades are plain steel with a brown lacquer that had to be scratched off before any detection was possible. A Blue Strike did as well as a modern stainless steel blade at 1.3 mV. The 1960s Gillette "Super Blue" blade fared slightly better that the war era Blue Blade, 1.2 mV compared to 1 mV. Both had to be scratched to work, though some detection was possible at the edges of some of the blades tested, presumably because there is no lacquer covering the edges. Ed Bourgault, in the navy photograph taken of him and his radio,[21] appears to be using a Gillette Blue Blade with a safety pin pressed against the edge.

The signal with the rest of the blades was barely audible at less than 1 mV, nine of them at .5 mV or less. A new clean steel nail gave .3 mV, even the spoon worked at .2 mV. The five Marlin blades tested ranged from .8 mV for the plain blue wrapper "Perfect Edge" to no signal at all for the one with the oval shaped center hole. Even the two "camouflage" Marlin blades gave different results, .5 mV for the one with the larger central diamond in its slot, .2 mV for the one with the smaller diamond, no better that the spoon. Whichever version of the Marlin blade Maxie Rupert was using would have made a significant difference.

Non-blue blades did well compared to blue blades using a safety pin. Half of the ten best performing blades were not blue, a good showing especially considering only six of the nineteen blades tested were non-blue. Though any obviously rusty areas were avoided, rectification may have been due to small spots of oxidation on the surface on the non-blue blades.

Using a pencil greatly improved signal strength, more so that any difference in the entire range of blades tested with safety pins. The worst performing blade and pencil combination, the Gillette camouflage blade with lacquer scratched off, gave 4.3 mV, more than twice the signal strength of the best blade and safety pin combination.

With a Pencil Lead

	mV
Gilt Edge	24.4
Gillette 1920s blade	20.2
Marlin "Perfect Edge" camo wrapper w large diamond	18.6
Marlin High Speed, lg. rectangle and "1122" in corners	17.8
Gillette "Blue Blade", scratched	16
Gillette Thin, scratched	15.7
a nail	15
Star, scratched	14.8
Marlin High Speed with large rectangle	14.5
Marlin "Perfect Edge" blue version of camo wrapper	14.3
Pal	14.3
Gem "Micromatic" single edge	14
Marlin oval center	14
Modern stainless blade	13.5
Gillette "Super Blue", scratched	13.2
Marlin "Perfect Edge" camo wrapper, small diamond	10.6
Club blue, scratched	6.9
Blu Strike	6
Durex	4.6
Gillette "camouflage", scratched	4.3
a spoon	1.5

How well a blade performed with a safety pin cat whisker was not necessarily an indicator of how well it would do with a pencil lead and vice versa. The Gilt Edge blade, which gave the best result at 24.2 mV, over twelve times stronger than the best blade and pin, was in the middle of the list with a pin. The Durex went from second best with pin to second worst with pencil.

Results for Marlin blades varied widely. Their "High Speed" blade marked "1 1 2 2" in the corners, the same blade used in at least one of Paul Cornell's radios, gave the fourth strongest signal of all blades at 17.8 mV, while the "camouflage" blade with a small diamond in the center of its slot only came in at 10.6.

The Marlin "1 1 2 2" High Speed, their regular High Speed, the Blu Strike and the Durex all have the same blade design and were likely made at the same facility around the same time. However, they gave a wide range of results at 17.8, 14.5, 6, and 4.6 mV respectively. This highlights just how different the results can be from batch to batch or from factors like shipping and storage.

Blue blades did no better that non-blue blades overall. Of the top ten best, 30% are non-blue, roughly the same percentage they are of all the blades tested. The second best results from a blade and pencil lead was with an old steel Gillette from the 1920s. Even a plain iron nail performed as well or better than 68% of all the blades tested. It was not surprising that plain steel worked well with a pencil lead considering Clark Pettingill's "novel detector"[22] of 1909 used carbon and plain steel, as did Pickard's carbon and needle detector and, much earlier, David Edward Hughes' original microphone detector. The setup was, of course, different, but the rectifying action came from the contact of carbon and steel. The right chunk of steel, clean and with little obvious corrosion, will work as well as a blade, blue or otherwise, with a pencil lead, as Corporal John Savacool found when he heard Axis Sally through a piece of shrapnel.[23]

Reception was mostly nonexistent using several pieces of rusty metal and rusty razor blades with either safety pin or pencil, although Reverend George Dobbs reported that the rusty samples he tried gave some of the best results.[24] Not all rust is the same, and some types likely would make good radio wave detectors. Finding out which ones would make an interesting experiment.

The sets

There were several basic types of foxhole radios and many subtle variations of each type. With a few exceptions, there were no measured drawings or standard specifications. Most were built from scant descriptions or the memory of a quick glance of someone else's set in a dark foxhole. But here and there details were written down or remembered later.

These descriptions are not intended to be instructions, though a working set could be made using them by anyone with some experience in making similar crystal sets. Instructions for making a basic foxhole radio can be found at the end of this chapter, and the reader is encouraged to experiment further.

The "Basic" set

This is essentially a bare bones crystal set, with a safety pin, pencil lead and razor blade detector. With or without a pencil lead, it was likely the most common type of foxhole radio at Anzio. It is the radio of Eldon Phelps and Maxie Rupert, William Ahrens, William Lloyd Wiley, Sapper Shelton[25] and the anonymous soldier photographed at

Anzio by *Yank*.[26] It was described in many articles during and after the war, nowhere with more clarity or fondness for the subject than Jack Gould's *All About Radio and Television*.[27]

The circuit is simple. One side of the coil connects to the antenna and half of the detector. The other half of the detector connects to the headphones, and then on to the other side of the coil and the ground.

In the context of a foxhole radio, a coil is multiple turns of insulated wire wrapped around a cardboard tube or other form. Of all the components it requires the most care and skill. The wire must be insulated so that the individual turns of wire do not connect electrically. At Anzio soldiers used whatever wire was available, insulated with cloth or enamel, in a variety of gauges. Some, like Ray McAllister, used coils of wire as they were found without rewinding them.[28]

The coil's diameter was never mentioned by the original Anzio foxhole radio builders. Many of them were likely built around heavy cardboard tubes that were used to ship grenades, artillery fuses, and electrical components like vacuum tubes. Coils wound around these tubes would have had a diameter of one to four inches or more. Toilet paper tubes would have made good coil forms, however most toilet paper at Anzio came in small waxed envelopes issued with rations rather than a roll. Jack Gould suggests a two-inch diameter coil form when describing Maxie Rupert's radio, likely referencing a toilet paper tube.[29] He also recommends using 28 or 30-gauge wire.

William Ahrens wrote that he used 80 turns of wire for his coil,[30] while Sapper Shelton only used 20 to 25 turns around a two-inch form.[31] William H. Rosee wrapped 75 feet of combat wire around a grenade container. Maxie Rupert's sketch showed 120 turns, a number that was fixed in the lore after Jack Gould printed it in the *Times*. Juston Garton's set in *QST*,[32] the *Superboy* set, even Ed Bourgault's set had 120 turns of wire in their coils.[33] There is nothing magic about 120. Little can be determined from it as far as the radio's selectivity, especially without knowing coil diameter, wire gauge and several other factors.

The baseboard, which all the other components attach to, is usually a flat piece of scrap lumber. Soldiers at Anzio would likely have used pieces from wooden packing crates, which were plentiful. The base needs to be large enough to mount the coil and detector and all the connection points, and small enough to be portable or fit neatly onto

)le bookshelf. It should be of soft wood, like pine, so that acks or nails can be easily inserted.

War era accounts of foxhole radios never go into any great discussion about the baseboard. Eldon Phelps only mentions that it is "a piece of dry wood" which says more about weather conditions at the beachhead and the relative scarcity of dry materials, at least early on. Dimensions are given in a few postwar articles. *Superboy #6*, for example, recommends six by six inches. Jack Gould's board is eight by six inches or more. Thumbtacks, nails, or screws[34] were usually used to attach coils and other components, though Ed Bourgault evidently preferred tape to hold his razor blade in place.[35]

The antenna is usually only described as being as long as practical. Ahrens did specify 100 feet, and Rosee 70 yards.

Figure 94 Model of the "standard" foxhole set, like those built by Eldon Phelps and Maxie Rupert.

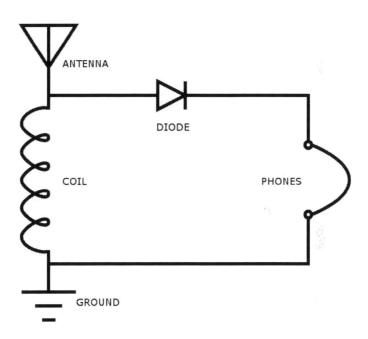

Figure 95 Schematic of the "standard" set.

The *Field Artillery Journal* set

Like the "Basic" set, Lieutenant Rosee's set[36] as printed in the July 1944 *Field Artillery Journal* used a microphone style detector with two carbon rods from flashlight batteries straddled by a razor blade. A flashlight battery in circuit between the detector and the headphones improved the detector's sensitivity and the radio's volume. A model built of this radio had greater volume than the "basic" set.

The detector uses two rods from zinc-carbon batteries, which are no longer as common as they were during WWII. Taking apart a zinc-carbon battery to get to the carbon core is not recommended. Graphite sticks and rods are readily available through art supply dealers and elsewhere. Rosee does not mention how the graphite rods are attached to the board but they may have been wired on or else carefully wedged between upright nails.

A razor blade worked well but, because it would not sit completely flat, it was somewhat difficult getting it into the right position. A needle was easier to set up, but it tended to roll out of place.

Rosee included more information about his radio's coil than most. He used 75 feet of "combat wire", likely referring to W-130 Assault Wire, a two conductor 22-gauge stranded communications wire. It was wrapped around a grenade container, and assuming he used the inner tube from a Mk 2 or similarly sized smoke grenade, it would have had a 2 3/4-inch diameter and a roughly 8 5/8-inch circumference, allowing for approximately 104 turns of wire. His antenna was one of the longer specified at 70 yards.

Many sets at Anzio used a microphone type detector. Rosee may have been the only one to specifically mention including a battery bias, but it is hinted at elsewhere.[37] Without it, the microphone detector works about as well as a razor blade and pencil lead in an otherwise similar radio.

Figure 96 Model of the "Rosee" set with microphone detector and battery bias

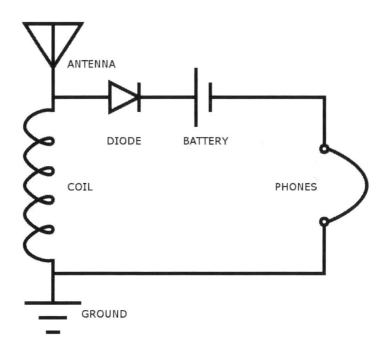

Figure 97 Schematic of the Rosee set.

The *Stars and Stripes* set

Private Ralph Evans' radio also used a microphone style detector and not much more. All that is known about it comes from a brief description and sketch in the June 1, 1944 issue of the Mediterranean Naples edition of *Stars and Stripes*.[38]

Two carbon sticks from flashlight batteries are stuck upright into a piece of wood, presumably into pre-drilled holes, far enough apart so that a razor blade can be balanced on top of them. The aerial, the article tells us, is attached to one carbon stick, and the ground to the other. Exactly how they are attached is not clear. The drawing shows the ground wire wound loosely on the left carbon, with four loops from bottom to top, and labeled "coil". The end of the wire is attached to one side of the headphones. The aerial wire is wrapped the same way, except from top to bottom, around the right-hand carbon. It attaches at the bottom to the other side of the headphones. Though it is not mentioned in the article, at least some of the insulation must have been removed from the coiled wires to allow for electrical contact with the carbons. A razor blade sits flat on the tops of the carbons and is adjusted until a signal can be heard.

A model built of this set was difficult to adjust, would usually hold a station for only a few seconds, and was nearly inaudible when it did. Granted, it was built using scanty instructions, but results were similar when the "coil" was given more turns or a different blade was used.

It is possible there is something missing or misinterpreted in the *Stars and Stripes* article that would otherwise make this a better receiver. The original, for example, may have had a battery bias, like the *Field Artillery Journal* radio, which may have improved performance. If the description in the article is complete and accurate, it is astonishing that Private Evans was able to hear anything on it at the beachhead. Either way, it is an interesting curiosity of foxhole radio lore.

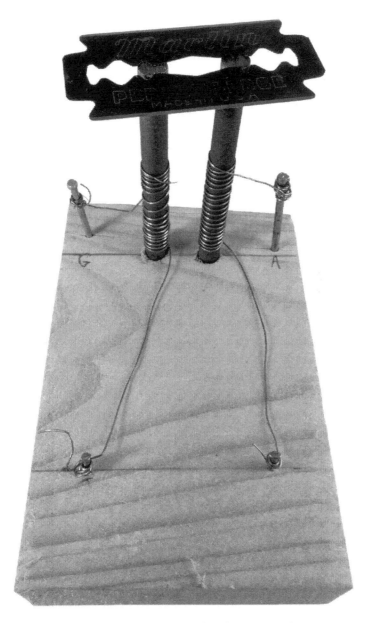

Figure 98 A model of Ralph Evans' set from Stars and Stripes.

The Cornell Set

Paul Cornell's radio is by far the most thoroughly described war era foxhole set. The clear illustrations and specific measurements, first printed in the September 1945 QST,[39] were copied at least six times in other publications.[40]

It is a cousin of the "basic" set, with a few distinctive features. The ground, rather than connecting directly to the coil, connects to a paper clip, unfolded and attached to the baseboard with a nail or screw so that it can pivot across the face of the coil in an arc, offering some degree of tuning. Cornell referred to it as the "switch arm". Enamel is sanded off the surface of the coil in an arc where the paper clip contacts it. This is tricky to do; remove too much, and the adjacent wires of the coil will short against each other.

The base is four inches square and 1/4-inch-thick, likely the thickness of wood from packing crates that Cornell was using. The coil, rather than being round, is made from a flat 3 3/4 by 2 by 1/4-inch board. Cornell never explained why he chose a flat piece of wood for his coil form, but it may have been easier to find than a cardboard tube, and it did result in a more compact and portable radio. Square or rectangular coils were used in some electronic projects of the day, which he would have been aware of. A drawing of a home-built rheostat from a 1945 children's book on electronics bears a striking resemblance to Cornell's receiver.[41]

The razor blade is attached with a thumbtack, as are two paperclips used for earphone jacks. The cat whisker is a pencil lead, without safety pin, wrapped directly with a wire leading from the earphone jack.

The Cornell set is a simple and elegant bit of improvisation that works well and is, along with the "basic" set, one of the classic foxhole radio designs.

Figure 99 A model of Paul Cornell's set.

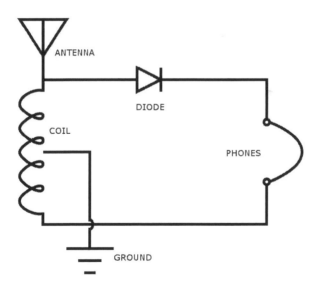

Figure 100 Schematic of the Cornell set.

The *Boys' Life* razor blade radio

The razor blade radio printed in the November 1959 *Boys' Life*[42] is so simple that it seems impossible that it would work at all. A screw and washer attach a razor blade, ground wire and one wire from a set of earphones to a small block of wood. A second screw and washer hold the antenna, the other earphone wire and a stiff wire wrapped around a pencil lead. It does work, but it is the weakest of all the published foxhole radio designs with the possible exception of the *Stars and Stripes* set. When another version of it was printed in the 1963 edition of *Elementary Electronics*, the author intended it as a detector component to be used "with a conventional circuit"[43] rather than as the whole radio.

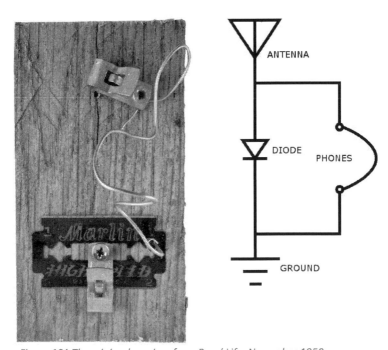

Figure 101 The minimal receiver from Boys' Life, November 1959.

This set might be dismissed as a post-war oddity if not for the similar set built by Pfc. Elias Vivero and Pfc. Huel Butler at Brooks Field.[44] Theirs used a safety pin instead of a pencil lead and must have been very difficult to hear, even with strong stations nearby.

288

Building a foxhole radio

A foxhole radio is not a very good radio. It is difficult to find a good spot on a razor blade for detection, and when one is found, the signal is often so weak that it is mostly drowned out by background noise. It is easily knocked out of place, or just drifts out of place undisturbed, and the same spot may never work again. Most cannot be tuned, so they are stuck on one station, or two or three if there are several nearby.

A foxhole radio is not a very good radio, but that is not the point of building one. There is the historical connection of making something that was made by servicemen in the field. And there is the satisfaction of crafting something from scrap that, after much effort, frustratingly and faintly, will work.

The instructions given here are for a "basic" foxhole radio with a coil. There was no standard foxhole design during the war. They were copied after a glimpse or a hasty description, evolving as they spread. There were a few published articles that here and there gave a dimension or two, or the number of turns of wire for the coil. But other than Paul Cornell's article in *QST*, there were no measured, detailed plans.

There was no need for precise detail. These sets were made in the field from whatever was on hand. Not everyone had 24-gauge enameled wire, or a two-inch diameter cardboard tube, or even a safety pin or pencil or razor. But if the basic components of the thing and how it all connected were understood, a set could be made from whatever was available.

Measurements are provided in these instructions only as a starting point to hopefully free the builder from fretting over the fitting of parts. Any numbers given have more to do with lore and tradition than engineering. Please feel free to experiment.

Heed all safety warnings. Ground wires should only be attached to grounding rods or metal cold water pipes, never gas pipes. Do not set up an antenna if there is even a chance of storms or lightning. And if you do use a razor blade for a detector, handle it carefully. A plain piece of steel, like a steel nail, is a safer alternative and will likely work just as well.

You will need

- Lumber scrap, preferably pine, approximately 6 x 6 inches, 1/2 to 1 inch thick
- A cardboard tube approximately 4 1/2 inches long, 1 1/2 to 2 inches wide
- 24 to 28-gauge enameled wire
- Safety pin
- Pencil
- Razor blade or another piece of steel
- Small nails
- Thumbtacks
- Crystal radio headphones or earphone
- Wire for the antenna, insulated, 100 feet or so
- Wire to connect the ground and other connections

To make the coil, poke two tiny holes about a quarter to half of an inch apart, one above the other, near the end of the tube using a pin or thumbtack. Push six to eight inches of the enameled wire through one hole from the outer side of the tube. Now push the wire back through the other hole. Pull tight and repeat, through the first hole and back out through the second. The idea is that there will be enough tension to hold the wire in place. There should now be about six inches of wire sticking out of one of the holes.

Holding the tube and keeping the six-inch free end of the wire out of the way, start carefully winding the coil. Each turn should lay tightly by the previous turn without overlapping. Take care not to kink the wire.

The turns will try to become disorderly and unravel. Keeping your thumb and fingers over them as you wind should help. It will be slow going and you may have to start over several times, but it will get easier once you get the hang of it. The number of turns in your coil matters in that it is one of the factors that determines what frequency your radio will receive; however, this radio has no capacitor and no real measurements or calculations and is more about trial and error and experimenting with different coil sizes and windings. Although there is no real reason to choose 120 turns, it is part of the lore and so is as good a place as any to start.

Once all the windings are complete, hold them in place and poke two more holes in the tube near where the windings end. Cut the wire, leaving eight inches or so loose on the coil. Push the end of the wire through one hole and back through the other, repeating as before. The coil should be tight without any overlaps and should be well secured enough on the ends that it is not in danger of unwinding. You can use a little transparent tape if it feels like it may unravel.

Attach the coil centered near the rear of the baseboard using two thumbtacks. Make sure the thumbtacks do not contact the wire of the coil.

The razor blade is attached next, in front of the coil and somewhat centered. Leave enough room so that the cat whisker can be adjusted without bumping into the coil. Fasten the blade to the board with two thumbtacks but do not push them all the way in yet. Keep in mind that other, less injurious bits of iron than a razor blade can be used and may work just as well or better. If a razor blade is used, make sure it is not lacquered.

To make the cat whisker, bend the head of the safety pin back so that, when it is held flat on the board, the point of the pin touches the board. Not all foxhole radios used pencil leads but you will have much better results if you do. The usual method was to tie a sharpened piece of lead to the point of the pin using a fine piece of wire. However, this is tricky to do and tends to slip out of place. A simpler method is to sharpen a wooden pencil and cut off the pointed end right were the paint begins. Then poke the safety pin into the back of the cut off point so that it rests between the wood and the graphite.

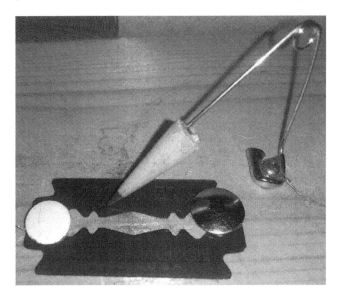

Using a small nail, attach the safety pin to the board so that the pencil lead contacts the razor blade. Do not drive the nail all the way in.

Drive two small, clean nails partway into the wood near both ends of the coil. These are the attachment points for the ground (right) and antenna (left) Drive two more nails side by side near the front right corner of the board. This is where the headphone will attach.

Using fine sandpaper, remove the enamel insulation from the loose end of the wire coming off the left end of the coil. Wrap the wire around the nail that is to the left of the coil, labeled "Antenna" in the illustration, so that it makes good electrical contact.

Note that Fahnestock clips are used for the radio in the illustration rather than nails. If available, they make things easier to hook up, but nails will work fine.

Wrap the end of another piece of wire around the same nail, then wrap the other end of that wire around one of the thumbtacks holding the razor blade in place, labeled "B".

Remove the insulation from the wire coming from the right end of the coil and wrap it around the nail that is to the right of the coil, labeled "Ground". Run another wire from this nail to the right most of the two nails at the front right of the board, "H2".

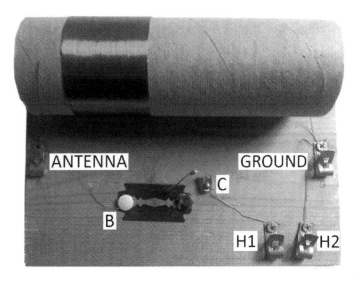

The final connection runs from the "H1" nail to the nail holding the safety pin, labeled "C" for cat whisker. Once connected, drive the nail holding the safety pin in a bit more but not so much that the safety pin cannot be rotated.

The antenna wire runs parallel to the ground and should be as long and high as possible. Some of the Anzio sets had antennae 100 feet or more. Use what space you have available. The ends of the antenna need to be isolated from whatever they are attached to by insulators. Typically, ceramic insulators would be used, but other nonconductive items were likely substituted at Anzio. The antenna needs to be strung so that it does not touch anything for its entire run. A bit of the antenna is left loose at one end, hanging from the insulator, so that it can connect to your radio at the "Antenna" nail. Make certain that your antenna is far from any power lines or electrical equipment, and never use it when there is a possibility of lightning.

A good ground is every bit as important as a good antenna. A cold water pipe is the classic recommendation for crystal radio grounds, but many houses today have plastic water pipes that will not work. Never use a gas pipe as a ground as this can potentially cause a fire or explosion. A narrow copper pipe or, better yet, a copper grounding rod driven into the earth will work well. Clamp one end of a wire to the grounding rod and attach the other end to the "Ground" connection on your radio. The ground will work better if the soil it is in is a little damp.

Modern headphones will not work with foxhole or crystal radios unless you build a converter.[45] Old crystal radio headphones are ideal if there happens to be a pair readily available in good working order. The simplest and least expensive route is a crystal earpiece. They are piezoelectric and tend to be cheaply made, and so the audio quality suffers, but they are easy to find,[46] as of this writing anyway, and work well enough with foxhole radios. Some of these earpieces have a small plug on the end, which can be snipped off. Strip off a half inch or so of insulation and attach it to the earphone connections on the radio.

Once everything is hooked up and the antenna and ground are in place, move the pencil point cat whisker across the razor blade until a station can be heard. It may be right away, or it may take a lot of adjusting. Remember that the signal may be faint, especially so if you are far from the transmitter. If nothing can be heard even after a lot of adjusting of the cat whisker, make sure everything is making good electrical contact where it should be. Check the antenna and ground. If one is available, substitute the detector with a 1N34A germanium diode or equivalent to make sure everything is hooked up correctly. Reception is generally better at night and waiting until dark can sometimes make a significant difference.

There are more sophisticated crystal radios than the foxhole radio. Some can pull in distant stations with impressive selectivity and volume. The crystal radio hobby is alive and well, and if building a foxhole radio has inspired you to pursue it, there is a wealth of information on the internet,[47] in radio and electronics magazines and books, and often through local radio clubs.[48]

Although it may not be the most sophisticated "crystal" radio, the foxhole radio is a fascinating artifact of radio lore and a testament to the resourcefulness of those who built it. Because it is a tangible and easily reproduced part of military lore, it has been a popular subject of radio enthusiasts almost since the first set was built at Anzio. There may be better choices for a first radio project, but few with as rich a history.

.

Appendix A

Squier and Lewis' Estimates

George Owen Squier's estimate to the Board of Ordnance for construction of radio equipment, George Owen Squier to J. C. Ayers, February 12, 1898, Records of the Board of Ordnance and Fortifications, National Archives and Records Administration.

Instruments

1 12 inch Induction Coil of latest design, with independent vibrator, parallel and series spark gap and interlocking reversing switch ... $185.00
2 Sets of 4 cells each Chloride Accumulators, portable type, at $45.00...
$90.00
1 Complete induction coil set, transmitter and receiver, Clarke type...
$75.00
2 Sets adjustable condensers, Marshall Type No. 15D at $40.00...
$80.00
6 Leyden jars, variable size... $20.00
2 Kelvin Electrostatic Multicellular Voltmeters No. 14 from 40 to 160 volts, and from 0 to 40 volts, at $60.00... $120.00
3 Special Marconi receiver tubes, with accessories [Squier is referring to coherers; this was six years before Fleming invented the diode vacuum tube.]... $80.00

Materials

For wire, zinc sheets, reflectors, brass, copper, aluminum, coils, etc...
$200.00

Labor & Construction

Special castings, labor for designing and constructing special transmitters
and receivers, with accessories ... $200.00

Total... $1050.00

Lewis' Bid, Isaac Newton Lewis to the board of ordnance and
fortification, February 13, 1898, Records of the Board of Ordnance
and Fortifications, National Archives and Records Administration.

Estimated Cost

One large Tesla Coil (oil insulation, condensers, rheostat, complete)...
$150.00

One rotary transformer for use with coil ... $75.00

One set, 6-inch brass balls, with mounting... $50.00

Once complete receiver (coherer, relay, battery, mounting, extra tubes, etc.)
$75.00

For machine work, materials, and original experimental apparatus...
$100.00

Total Cost... $450.00

Appendix B

Instructions for setting up the Clarke wireless apparatus, 1898. Sent by William J. Clarke of the United States Electrical Supply Company to George Owen Squier, May 9, 1898. Courtesy the United States Air Force Academy Library.

Directions for operating wireless telegraphy apparatus.

   Place the transmitter upon the table upon your right hand and the receiver upon your left, in such a position that the lettering on the name plates of the apparatus will appear to you right side up. Connect the carbon of one cell of dry battery to the binding post marked "1" in drawing, and the zinc to post marked "2". Now connect twelve cells of dry battery to the posts marked "3" and "4", and after seeing that all connections are secure and tight, loosen up the binding screws at each end of the Coherer or glass tube, an also check nuts on the inside of the brass posts near to the end of the glass tube. This will permit the spiral springs to draw out the plugs in the tube which they should be allowed to do until they are about 3/16 of an inch apart, this will completely open the circuit of one cell of dry battery. Now press the armature of the relay "R" up against its contact, and the sounder should immediately sound, and the de-coherer "D" (which is in multiple with it) should begin to vibrate rapidly. If this does not occur it is possible that the relay armature does not strike its contact on account of the magnet cores being too far forward. The magnet should be adjusted so that the armature will just strike its contact and close the local circuit without touching the cores of the magnet.

As soon as you find that the armature makes proper connection and sounds the other two instruments you can begin to operate the key "K", and will slacken up the armature spring of the relay "R", until such time as the pressing of the key "K" will cause the current from the one end of battery to operate relay "R", and sound the other apparatus every time the key is pressed. Continue the adjustment both of the relay and sounder until Morse signals can be readily transmitted, and then tighten up the check nuts at each end of the coherer until the plugs in the glass tube begin to press upon the metallic powder, when it will be found that the circuit will close and immediately open again on account of the de-coherer "D" tapping upon the tube. Continue screwing up until such time as the circuit refuses to open after closing, and then slowly loosen one of the check nuts until the circuit opens when your apparatus should be in proper adjustment, then tighten up the two screws which bind the plugs in the glass tube so that they cannot move.

Now try the key K again, and if the circuit is inclined to keep closed the plugs in the tube should be separated a trifle more, in other words the receiver should promptly respond to Morse signals sent by the key "K", and at the same time have the plugs in the tube as close together as possible without being close enough to interfere with proper signals from key "K".

If your transmitter is a small size one connect it up with 6 cells of a dry battery and adjust the vibrator so that it will operate whenever the Morse key of the transmitter is depressed. Then adjust the distance between the two bass balls until sparks readily pass across on pressing the key, and you should find that the receiver should respond instantly to every impulse of the transmitter.

The two switches of the receiver S & S1 are intended to cut off both local and main battery, as if these are left on when the instrument is not in use, they will exhaust themselves rapidly by continually working through the resistance coils which are placed in the base of the instrument.

When operating it at a greater distance than across the table it will be found necessary to connect post "G" of the receiver to ground, and also one of the posts G of the transmitter. Ascertain by experiment which one of these posts gives the best result. For still greater distances the remaining post of the transmitter should be connected to a large metallic plate placed high in the air carefully insulated and connected by a wire which is insulated thoroughly. The same kind of plate and wire should be connected to post P of the receiver.

As this class of apparatus is something entirely new, you should not be discouraged if you find it difficult to properly adjust it at first. In fact it might take several weeks before you have properly mastered all the details, and then you will feel that it is indeed an easy matter.

The small transmitter is only intended for signaling [sic] to a distance of a couple of hundred feet, whereas the larger one is capable of transmitting to a distance of ten or more miles. Should you have any trouble whatever with the instruments please communicate with us, and we will do all in our power to assist you.

Yours very truly,
U. S. Electrical Supply Co.
per
William J. Clarke

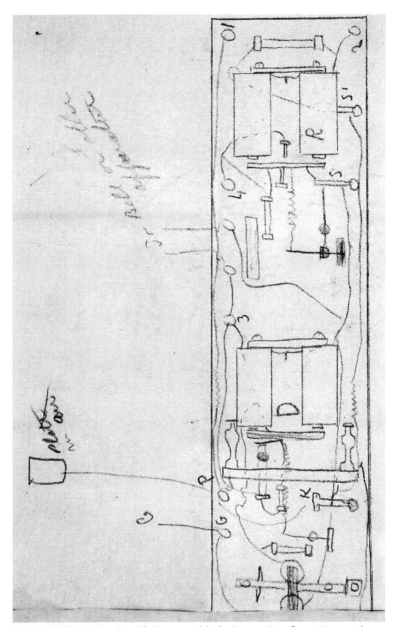

Figure 102 Illustration that Clarke sent with the instructions for setting up the wireless apparatus, 1898. Courtesy the United States Air Force Academy Library.

Notes

Chapter 1
A New and Astonishing World

1. Lt. Julian McAllister to Col. H. K. Craig, Chief of Ordnance, June 22, 1855, Record Group 77, Entry 1201, Volume 1, National Archives - Philadelphia.
2. Major J. G. Martin to Colonel H. K. Craig, June 22, 1855, Record Group 77, Entry 1201, Volume 1, National Archives - Philadelphia.
3. John Paul Graham and M. B Gatza, *The Architectural Heritage of Fort Monroe: Inventory and Documentation of Historic Structures Undertaken by the Historic American Buildings Survey*, vol. 2 (Washington, D.C.: Historic American Buildings Survey/Historic American Engineering Record, National Park Service, Dept. of the Interior, 1987), 61.
4. T. C. Martin to George O. Squier, November 22, 1898, Correspondence Pertaining to Communications Experiments, Jul. - Dec. 1898, McDermott Library Special Collections, United States Air Force Academy Libraries.
5. James Clerk Maxwell, "On Physical Lines of Force," *The London, Edinburgh and Dublin Philosophical Magazine and Journal of Science*, March 1861, continued April and May 1861, January and February 1862.
6. Most of what is known to survive of Hertz's original apparatus is preserved in the Deutsches Museum, Munich.
7. Hertz's original paper, "*Ueber sehr schnelle electrische Schwingungen*", was published in Annalen der Physik 267, no. 7 (May 1887): 421-448. An English translation, "On Very Rapid Electric Oscillations", appears in a collection of Hertz's work, *Electric Waves*, printed, most recently, by Cornell University Press.

8. William Crookes, "Some Possibilities of Electricity," *Fortnightly Review*, February 1, 1892, 173–81.

9. Oliver Lodge, "The Work of Hertz," *The Electrician* 33 (July 6, 1894): 271–72.

10. Heinrich Hertz and Daniel Evan Jones, *Electric Waves: Being Researches on the Propagation of Electric Action with Finite Velocity through Space* (London: Macmillan, 1893).

11. C. F. Guitard, "Condensation by Electricity," *The Mechanic's Magazine*, 1850, 346.

Chapter 2
This Important Phenomena

1. Squier, George Owen and Albert Crehore, "London Notes" (Diary, 1897), Bentley Historical Library, University of Michigan.

2. Albert C. Crehore, *Autobiography* (Gates Mills, Ohio: W.G. Berner, 1944), 79.

3. George Owen Squier to the Adjutant, Fort Monroe, January 14, 1898, Correspondence Pertaining to Communications Experiments, Jan. - Jun. 1898, McDermott Library Special Collections, United States Air Force Academy Libraries.

4. United States. et al., *Report of the Board on Fortifications or Other Defenses Appointed by the President of the United States under the Provisions of the Act of Congress Approved March 3, 1885*, 49th Congress, 1st Session, House Executive Document Number 49 (Washington: U.S. Government Printing Office, 1886).

5. United States, *The Statutes at Large of the United States of America, from December 1887 to March 1889*, vol. XXV (Washington, D.C.: United States Government Printing Office, 1889), 491.

6. United States War Department, *Annual Report of the Chief Signal Officer for the Year 1887* (Washington, D.C.: U.S. Government Printing Office, 1887), 142.

7. United States War Department, 142.

8. United States War Department, 142.

9. United States War Department, *Annual Report of the Chief Signal Officer for the Year 1890* (Washington, D.C.: U.S. Government Printing Office, 1890), 52.

10. United States War Department, *Annual Report of the Chief Signal Officer for the Year 1898* (Washington, D.C.: U.S. Government Printing Office, 1898), 59.

11. United States War Department, *Report of the Chief Signal Officer to the Secretary of War for the Fiscal Year Ending June 30, 1899* (Washington, D.C.: U.S. Government Printing Office, 1899), 4.

12. Squier to the Adjutant, Fort Monroe, January 14, 1898.
13. Squier to the Adjutant, Fort Monroe.
14. Squier to the Adjutant, Fort Monroe.
15. Isaac Newton Lewis to The Board of Ordnance and Fortification, December 8, 1897, Records of the War Department General and Special Staffs, Board of Ordnance and Fortifications, National Archives and Records Administration.
16. "Laying a Cable in the Narrows," *The Telegraphic Journal and Electrical Review* 11, no. 254 (October 7, 1882): 286.
17. "Executive Document Number 168," *United States Congressional Serial Set* 51st Congress, 1st Session (June 27, 1890).
18. "The Report of the Sixty-Third Annual Reunion of the Association of the Graduates of the United States Military Academy," June 9, 1932.
19. Lewis to The Board of Ordnance and Fortification, December 8, 1897.
20. Squier to the Adjutant, Fort Monroe, January 14, 1898.
21. Lewis to The Board of Ordnance and Fortification, December 8, 1897.
22. "Proceedings of the Board of Ordinance and Fortification," January 20, 1898, Records of the War Department General and Special Staffs, Board of Ordnance and Fortifications, National Archives.
23. H. L. Chadbourne, "William J. Clarke and the First American Radio Company" (1982), Bancroft Library, U. C. Berkley Libraries.
24. "New York Notes," *The Electrical Engineer* 24, no. 483 (August 5, 1897): 123.
25. Chadbourne, "William J. Clarke and the First American Radio Company," 8.
26. "Marconi Wireless Telegraphy in America," *The Electrical Engineer* 24, no. 500 (December 2, 1897): 532.
27. "Marconi Wireless Telegraphy in America."
28. "Clarke on Wireless Telegraphy," *Transactions of the American Institute of Electrical Engineers* XIV (1897): 607–13.
29. For a description and illustrations of Clarke's apparatus see "Wireless Telegraphy," *Scientific American*, April 2, 1898, 213–14.
30. "Clarke's Apparatus for Wireless Telegraphy," *The Electrical Engineer* XXV, no. 519 (April 14, 1898): 391–93.
31. William J. Clarke to George Owen Squier, January 31, 1898, Correspondence Pertaining to Communications Experiments, Jan. - Jun. 1898, McDermott Library Special Collections, United States Air Force Academy Libraries.
32. J. C. Ayers to George Owen Squier, February 17, 1898, Correspondence Pertaining to Communications Experiments, Jan. - Jun. 1898, McDermott Library Special Collections, United States Air Force Academy Libraries.

33. George Owen Squier to J. C. Ayers, March 13, 1898, Correspondence Pertaining to Communications Experiments, Jan. - Jun. 1898, McDermott Library Special Collections, United States Air Force Academy Libraries.
34. Squier to Ayers.
35. "Proceedings of the Board of Ordinance and Fortification," March 16, 1898, Records of the War Department General and Special Staffs, Board of Ordnance and Fortifications, National Archives.
36. United States War Department, "Report of the Board of Ordnance and Fortification," in *Annual Report of the Secretary of War for the Year 1898* (Washington, D.C.: U.S. Government Printing Office, 1898).
37. Similar equipment built by Clarke is described in "Clarke's Apparatus for Wireless Telegraphy."
38. William J. Clarke to George Owen Squier, May 9, 1898, Correspondence Pertaining to Communications Experiments, Jan. - Jun. 1898, McDermott Library Special Collections, United States Air Force Academy Libraries The complete instructions are reprinted in the appendix of this book.
39. Albert C. Crehore to George Owen Squier, May 24, 1898, Correspondence Pertaining to Communications Experiments, Jan. - Jun. 1898, McDermott Library Special Collections, United States Air Force Academy Libraries.

Chapter 3
With More Perfect Adjustment

1. United States War Department, *Report of the Chief Signal Officer to the Secretary of War for the Fiscal Year Ending June 30, 1899* (Washington, D.C.: U.S. Government Printing Office, 1899), 28.
2. "Squier Again Tests Marconi's Telegraphy," *New York World*, April 11, 1899.
3. "Wireless Telegraphy," *San Antonio Light*, April 15, 1899.
4. "Wireless Telegraphy," *Portsmouth Herald*, May 1, 1899.
5. "Wireless Telegraphy," *Harper's Weekly*, May 20, 1899.
6. Squier made photographs of his 1898 transmitter and receiver but they have not been located.
7. "Wireless Telegraphy," May 20, 1899.
8. "Wireless Telegraphy," *The North Adams (Massachusetts) Evening Transcript*, May 15, 1899.
9. "Wireless Telegraphy."
10. "Wireless Telegraphy."
11. "Editorial," *The Electrical World* 30, no. 2 (July 10, 1897): 29–30.

12. United States War Department, *Annual Report of the Secretary of War for the Year 1901*, vol. 1 (Washington, D.C.: United States Government Printing Office, 1901), 937.
13. Captain L. S. Howeth, *History of Communications-Electronics in the United States Navy* (Washington: United States Government Printing Office, 1963), 25.
14. Howeth, 22.
15. H. L. Chadbourne, "William J. Clarke and the First American Radio Company" (1982), Bancroft Library, U. C. Berkley Libraries.
16. Howeth, *History of Communications-Electronics in the United States Navy*, 34.
17. For insight into the navy's slow acceptance of radio and technology in general before WWI, see Susan J. Douglas, "Technological Innovation and Organizational Change: The Navy's Adoption of Radio, 1899-1919," in *Military Enterprise and Technological Change: Perspectives on the American Experience* (Cambridge, Mass.: MIT Press, 1985), 117–73.
18. Howeth, *History of Communications-Electronics in the United States Navy*, 35.
19. "Use of Marconi Wireless in America," The Electrical World and Engineer, 34, no. 20 (November 11, 1899): 743.
20. "Army Wireless Telegraphy," *New York Times*, November 25, 1899.
21. "Wireless Telegraph Stations," *New York Times*, July 1, 1900.
22. United States War Department, *Annual Reports of the War Department for the Fiscal Year Ended June 30, 1900*, vol. 1 (Washington, D.C.: United States Government Printing Office, 1900), 953.
23. Vivian J. Phillips, *Early Radio Wave Detectors* (Stevenage, Hertfordshire, England: P. Peregrinus in association with the Science Museum, London, 1980), 69.
24. Greenleaf Whittier Pickard, "The 1901 Yacht Race" (unpublished manuscript, n.d.), Estate of Greenleaf Whittier Pickard, courtesy Ben Pickard.
25. Greenleaf Whittier Pickard to George H. Clark, May 26, 1931, Estate of Greenleaf Whittier Pickard, courtesy Ben Pickard.
26. Pickard, "The 1901 Yacht Race."
27. Pickard to George H. Clark, May 26, 1931.
28. "Wireless Telegraphy That Sends No Messages except by Wire," *The New York Herald*, October 28, 1901.
29. "Wireless Telegraphy!," *The Washington Globe*, November 10, 1901.
30. Lee de Forest spelled his family name with a lower case "d" but all businesses bearing his name used a capital "D".
31. Lee deForest, Diary (February 9, 1902), Lee deForest Papers, Library of Congress.
32. Lt. J. M. Hudgins, *Instructions for the Use of Wireless-Telegraph Apparatus* (Washington, D.C.: United States Government Printing Office, 1903).

33. United States War Department, *Annual Report of the Chief Signal Officer for the Year 1903* (Washington, D.C.: U.S. Government Printing Office, 1903), 20.
34. United States War Department, 20.
35. *Wireless Telegraphy: Report of the Inter-Departmental Board Appointed by the President to Consider the Entire Question of Wireless Telegraphy in the Service of the National Government* (U.S. Government Printing Office, 1905), 9.
36. United States War Department, *Annual Report of the Chief Signal Officer for the Year 1905* (Washington, D.C.: U.S. Government Printing Office, 1905), 36.
37. United States War Department, *Annual Report of the Chief Signal Officer for the Year 1904* (Washington, D.C.: U.S. Government Printing Office, 1904), 39.
38. United States War Department, 40.

Chapter 4
What Wireless Will Do

1. United States War Department, *Annual Report of the Chief Signal Officer for the Year 1905* (Washington, D.C.: U.S. Government Printing Office, 1905), 37.
2. United States War Department, 37.
3. William Mitchell, *US Army Signal Corps Portable/Radio Communication Equipment: Two Open Boxes Containing Wireless Transmitting and Receiving Equipment*, n.d., Photograph, n.d., Lot 6070, Library of Congress Prints and Photographs Division.
4. William Mitchell, *US Army Signal Corps Portable/Radio Communication Equipment: Open Boxes Mounted on Pack Mules*, n.d., Photograph, n.d., Lot 6070, Library of Congress Prints and Photographs Division.
5. *Signal Corps Set Made by Sgt. King*, n.d., Photograph, n.d., author's collection.
6. United States War Department, *Report of the Chief Signal Officer 1905*, 32.
7. "Wireless at the Post," *The Leavenworth Post*, December 27, 1905.
8. *Leavenworth Times*, October 29, 1905.
9. "Wireless at the Post."
10. "Wireless at the Post."
11. "What Wireless Will Do," *Leavenworth Post*, October 30, 1905.

Chapter 5
A Novel Detector

1. Greenleaf Whittier Pickard, "How I Invented the Crystal Detector," *The Electrical Experimenter*, August 1919.
2. Sir Jagadis Chandra Bose, Detector for Electrical Disturbances, US755840 A, filed September 30, 1901, and issued March 29, 1904.
3. Carl Kinsley, "Coherers Suitable for Wireless Telegraphy," *Physical Review (Series I)* 12, no. 3 (1901): 177–83.
4. William Henry Eccles, Electrical Engineering, 1 (1907): 241. Quoted in Vivian J. Phillips *Early Radio Wave Detectors* (London: Peter Peregrinus, 1980).
5. For a detailed account see Vivian J. Phillips, *Early Radio Wave Detectors* (Stevenage, Hertfordshire, England: P. Peregrinus in association with the Science Museum, London, 1980).
6. Leslie Miller, "The New Wireless Telegraphy," *The Model Engineer and Electrician*, 1898.
7. A. Frederick Collins, "How to Construct an Efficient Wireless Telegraph Apparatus at a Small Cost," *Scientific American*, September 14, 1901, 170–71.
8. Clark Pettingill, "Novel Detector," *Modern Electrics*, January 1909, 352.
9. William Crookes, "Some Possibilities of Electricity," *Fortnightly Review*, February 1, 1892, 173–81.
10. J. J. Fahie, *A History of Wireless Telegraphy: Including Some Bare-Wire Proposals for Subaqueous Telegraphs* (New York: Dodd, Mead, 1902), 305.
11. Fahie, 310.
12. Fahie, 307.
13. "Professor D. E. Hughes's Researches in Wireless Telegraphy," *The Electrician*, May 5, 1899, 40–41.
14. Fahie, *A History of Wireless Telegraphy*.
15. Harry Shoemaker and Greenleaf W. Pickard, Wave-detecting Device, US707266 A, filed June 2, 1902, and issued August 19, 1902.
16. Alfred Powell Morgan, *Wireless Telegraph Construction for Amateurs* (New York: D. Van Nostrand Co., 1910).
17. Alfred Powell Morgan, "A Microphone Detector," *Modern Electrics*, March 1909, 428.
18. Morgan.
19. Walter Wentworth Massie, Oscillaphone, US769005 A, filed July 14, 1904, and issued August 30, 1904; Walter Wentworth Massie, Oscillaphone, US819779 A, filed August 18, 1905, and issued May 8, 1906.
20. See A. Hyatt Verrill, *Harper's Wireless Book* (New York and London: Harper & Bros., 1913), 35.

21. Walter Wentworth Massie and Charles Reginald Underhill, *Wireless Telegraphy and Telephony Popularly Explained* (D. Van Nostrand Co., 1908), 27.
22. A. Frederick Collins, *The Book of Wireless* (New York: D. Appleton and Company, 1915), 16–18.
23. "A Wireless Receiving Station at Small Cost," *St. Nicholas*, April 1917, 559–60.

Chapter 6
Materially Clearer

1. Greenleaf Whittier Pickard, "The Who's Who Of It" (Unpublished manuscript, n.d.), Estate of Greenleaf Whittier Pickard, courtesy Ben Pickard.
2. Pickard to George H. Clark, May 26, 1931.
3. Greenleaf Whittier Pickard to George H. Clark, March 12, 1944, Estate of Greenleaf Whittier Pickard, courtesy Ben Pickard.
4. Pickard to George H. Clark, May 26, 1931.
5. Pickard to George H. Clark.
6. Amos Dolbear, "The Cricket as a Thermometer," *The American Naturalist* 31, no. 371 (November 1897): 970–71. Dolbear never specified which cricket's chirps he was counting but some later researchers speculate that it was *Oecanthus fultoni*. The formula, $T_F = 50 + \left(\frac{N_{60}-40}{4}\right)$, where T_F is the temperature in degrees and N_{60} is the number of chirps for minute, works fairly well for common field crickets (Gryllinae), though factors other than temperature can affect the chirp rate.
7. Pickard to George H. Clark, March 12, 1944.
8. Greenleaf Whittier Pickard to George H. Clark, February 20, 1944, George H. Clark Radioana Collection, Archives Center, National Museum of American History, Smithsonian Institution.
9. Greenleaf Whittier Pickard to Paul I. Murphy, July 11, 1948, Estate of Greenleaf Whittier Pickard, courtesy Ben Pickard.
10. Ben Pickard, "G. W. Pickard," E-mail, April 15, 2008.
11. Greenleaf Whittier Pickard, "How I Invented the Crystal Detector," *The Electrical Experimenter*, August 1919.
12. Pickard.
13. Pickard.
14. Pickard.
15. Greenleaf Whittier Pickard, Laboratory notebook (May 29, 1902), George H. Clark Radioana Collection, Archives Center, National Museum of American History, Smithsonian Institution.
16. Pickard to Paul I. Murphy, July 11, 1948.
17. Pickard to Paul I. Murphy.

18. George H. Clark, "G. W. Pickard SRM 4 938" (Unpublished manuscript, July 2, 1942), 938, George H. Clark Radioana Collection, Archives Center, National Museum of American History, Smithsonian Institution.
19. Pickard, "How I Invented the Crystal Detector."
20. Ferdinand Braun, "Uber Die Stromleitung Durch Schwefelmetalic," Annalen Der Physik and Chemie 153, no. 4 (1874): 556–63.
21. Silvanus P. Thompson and Oliver J. Lodge, "On Unilateral Conductivity in Tourmaline Crystals," The Telegraphic Journal 6, no. 135 (September 15, 1878): 381.
22. Sir Jagadish Chandra Bose, "On Polarisation of Electric Rays by Double-Refracting Crystal," Journal of the Asiatic Society of Bengal 64, no. 2 (1895): 291–96.
23. George H. Clark, "SRM4 1188" (Unpublished manuscript, 1944), George H. Clark Radioana Collection, Archives Center, National Museum of American History, Smithsonian Institution.
24. Clark, "G. W. Pickard SRM 4 938."
25. Greenleaf Whittier Pickard, "Notes on the Wireless Specialty Apparatus Company" (unpublished manuscript, n.d.), Estate of Greenleaf Whittier Pickard, courtesy Ben Pickard.
26. Pickard to Paul I. Murphy, July 11, 1948.

Chapter 7
New and Useful Improvements

1. Sir Jagadis Chandra Bose, Detector for Electrical Disturbances, US755840 A, filed September 30, 1901, and issued March 29, 1904.
2. Henry H. C. Dunwoody, Wireless Telegraph System, 837616, filed March 23, 1906, and issued December 4, 1906.
3. "Inventor of 'Heart of Radio' Is a Former Fairfield Citizen," Fairfield Weekly Ledger-Journal, August 30, 1928.
4. Sixty-Fourth Annual Report of the Association of the Graduates of the United States Military Academy, 1953.
5. "Famed as a Prophet," Chicago Inter Ocean, June 7, 1895.
6. "Wireless Telegraphy for Forts," New York Times, August 6, 1902.
7. "Army Posts Wireless Tests," New York Times, March 12, 1903.
8. "Government's Wireless Contract Arranged," Baltimore Morning Herald, July 27, 1904.
9. "Propriety Questioned," The Pittsburg Daily Post, July 27, 1904.
10. Alexander Graham Bell, "The Tetrahedral Principle in Kite Structure," The National Geographic Magazine 14, no. 6 (June 1903): 218–51.
11. "Kites Get Messages," Washington Post, March 28, 1906.

12. "Oversea Wireless Is a Fact, Says De Forest," *The New York Times*, April 8, 1906.
13. F. J. Tone, "Production of Silicon in the Electric Furnace," *Transactions of the American Chemical Society* 7 (1905): 243–49.
14. Dunwoody, Wireless Telegraph System.
15. Greenleaf Whittier Pickard to L. S. Hillegas Baird, August 10, 1950; reprinted in Thorn L Mayes, *Wireless Communication in the United States: The Early Development of American Radio Operating Companies* (East Greenwich, R.I.: New England Wireless and Steam Museum, 1989), 219–20.
16. Greenleaf Whittier Pickard, Oscillation Detector and Rectifier, US912613 A, filed September 3, 1907, and issued February 16, 1909.
17. "A Prodigy in Electricity," *The Ada Evening News*, March 22, 1907.
18. "A Prodigy in Electricity."
19. "Affidavit of Greenleaf Whittier Pickard," Pickard vs. Ashton & Curtis, Interference No. 31,649 (United States Patent Office, November 1911), Courtesy Alan Douglas.
20. A. Frederick Collins, "Carborundum and Silicon Detectors for Wireless Telegraphy," *Scientific American*, March 16, 1907, 234.
21. "Affidavit of Miram Oliver Pickard," Pickard vs. Ashton & Curtis, Interference No. 31,649 (United States Patent Office, November 1911), Courtesy Alan Douglas.
22. Lee deForest, "Carborundum Wireless Receivers," *Electrical World*, September 8, 1906, 491.
23. H. J. Round, "Carborundum as a Wireless Telegraph Receiver," *Electrical World* 58, no. 8 (August 25, 1906): 370–71.
24. Greenleaf Whittier Pickard, "The Carborundum Wireless Detector," *Electrical World*, November 24, 1906.

Chapter 8
Stable and Sensitive

1. Greenleaf Whittier Pickard, "How I Invented the Crystal Detector," *The Electrical Experimenter*, August 1919.
2. Greenleaf Whittier Pickard to Paul I. Murphy, July 11, 1948, Estate of Greenleaf Whittier Pickard, courtesy Ben Pickard.
3. F. J. Tone, "Production of Silicon in the Electric Furnace," *Science Abstracts, Section B Electrical Engineering* 8 (November 1905): 582–83.
4. "Affidavit of Greenleaf Whittier Pickard," Pickard vs. Ashton & Curtis, Interference No. 31,649 (United States Patent Office, November 1911), Courtesy Alan Douglas.
5. Pickard to Paul I. Murphy, July 11, 1948.

6. George H. Clark, "G. W. Pickard SRM 4 938" (Unpublished manuscript, July 2, 1942), George H. Clark Radioana Collection, Archives Center, National Museum of American History, Smithsonian Institution.

7. Greenleaf Whittier Pickard, "Notes on the Wireless Specialty Apparatus Company" (unpublished manuscript, n.d.), Estate of Greenleaf Whittier Pickard, courtesy Ben Pickard.

8. George H. Clark, unpublished manuscript (n.d.), George H. Clark Radioana Collection, Archives Center, National Museum of American History, Smithsonian Institution.

9. There are different versions of this number. A typewritten *History of the Wireless Specialty Apparatus* in the Clark Collection, Smithsonian Institution, likely written by Clark from Pickard's notes, reports 35 silicon detectors ordered by the army.

10. F. J. Tone, "Carborundum," *The Mineral Industry, Its Statistics, Technology, and Trade during 1907* 17 (1908): 149–56.

11. Tone.

12. U. S. Congress. House., *Report of the Secretary of Commerce and Labor Concerning Patents Granted to Officers and Employees of the Government* (60th Congress, 1st session, 1907) Doc. 914, 25.

13. Benjamin J. Miessner, Detector for wireless apparatus., US1104065 A, filed October 5, 1910, and issued July 21, 1914.

14. George H. Clark, "History of the Fine Wire Flexible Contact for the Crystal Detector" (unpublished manuscript, July 7, 1938), Estate of Greenleaf Whittier Pickard, courtesy Ben Pickard.

15. George H. Clark to W. C. White, June 29, 1938, Estate of Greenleaf Whittier Pickard, courtesy Ben Pickard.

16. Alfred Powell Morgan, "Building a 'Pericon' Detector," *Popular Electricity and the World's Advocate* 2, no. 1 (May 1909): 107.

17. "'Cat Whisker' Detector," *Popular Electricity and the World's Advance* 6, no. 5 (September 1913): 585.

18. Pickard to Paul I. Murphy, July 11, 1948.

19. Ben Pickard, "G. W. Pickard," E-mail, April 15, 2008.

20. The Amador Hotel still stands. It is the oldest public building in Las Cruces, and as of this writing is undergoing a renovation.

21. *Sixty-Fourth Annual Report of the Association of the Graduates of the United States Military Academy*, 1953.

22. Greenleaf Whittier Pickard to L. S. Hillegas Baird, August 10, 1950; reprinted in Thorn L Mayes, *Wireless Communication in the United States: The Early Development of American Radio Operating Companies* (East Greenwich, R.I.: New England Wireless and Steam Museum, 1989), 219–20.

23. Lee deForest to L. S. Hillegas Baird, December 6, 1948; reprinted in Mayes, *Wireless Communication in the United States: The Early Development of American Radio Operating Companies*, 222–23.

24. Harold H. Dunwoody to the author, "HHC Dunwoody," August 12, 2008.
25. George Washington Pierce, "Crystal Rectifiers for Electric Currents and Electric Oscillations, Part I," *The Physical Review* 28, no. 1 (July 1907): 31–60, continued as part II in March 1909 and part III in November 1909.
26. "Wireless Telegraph Plant Operated by Boys," *Carroll (Iowa) Times*, December 6, 1906.
27. "Yale Astonished by Boy's Wireless," *The Portsmouth Herald*, October 21, 1906.
28. Milton Rochkind, "A Potato Detector," *The Electrical Experimenter*, July 1915, 110.

Chapter 9
A Pure, Sharp Wave

1. H. W. Daly, *Manual of Instruction in Pack Transportation, Adapted for the Use of the Cadets at the United States Military Academy* (West Point, N.Y., 1901).
2. H. W. Daly, *Pack Transportation* (Washington, D.C.: United States Government Printing Office, 1908).
3. "H. W. Daly, Chief Packer, Writes Valuable Book," *The Leavenworth Times*, February 21, 1908.
4. Bolling W. Smith, "Radio and Coast Defense in the Endicott-Taft Era, 1899-1916," *The Coast Defense Study Group Journal*, May 1977, 33; United States War Department, *Annual Report of the Chief Signal Officer for the Year 1906* (Washington, D.C.: U.S. Government Printing Office, 1906), 26.
5. George A. Wieczorek, "Field Wireless Operations in Cuba," *Journal of the United States Cavalry Association* 17, no. 63 (January 1907): 526–29.
6. Wieczorek.
7. Wieczorek.
8. *Washington Post*, May 19, 1907.
9. *Washington Post*, June 16, 1907.
10. R. H. White, "A New Government Portable Wireless Apparatus," *Electrician and Mechanic*, 1907.
11. United States Army Signal Corps, *Storage Catalogue* (U.S. Government Printing Office, 1920), 387–88.
12. United States Army Signal Corps, *Property and Disbursing Regulations, Including Miscellaneous General Regulations* (Washington, D.C.: U.S. Government Printing Office, 1907), 122.
13. Edgar Russel, *Weapons and Munitions of War: Field Equipment for Signal Troops* (Fort Leavenworth, Kansas: Staff College Pres, 1908).
14. "Wireless Shows Value to Army," *The Topeka Daily Capital*, July 24, 1911.

15. War Department, *Drill Regulations for Field Companies of the Signal Corps (Provisional) 1911* (Washington, D.C.: United States Government Printing Office, 1911).
16. Lt. J. M. Hudgins, *Instructions for the Use of Wireless-Telegraph Apparatus* (Washington, D.C.: United States Government Printing Office, 1903).
17. Hudgins, 3.
18. S. S. Robinson, *Manual of Wireless Telegraphy for the Use of Naval Electricians* (Washington: U.S. Government Printing Office, 1906).
19. S. S Robison and Stanford Caldwell Hooper, *Robison's Manual of Radio Telegraphy and Telephony for Use of Naval Radiomen,* (Annapolis, Md.: United States Naval Institute, 1928).
20. William Maver, *Maver's Wireless Telegraphy: Theory and Practice* (New York: Maver Publishing Company, 1904).
21.. Mitchell's "Field Signal Communications" (1905), Squier's "Field Equipment of Signal Troops" (1907), Saltzman's "Weapons and Munitions of War" (1907), Allison's "The Use of the Signal Corps as an Aid to Maneuvers" (1908), and Russel's "Weapons and Munitions of War" (1908) all cover the use of wireless. All have been digitized and can be located by searching the Combined Arms Research Library catalog, currently at http://usacac.army.mil/organizations/cace/carl
22. George A. Wieczorek, *Notes on Wireless Telegraph Stations* (Fort Wood N.Y.H., 1909).
23. James Allen, *Regulations for United States Military Telegraph Lines, U.S. Signal Corps* (Washington: Govt. Print. Off., 1909).
24. War Department, *Drill Regulations for Field Companies of the Signal Corps (Provisional) 1911.*
25. Office of the Chief Signal Officer, *Radiotelegraphy, Circular No. 1, 1914* (Washington, D.C.: U.S. Government Printing Office, 1914).
26. United States War Department, *Compilation of General Orders, Circulars, and Bulletins Issued Between February 15, 1881, and December 31, 1915* (U.S. Government Printing Office, 1916), 563.
27. L. L Fordred, "Wireless in the Second Anglo Boer War 1899-1902," *Transactions - The South African Institute of Electrical Engineers* 88, no. 3 (1997): 61.
28. "Wireless for Border Patrol," *The New York Times*, February 10, 1911; "The Army," *Army and Navy Register*, February 25, 1911.
29. John J. Pershing, "Report by Major General John J. Pershing, Commanding, of the Punitive Expedition" (Colonia Dublán, Mexico, 1916), 2.
30. Pershing, 44.
31. Pershing, 82.
32. Pershing, 82.
33. Pershing, 44.

Chapter 10
Hell Tore Loose

1. George Bennett Ferree, "Memories from My Old Diary Covering from August 25, 1918 to November 11, 1918" (1918), entry from October 11, 1918.
2.. During WWI radio was still generally referred to in terms of wavelength, the measurement of distance between two consecutive wave peaks, rather than frequency, the number of wave cycles per second. Wavelength can be converted to frequency with the formula $f = c/\lambda$ where f = frequency in hertz (cycles per second), c = the speed of light in meters, or 3 x 108, and λ = wavelength in meters. So a 2,200 meter wave is about 136,000 hertz or 136 KHz.
3. George Bennett Ferree, "George Bennett Ferree Papers" (1961), 6.
4. Frederic Louis Huidekoper, *The History of the 33rd Division, A.E.F.* (Illinois State Historical Library, 1921), 317.
5. Ferree, "Papers," 6.
6.. Adolf, Berta, Cäsar, David, Emil, Frederick, Gustav, Heinrich, Isidor, Jakob, Karl, Ludwig, Moritz, Nathan, Otto, Paula, Quelle, Richard, Siegfried, Theodor, Ursula, Viktor, Willi, Xantippe, Ypsilon, and Zacharias. The United States Army in France used, according to the 1919 *Signal Communications for All Arms*, Ack, Boy, Cat, Don, E, F, George, H, I, Jig, K, L, Emma, N, O, Pip, Quash, R, Esses, Toc, U, Vic, W, X, Yoke, and Zed.
7. Ferree, "Memories from My Old Diary", entry for September 26, 1918.
8. Rupert Stanley, *Text Book on Wireless Telegraphy* (Longmans, Green, 1914), 339.
9. Division Signal School, 40th Division, "Liaison Signals by Radiotelegraphy," 1918, 9–10.
10. Ferree, "Memories from My Old Diary", entry for September 12, 1918.
11. Ferree, entry for September 20, 1918.
12. United States War Department, *Annual Report of the Chief Signal Officer for the Year 1919* (Washington, D.C.: U.S. Government Printing Office, 1919), 162. This is by far the longest of the Chief Signal Officer's Annual Reports and gives an exhaustive account of the Corps' activities and equipment during WWI.

Chapter 11
Small Favors

1. United States War Department, *Annual Report of the Chief Signal Officer for the Year 1919* (Washington, D.C.: U.S. Government Printing Office, 1919), 267–68.

2. The Finnish inventor Eric Tigerstedt developed a similar tube, also in 1914, to amplify sound in his sound-on-film motion picture experiments. A cylindrical anode surrounded a cylindrical grid which in turn surrounded the cathode. Because more electrons could be captured by the anode, it was a substantially better amplifier than tubes based on the de Forest triode design. Since they were only used for a specific experimental application, only a few of Tigerstedt's tubes were built.

3. United States War Department, *Report C.S.O. 1919*, 267.

4. United States War Department, 6.

5. *Airplane Radio Transmitter SCR-65*, S. C. R. Pamphlet No. 5 (Office of the Chief Signal Officer, 1918), 1.

6. Second Corps Signal School, A. E. F., "Instruction Paper on Type 'A' 1 Receivers" (March 18, 1918), 1.

7. Second Corps Signal School, A. E. F., 2.

8. Second Corps Signal School, A. E. F., 3.

9. Second Corps Signal School, A. E. F., 2.

10. Second Corps Signal School, A. E. F., 6.

11. *Ellington 1918* (Houston, Texas: Ellington Field, 1918), 87. "Archie" was British (and later American) slang for anti-aircraft guns.

12. George A. Wieczorek, "Notes from the Second Corps Signal School" (1918).

13. George Bennett Ferree, "Memories from My Old Diary Covering from August 25, 1918 to November 11, 1918" (1918), entry for October 27, 1918.

14. Ferree, entry for October 27, 1918. Ferree is likely referring to the civilian *Cimetière Romagne-Sous-Montfaucon*. Romagne-sous-Montfaucon would later be the location of the Meuse-Argonne American Cemetery as well as a smaller German war cemetery.

15. Ferree, entry for October 27, 1918.

16. Ferree, entry for October 7, 1918.

17. Ferree, entry for October 11, 1918.

18. Ferree, entry for October 10, 1918.

19. *History of the 314th Field Artillery*, 1929, 50.

20. Albert Marple, "Wireless Music for Wounded Soldiers," *The Wireless Age*, April 1918, 590, 593.

Chapter 12
Unbelievable Silence

1. Woodrow Wilson, "Executive Order 2605A - Taking Over Necessary and Closing Unnecessary Radio Stations," April 30, 1917, http://www.presidency.ucsb.edu/ws/index.php?pid=75415.

2. "The Feminine Wireless Amateur," *The Electrical Experimenter*, October 1916, 396–97, 452.
3. "CHIPS Articles: Celebrating the First Women to Join the Naval Reserve Force," accessed August 31, 2016, http://www.doncio.navy.mil/CHIPS/ArticleDetails.aspx?ID=6140.
4. Edwin Howard Armstrong, "Report on Tests of American Artillery Receiver, A. R. 4." (Division of Research and Inspection, Research Section, 1917), retrieved from http://users.erols.com/oldradio/eha7.htm.
5. Office of the Chief Signal Officer, *Radiotelegraphy, Circular No. 1, 1914* (Washington, D.C.: U.S. Government Printing Office, 1914), 109.
6. Office of the Chief Signal Officer, *Radiotelegraphy, Circular No. 1, 1914*.
7. Office of the Chief Signal Officer, *Radiotelegraphy, Circular No. 1, 1915* (Washington, D.C.: U.S. Government Printing Office, 1915), 102.
8. Office of the Chief Signal Officer, *Radiotelegraphy, Circular No. 1, 1916* (Washington, D.C.: U.S. Government Printing Office, 1916), 105.
9. For a complete list of all included components see United States Army Signal Corps, Training Section, *Radio Receiving Sets, Type SCR-54, Type SCR-54-A and Detector Equipment, Type DT-3-A* (Signal Corps, U.S. Army, 1918). The designations "SCR" and "BC" can sometimes cause confusion and with good reason. A receiver may have printed instructions for "Type SCR-54-A" glued into its lid, while the metal plate on the lid seems to identify the same equipment as a "BC-14-A". "BC" means "basic component" and in this case refers to "a wooden box with a hinged waterproof cover 3 7/16 inches deep; bakelite operating panel; the box contains primary and secondary tuned circuits inductively coupled and each comprising adjustable inductance and capacitance; coupling adjustable, the secondary may be made aperiodic, and it comprises a crystal detector and a double telejack," and is "used in Set, type SCR-54-A" (Signal Corps Storage Catalogue, U.S. Government Printing Office, 1920., p. 553). In other words, it is the receiver component for the SCR-54-A. "SCR" is a group of components, and the SCR-54-A includes the BC-14-A receiver, as well as all the antennae, batteries, crystals, headsets, boxes, bags, wire, tools, and everything else issued with it.
10. Captain L. S. Howeth, *History of Communications-Electronics in the United States Navy* (Washington: United States Government Printing Office, 1963), 218–19.
11. United States War Department, *Annual Report of the Chief Signal Officer for the Year 1919* (Washington, D.C.: U.S. Government Printing Office, 1919), 250.
12. George Bennett Ferree, "Memories from My Old Diary Covering from August 25, 1918 to November 11, 1918" (1918), entry for October 26, 1918.

13. Paul Levin, "World War 1 Crystal Radio Set Donated by Chenoan to Army," *The Pantagraph*, February 23, 1975.
14. "CQ" is radio code for "general call", or "calling all stations". "FL" was the call sign for the Eiffel Tower station.
15. Victor Giraud, *Histoire de la Grande Guerre* (Hachette, 1920), 688.
16. This is how the message appears in George B. Ferree's journal entry for the day, which is slightly different from the version he later affixed to the radio, "CQ CQ de de FL FL to the commander in chief. Hostilities will cease on the whole front from the eleventh November eleven o'clock French o'clock. The allied troops will not cross until further order the line reached on that date and that hour. Marshall Foch." The version usually printed in division histories and other accounts of the war has "French time" rather than "French o'clock", for example "Hostilities will cease upon the whole front from the eleventh November eleven o'clock, French time. The Allied troops will not cross until a further order the line reached on that date and that hour. Marshal Foch, Commander in Chief." - Frank Palmer Sibley, *With the Yankee Division in France* (Little, Brown, 1919), 338.
17. "Guns along the Meuse Roar Grand Finale of Eleventh Hour," *The Stars and Stripes* 1, no. 41 (November 15, 1918).
18. Ferree, "Memories from My Old Diary", entry for November 11, 1918.
19. Frank Palmer Sibley, *With the Yankee Division in France* (Little, Brown, 1919), 340.
20. Sibley, 340–41.
21. Lieutenant Commander L. B. Bye, "U. S. Naval Railway Batteries," *Naval Institute Proceedings* 45, no. 6 (June 1919): 955.
22. George H. English, *History of the 89th Division, U.S.A.* (Smith-Brooks Printing Company, 1920), 243.
23. Ferree, "Memories from My Old Diary", entry for November 11, 1918.
24. Robert Casey, *The Cannoneers Have Hairy Ears: A Diary of the Front Lines* (New York: J.H. Sears & Co., 1927), 329.
25. Robert Casey, *The Cannoneers Have Hairy Ears, with Annotation by George B. Ferree* (New York: J.H. Sears & Co., 1927), 329.
26. English, *History of the 89th Division*, 243.
27. "Guns along the Meuse."
28. Casey, *The Cannoneers Have Hairy Ears*, 1927, 329–30.
29. English, *History of the 89th Division*, 244.
30. Fred Young, "No Substitute for Football," *The Pantagraph*, November 5, 1942.
31. Catalog # MON 1622.1 / CCN: 277040

Chapter 13
Into the Air Again

1. Hugo Gernsback, "Amateur Radio Restored," *The Electrical Experimenter*, June 1919, 131.
2. "At Last!," *QST*, November 1919, 13.
3. "At Last!"
4. H. P. Davis, "The Early History of Broadcasting in the United States," in *The Radio Industry* (Chicago: A.W. Shaw and Co., 1928), 194.
5. The Pirates won, 8-5.
6. United States Treasury Department, *Statistics of Income from Returns of Net Income for 1922* (Washington, D.C.: United States Government Printing Office, 1925), 2.
7. Power companies in the 1930s had little interest in investing in power plants and installing lines for sparsely populated areas. The REA was very successful; by 1942 nearly 50% of farms had power, and by 1952 nearly all were connected.
8. "Razor Blade Radio Tunes Sharply, Cuts out Static," *Oakland Tribune*, September 9, 1927, sec. D.
9. Clark Pettingill, "Novel Detector," *Modern Electrics*, January 1909, 352.
10. Clark Pettingill, "An Audible Detector," *Modern Electrics*, January 1911, 577.
11. Hugo Gernsback, "Wanted: - Inertialess Speakers," *Radio-Electronics* 24, no. 10 (October 1953): 33.
12. "Razor Blade Used," *Oakland Tribune*, February 11, 1923.
13. "Junior Constructor," *Radio News*, June 1921, 881.
14. John H. Schalek, "Safety-Razor Blade Replaces 'Catwhisker,'" *Popular Science*, September 1922, 75.
15. "Emergency Crystal Detector," *Radio News*, June 1925, 2260.
16. "Sparks Electric," *Grand Rapids Tribune*, December 21, 1921.
17. "Radio Digest," *Lincoln Sunday Star*, December 6, 1925.
18. "Ask Hank, He Knows!," *Elementary Electronics*, July 1975, 16.
19. "The Radio Experimenter," *Dallas Morning News*, August 13, 1922.
20. United States War Department, *Field Service Regulations, United States Army* (Washington, D.C.: U.S. Government Printing Office, 1923), 19; as reprinted in Rebecca Robbins Raines, *Getting the Message Through: A Branch History of the U.S. Army Signal Corps* (Washington, D.C.: Center of Military History, U.S. Army, 1996), 229.
21. Raines, *Getting the Message Through*, 231.22
22.. There were 29,400,000 US homes with radios in January 1941 and 30,300,000 January 1942 according to the 1942 *Broadcasting Yearbook*, p 14. 81 percent of those were listening to Roosevelt's speech on December 7, 1941, approximately 24,500,000.

Chapter 14
That Damned Anzio

1. Ernie Pyle, *Brave Men* (New York: H. Holt and Company, 1944), 233.
2. Leroy D. Good to the author, June 18, 2011.
3. Edmund F. Ball, *Staff Officer with the Fifth Army* (New York: Exposition Press, 1958), 299.
4. George A. Mackie to Florence Stevens, August 30, 1944.
5. W. E. Bakersmith to Elva Bakersmith, February 20, 1944.
6. Robert W. Albro to Mrs. W. L. Albro, February 28, 1944.
7. *Anzio Beachhead, 22 January - 25 May 1944*, American Forces in Action Series (Historical Division, Department of the Army, 1948), 113.
8. Wynford Vaughan-Thomas, *Anzio* (London: Longmans, 1961), 190.
9. Fred Sheehan, *Anzio, Epic of Bravery* (Norman, Oklahoma: University of Oklahoma Press, 1964), 166.
10. Willard E. Purdy to Mr. and Mrs. H. A. Henderson, July 27, 1944.
11. Don Welling, interview by the author, January 10, 2011.
12. Sheehan, *Anzio, Epic of Bravery*, 173.
13. Vaughan-Thomas, *Anzio*, 210.
14. *Anzio Beachhead*, 114.
15. Sheehan, *Anzio, Epic of Bravery*, 171.
16. Sheehan, 171.
17. Bill Harr, "Six-By-Six Cops First Anzio Derby," *45th Division News*, May 18, 1944.
18. A thorough account of the Anzio Derby can be found in Bill Harr, *Combat Boots: Tales of Fighting Men, Including the Anzio Derby* (New York: Exposition Press, 1952).
19. Vaughan-Thomas, *Anzio*, 196.
20. "Manchester Eighth Army Veterans Association," May 9, 2006, https://web.archive.org/web/20060509005220/http://www.eavm.co.u k/Articles/Anzio.htm.
21. Royal Army Service Corps, *The Story of the Royal Army Service Corps, 1939-1945* (Published under the direction of the Institution of the Royal Army Service Corps by G. Bell, 1955), 274.
22. "By the Right Flank!," *45th Division News*, April 15, 1944.
23. Sheehan, *Anzio, Epic of Bravery*, 170.
24. "Barrage, Egg, Save the Life of Lucky Hen," *45th Division News*, April 28, 1944.
25. "By the Right Flank!," *45th Division News*, May 6, 1944.
26. Sheehan, *Anzio, Epic of Bravery*, 174.
27. Don Robinson, *News of the 45th* (New York: Grosset & Dunlap, 1944), 46.
28. Ivy Howard, "Roland E. Ormsby," September 27, 2017.

29. United States Adjutant-General's Office, "War Department General Order No. 46," July 25, 1895.
30. *Hearings Before the Committee on Military Affairs* (Washington, D.C.: United States Government Printing Office, 1912), 203.
31. "Radio Industry Comes Thru with Ideal Service Men's Kit," *Radio Daily*, May 5, 1942.
32. For a detailed description of the contents of each kit, see War Department, *FM 28-105 The Special Service Company* (Washington, D.C.: U.S. Government Printing Office, 1944), https://archive.org/details/Fm28-105.
33. "Men on Anzio Beachhead Print Own News Sheets; Delivery Each Morning," *Joplin Globe*, May 14, 1944.
34. George Anthony Avery to the author, January 25, 2011.
35. Anthony S. D'Angelo to the author, January 18, 2011.
36. "'The Nuffield Trust for the Forces of the Crown - 'The First Fifty Years,'" http://www.nuffieldtrust.org/fifty.htm.
37. Theodore Stuart DeLay, "An Historical Study of the Armed Forces Radio Service to 1946" (Dissertation, University of Southern California, 1951), 290.
38. "Receiver R-100/URR Radio," accessed March 29, 2017, http://www.radiomuseum.org/r/military_morale_builder_radio_r_10.html.
39. DeLay, "An Historical Study of the Armed Forces Radio Service to 1946," 294.
40. Norris J. Dupre, interview by the author, January 11, 2011.
41. Corporal Melvin F. Diamond, "Foxhole Radio Chain Makes with Schmaltz," *Stars and Stripes Mediterranean Algiers Edition*, May 6, 1944.
42. Welling, interview.
43. Bryan Compton, interview by the author, January 13, 2011.
44. Goldie Phelps to the author, February 1, 2006.
45. Goldie Phelps, interview by the author, April 11, 2015.
46. Sicily, July 10, 1943; Salerno, September 10, 1943; Anzio, January 22, 1944; France, August 15, 1944.
47. "Music Helps in a Foxhole," *The Salt Lake Tribune*, April 28, 1944. The article was printed in many newspapers across the U. S.
48. "Flashes from the Italian Front Lines," *Stars and Stripes, Mediterranean Algiers Edition*, May 6, 1944. The article was also printed in the May 12, 1944 Tunis edition and possibly others.
49. "Foxhole Radio," *Stars and Stripes, Sicily Edition*, May 26, 1944.

Chapter 15
Digging In

1. It has been possible to be in a "blue funk" since the 1860s at least, according to the *Oxford English Dictionary*.
2. "Tactical Notes," *The Military Historian and Economist* II, no. 1 (January 1917): 250.
3. W. E. Collinson, "German 'War Words,'" *Modern Language Review* 14 (January 1919): 87–93.
4. General Headquarters, American Expeditionary Forces, Second Section, General Staff, "'Stellungs' and 'Fox-Holes,'" *Summary of Information*, no. 216 (November 3, 1918).
5. Robert Debs Heinl, *Soldiers of the Sea: The United States Marine Corps, 1775-1962* (Annapolis, Maryland: United State Naval Institute, 1962), 203.
6. G-2-C, 1st Army Corps U.S., *Information from Captured German Maps, Prisoner's Statements and Recent Aeroplane Photographs*, 1:20000 (G-2-C, 1st Army Corps U.S., October 2, 1918).
7. G-2-C, 1st Army Corps U.S., *Enemy Information from Airplane Photos, Prisoners Statements, Plan Directeurs, Observations Etc.*, 1:20000 (G-2-C, 1st Army Corps U.S., October 25, 1918).
8. General Headquarters, American Expeditionary Forces, Second Section, General Staff, "Enemy's Defenses," *Summary of Information*, no. 213 (October 31, 1918).
9. "Big German Guns Fail to Shatter Fortress of Sand," *The (New York) Evening World*, November 12, 1915.
10. "Furious Russian Gun Fire Blows Victims to Shreds," *New York Tribune*, July 31, 1916.
11. "Rain Causes Lull in Fighting along U.S. Aisne Front," *New York Tribune*, September 9, 1918.
12. Arthur McKeogh, *The Victorious 77th Division (New York's Own) in the Argonne Fight* (New York: John H. Eggers Company, 1919), 15–16.
13. Joint War History Commissions of Michigan and Wisconsin, *The 32nd Division in the World War, 1917-1919* (Milwaukee, Wisconsin: Wisconsin Printing Company, 1920), 313.
14. Martin Lindsay, *So Few Got through: The Personal Diary of Lieut-Col. Martin Lindsay* (Collins, 1946), 114.
15. P. S. Bond, *The R. O. T. C. Manual, Senior Course* (Baltimore, Maryland: The Johns Hopkins Press, 1921), 214.
16. P. S. Bond et al., *Field Engineering: A Practical Exposition of the Organization of the Ground for Defense as Developed by the U.S. Army in the World War*, 1st ed. (New York: The American Army and Navy Journal, 1922), 21.
17. Bond et al., 15.

18. Brandt, *"Ist Der Frontale Infanterieangriff Noch Durchführbar?,"* Militär-Wochenblatt, March 25, 1935. Reprinted in *English in Review of Military Literature*, December 1935, Vol XV no 59, p. 129.

19. Marine Corps Schools, *Tentative Manual for Defense of Advanced Bases* (Quantico, Virginia: Marine Corps Schools, 1936), 106.

20. United States Army Corps of Engineers, *FM 5-15 Field Fortifications 1940* (Washington, D.C.: United States Government Printing Office, 1940), 63.

21. United States Army Corps of Engineers, 65.

22. United States War Department, *FM 5-15 Field Fortifications 1944* (Washington, D.C.: United States Government Printing Office, 1944), 47.

23. United States War Department, 48.

24. United States War Department, 47.

25. United States War Department, 49.

26. United States War Department, 52–53.

27. United States War Department, *FM 20-205 Dictionary of United States Army Terms* (Washington: United States Government Printing Office, 1944).

28. Department of the Army, *FM 5-15 Field Fortifications 1949* (Washington, D.C.: United States Government Printing Office, 1949), 50.

29. Department of the Army, 61.

30. Department of the Army, 62.

31. Department of the Army, 65.

32. Ernie Pyle, "Anzio: Dugout Luxury - Until Shell Comes Through Roof," *Dallas Morning News*, June 11, 1944.

33. Pyle.

34. "Men and Women in Service," *Dubuque Telegraph Herald*, May 21, 1944.

35. Dr. Ray McAllister, interview by the author, January 23, 2006.

36. Saburo Nishime, "Memories: From Anzio To Civitavecchia," accessed December 14, 2016, http://www.100thbattalion.org/archives/puka-puka-parades/european-campaigns/italian-campaign/anzio/memories-from-anzio-to-civitavecchia/.

37. McAllister, interview.

38. Edward L. Josowitz, *An Informal History of the 601st Tank Destroyer Battalion* (Salzburg, 1945), 28.

39. *Anzio Beachhead, 22 January - 25 May 1944*, American Forces in Action Series (Historical Division, Department of the Army, 1948), 113–14.

40. "Front Line Radio," *Daily Boston Globe*, May 24, 1944.

41. "Soldier Makes Radio of Odds and Ends," *Biloxi Daily Herald*, May 31, 1944.

42. Marvin Peterson, "With Uncle Sam," *Chicago Daily Herald*, June 16, 1944.

43. "Fifth Army Has Radios in Foxholes," *The Austin Statesman*, June 30, 1944.

44. "Fifth Army Has Radios in Foxholes."
45. Charles Myrick to the author, November 18, 2006.
46. *Photograph 111-SC-282168 U. S. Fifth Army Mobile Unit Programs Can Be Heard over Razor Blade Sets*, 1945, 1945, 282168, Records of the Office of the Chief Signal Officer, Record Group 111, National Archives at College Park, College Park, Maryland.
47. *Photograph Showing a Foxhole Radio at Anzio*, 1944, 1944, courtesy Waldon Johnson.
48. Waldon H. Johnson to the author, January 19, 2011.
49. Fred Sheehan, *Anzio, Epic of Bravery* (Norman, Oklahoma: University of Oklahoma Press, 1964), 169.
50. Warren C. Garman, interview by the author, January 10, 2011.
51. Leroy D. Good to the author, June 18, 2011.
52. Don Welling, interview by the author, January 10, 2011.
53. "A Safety Pin Detector," *Radio Amateur News*, January 1920, 367.

Chapter 16
Short and Neatly Trimmed

1. Most famously, Joseph Palmer, a veteran of the War of 1812, whose beard made him the object of ridicule by the residents of Fitchburg, Massachusetts. In 1830 he was attacked by four men with scissors and razors intent on shaving him. He managed to defend himself with a jackknife. He was fined for injuring two of the assailants and imprisoned for refusing to pay the fine on principal, all the while managing to save his beard.
2. Friedrich Wilhelm von Steuben, *Regulations for the Order and Discipline of the Troops of the United States Part I* (Philadelphia: Styner and Cist, 1779), 88.
3. George Washington, "George Washington, August 19, 1780, General Orders" (August 19, 1780), George Washington Papers, Series 3, Varick Transcripts, 1775-1785, Subseries 3G, General Orders, 1775-1783, Letterbook 5: April 11, 1780 - Sept. 5, 1781, Library of Congress.
4. General Winfield Scott, *General Regulations for the Army, or, Military Institutes* (Philadelphia: M. Carey and Sons, 1821), 48.
5. United States War Department, *Regulations for the Uniform and Dress of the Army of the United States* (Washington, D.C.: J. Gideon, Printer, 1839), 24.
6. "Bathing is recommended, and where conveniences for it are to be had, the men should be made to bathe at least once a week. The feet to be washed always at least twice a week." United States War Department, *General Regulations for the Army of the United States* (Washington, D.C., 1835), 13.

7. Texas War Department, *General Regulations for the Government of the Army of the Republic of Texas* (Houston: Intelligencer Office - S. Whiting, printer, 1839), 11.
8. Headquarters of the Army, Adjutant General's Office, "Circular Issued May 31, 1843," May 31, 1843.
9. War Department, Adjutant General's Office, "General Order No. 35 of 1848," July 6, 1848.
10. Head Quarters of the Army, Adjutant General's Office, "General Order No. 2 of 1853," January 6, 1853.
11. United States War Department, *Revised Army Regulations of 1861*, 1863, 481.
12. Confederate States of America, War Department, *Regulations for the Army of the Confederate States, 1863* (Richmond: West & Johnston, 1863), 406.
13. W. H. Van Buren and United States Sanitary Commission, *Rules for Preserving the Health of the Soldier* (Washington, D.C.: Sanitary Commission, 1861).
14. United States War Department, *Regulations for the Army of the United States, 1895* (Washington, D.C.: U.S. Government Printing Office, 1895), 38.
15. United States War Department, *Regulations for the Army of the United States. 1901: With Appendix, Separately Indexed, Showing Changes to June 30, 1902* (Washington, D.C.: U.S. Government Printing Office, 1902), 44.
16. British War Office, *The King's Regulations and Orders for the Army, 1912: Reprinted with Amendments Published in Army Orders up to 1st August, 1914* (London, 1914), 325, paragraph 1696. "The hair of the head will be kept short. The chin and under-lip will be shaved, but not the upper lip. Whiskers, if worn, will be of moderate length."
17. United States War Department, *Regulations for the Army of the United States, 1913, Corrected to April 15, 1917* (Washington, D.C.: U.S. Government Printing Office, 1917), 286.
18. United States Navy, *Regulations for the Government of the Navy of the United States (Navy Regulations) 1913* (Washington, D.C.: United States Government Printing Office, 1913), 157.
19. Lt. Norman R. Van Der Veer, *The Bluejackets' Manual*, 6th ed. (New York: Military Pub. Co., 1918), 179.
20. United States Marine Corps, *Uniform Regulations, United States Marine Corps: Together with Uniform Regulations Common to Both U.S. Navy and Marine Corps* (Washington, D.C.: U.S. Government Printing Office, 1917), 12–13.
21. Headquarters, American Expeditionary Forces, *Defensive Measures Against Gas Attacks* (France, 1917), 8; reiterated in Army War College, *Gas Warfare Part II: Methods of Defense Against Gas Attacks* (Washington, D.C.: United States Government Printing Office, 1918), 62.
22. Headquarters, American Expeditionary Forces, *Defensive Measures Against Gas Attacks*, 38.

23. "The Gillette Safety Razor Company," *The Commercial and Financial Chronicle* 110, no. 2853 (February 21, 1920): 773.
24. "The Gillette Safety Razor Company," *The Commercial and Financial Chronicle* 112, no. 2903 (February 12, 1921): 664.
25. "The Gillette Safety Razor Company," *The Commercial and Financial Chronicle* 114, no. 2956 (February 18, 1922): 731.
26. Paragraph 7 of "Military Hygiene and Sanitation", Army Regulation 40-205, December 15, 1924, with changes to 1942, December 31, 1942. "Every member of a command will bathe once daily while in garrison, and in the field at least once weekly. The hands will be washed before each meal and immediately after visiting a latrine. Teeth will be cleaned with a brush at least once a day. Fingernails will be cut short and kept clean. The hair will be kept short and the beard neatly trimmed. Clothing and bedding will be kept clean. Soiled clothing will be kept in barrack bags. At prescribed physical inspections particular attention will be given to personal cleanliness."
27. United States Navy, *The Bluejackets' Manual*, 11th ed. (Annapolis, Maryland: United States Naval Institute, 1943), 204 "The hair, beard, and mustache must be worn neatly trimmed. The face must be kept clean shaved, except that a mustache or beard and mustache may be worn at discretion. No eccentricities in the manner of wearing the hair, beard, or mustache are allowed."
28. William H. Pine, *Paramount Victory Short No. T2-1: A Letter from Bataan* (Paramount, 1942).
29. Maxie L. Rupert to the Marlin Razor Blade Division, May 9, 1944. Courtesy Maxie L. Rupert.
30. Maxie L. Rupert to the author, January 14, 2008.
31. "Our publicity client has received letter your son dated May Ninth Anza [sic] beach head telling how he has made radio receiving set using Marlin razor blades. We wish to make story public to press Tuesday June 6th & will appreciate by telegraph collect information regarding Lt Ruppert [sic] such as age where educated previous interest in radio married or engaged and other information up to 100 words you think would be of interest in press story also rush his picture air mail special delivery to me care Baldwin Mermey 205 East 42 St New York New York= Phillys Schuyler." Phillys Schuyler to George Rupert, telegram, June 2, 1944, courtesy Maxie Rupert.
32. Baldwin and Mermey, "Press Release Prepared for the Marlin Firearms Company," June 9, 1944.
33. According to Marlin promotional material, courtesy Maxie L. Rupert.
34. Jack Gould, "One Thing and Another Along Radio Row," *New York Times*, June 25, 1944.
35. James H. Pitman, "It Even Works in Newark," *New York Times*, July 2, 1944.

36. From Marlin promotional material, courtesy Maxie L. Rupert.
37. "Foxhole Razor Blade Radio Set," *Broadcasting*, June 19, 1944, 67.
38. "Beachhead Gadget," *Time Magazine*, July 17, 1944, 88.
39. "Letters," *Time Magazine*, August 7, 1944, 4, 7.
40. "Razor-Blade Radios," *Electronics*, August 1944, 294–96.
41. "A Razor Blade and Cat Whisker," *Electronics*, September 1944, 332.
42. "Unbiased," *Wireless World*, September 1944, 302.
43. "Radio Made Out of a Razor Blade," *Popular Mechanics*, October 1944, 11.
44. John W. Campbell Jr., "Radio Detectors and How They Work," *Popular Science*, October 1944, 206.
45. *Popular Science*, August 1944, 53.
46. "Officer Makes Foxhole Radio out of Razor Blade," *Illustrated Current News*, 1944.
47. Thomas P. Smith, "The 'Fox-Hole' Radio," *Radio-Electronics*, July 1987, 14.
48. Maxie L. Rupert to the author, January 14, 2008.
49. Maxie L. Rupert to the author, January 30, 2008.

Chapter 17
How the Dam Thing Worked I'll Never Know

1. Private Ralph E. Evans, "Radio in a Nutshell," *Stars and Stripes Mediterranean Naples Edition*, June 1, 1944.
2. Lt. William H. Rosee, "Music (?) For Your Dugout," *Field Artillery Journal*, July 1944.
3. A. Frederick Collins, *The Book of Wireless* (New York: D. Appleton and Company, 1915), 20.
4. Alfred Powell Morgan, "A Microphone Detector," *Modern Electrics*, March 1909, 428.
5. Clark Pettingill, "Novel Detector," *Modern Electrics*, January 1909, 352.
6. "A Wireless Receiving Station at Small Cost," *St. Nicholas*, April 1917, 559–60.
7. Leroy D. Good to the author, June 18, 2011.
8. Douglas M. Bailey to the author, "Fox Hole Radio," November 7, 2007.
9. George Anthony Avery to the author, January 25, 2011.
10. Harry Evans W2MIB, "Strays," *QST*, June 1945, 50.
11. Warren C. Garman, interview by the author, January 10, 2011.
12. Stuart B. Hunt, "Build This Receiver," QRP-L E-Mail List Archive from lehigh.edu, January 24, 1998, http://qrp.kd4ab.org/1998/980124/0024.html.
13. Joseph A. Springer, *The Black Devil Brigade: The True Story of the First Special Service Force* (Pacifica Military History, 2004), 172.

14. Aubrey Eugene Thomas, "Army Years" (n.d.), courtesy Catherine Thomas.
15. Thomas.
16. Garman, interview.
17. Hunt, "Build This Receiver."
18. Douglas M. Bailey, "Diary Entry, May 11, 1944," The 463rd Parachute Field Artillery Official Website, http://www.ww2airborne.net/463pfa/trooper_bailey.html.
19. Thomas Daniel Murphy, *Ambassadors in Arms: The Story of Hawaii's 100th Battalion* (Honolulu: University of Hawaii Press, 1955), 181.

Chapter 18
Be Kind to Your Sets, Boys

1. Warren L. Nicely to the author, January 12, 2011.
2. "Berlin Bessie Had Revenge in Yank Dead," *The Stars and Stripes - Germany Edition*, June 18, 1945.
3. Bill Oden to Mr. and Mrs. G. E. Oden, March 17, 1944.
4. *Propaganda Leaflet AI-038a-2-44* (Nazi Germany, 1944).
5. Hidenobu Hiyane to the author, January 17, 2007.
6. AP Wire Photo, *"Axis Sally" Wears a Helmet*, 1944, Photograph, 1944.
7. John Zappitello to the author, February 7, 2012.
8. Edward George Butwell to the author, March 3, 2011.
9. Dr. Ray McAllister, interview by the author, January 23, 2006.
10. Dr. Russel Weiskircher to the author, January 11, 2011.
11. Vere "Tarzan" Williams, "Autobiography of Vere Williams, 157th Infantry Regiment, Part 3," n.d., http://www.45thdivision.org/Veterans/VWilliams2.htm.
12. Lee Palmer to the author, January 24, 2011.
13. Edmund F. Ball, *Staff Officer with the Fifth Army* (New York: Exposition Press, 1958), 301.
14. Joe C. Nemec to Mr. and Mrs. Joseph Nemec, June 15, 1944.
15. Stuart B. Hunt, "Build This Receiver," QRP-L E-Mail List Archive from lehigh.edu, January 24, 1998, http://qrp.kd4ab.org/1998/980124/0024.html.
16. Letter from Lt. Thomas Peter Welch to his mother, May 14, 1944, reprinted in Victor Failmezger, *American Knights: The Untold Story of the Men of the Legendary 601st Tank Destroyer Battalion* (Osprey, 2015), 162.

Chapter 19
In the Field with the Fifth Army

1. Rebecca Robbins Raines, *Getting the Message Through: A Branch History of the U.S. Army Signal Corps* (Washington, D.C.: Center of Military History, U.S. Army, 1996), 274.
2. American Forces Radio and Television Service, *History of AFRTS: The First 50 Years* (American Forces Information Service and Armed Forces Radio and Television Service, 1993), 7.
3. Lawrence Strauss, "Community Radio: Old Tradition for Sitkans," *Sitka Sentinel*, May 14, 1982.
4. Patrick Morley, *"This Is the American Forces Network": The Anglo-American Battle of the Air Waves in World War II* (Westport, Connecticut: Praeger, 2001), 61.
5. American Forces Radio and Television Service, *History of AFRTS*, 9.
6. American Forces Radio and Television Service, 9.
7. Russell Oliver Fudge, "The Armed Forces Radio Service" (Thesis, University of Missouri, 1949), 22.
8. "World's First Army [Radio] Station Is Approved," *Kodiak Bear*, July 22, 1942; as reprinted on "Kodiak Military History, Armed Forces Radio," http://www.kadiak.org/radios/wvcq_bear_article_19420722.html.
9. "Rotarians at Kodiak, Alaska, 'Godfather' an Army Radio Station," *The Rotarian* 63, no. 1 (July 1943): 45.
10. Strauss, "Community Radio."
11. American Forces Radio and Television Service, *History of AFRTS*, 9.
12. Strauss, "Community Radio."
13. Fudge, "The Armed Forces Radio Service," 3.
14. American Forces Radio and Television Service, *History of AFRTS*, 19.
15. It was determined, for example, that peak listening periods occurred in the morning from 6:15 to 7:00 am, midday, and 7:00 to 8:30 pm, and that favored program types were dance music and news. Serial dramas and classical music were at the bottom of the list.
16. American Forces Radio and Television Service, *History of AFRTS*, 19.
17. Fudge, "The Armed Forces Radio Service," 60.
18. American Forces Radio and Television Service, *History of AFRTS*, 25.
19. Vern Carstensen's son, Jim, has put together an excellent website about the Fifth Army Mobile Station at http://www.fiftharmymobileradio.com/ which has been archived by the Library of Congress at https://www.loc.gov/item/lcwa00096722/
20. Vern Carstensen, interview by Les Tremayne for the Pacific Pioneers Broadcasters, February 10, 1992.
21. Station KROS first broadcast on September 28, 1941.
22. Carstensen, interview.

23. Vern Carstensen, "Movement Log," 1945. Courtesy Jim Carstensen.
24. Vern Carstensen, "Proposed Mobile Radio Station," 1944. Courtesy Jim Carstensen.
25. Carstensen, interview.
26. The staff included, with a few changes during their sixteen months on the road, Lieutenant Vern Carstensen, station manager; T/5 Warren J. Ostrode, editor and assistant station manager; T/4 Harold Tucker, T/5 Lloyd Murray, and Private John Rapp, a former writer for Eddie Cantor, made up the production team; and T/4 Edward Reicher was chief clerk. Announcers included Carstensen, Sergeant Dick Wesson, who was a CBS announcer from Oregon City, Oregon, T/4 Bill Griskey, who worked as an announcer with NBC in New York, T/5 Russell W. Shepherd, and T/5 Harold Klein. The music department was headed by Sergeant Early Cady, who had been a musician in Akron. Staff Sergeant Walter Kirk served as the chief engineer, T/3 Leroy Hathon, who ran a radio repair shop in Owosso, Michigan, T/3 George Piros, and Private Charles Range, former sound engineer with CBS, rounded out the engineering department.
27. Dave Kaufman, "The Fifth Army Mobile Radio Station," *The Trading Post: American Society of Military Insignia Collectors* 58, no. 1 (January 1999): 11–17.
28. Carstensen, interview.
29. Kaufman, "The Fifth Army Mobile Radio Station."
30. The 1944 World Series was the last World Series where both teams, the St. Louis Cardinals and The St. Louis Browns, had the same home field. According to Carstensen, GIs tended to favor the Cardinals, who won the series 4 games to 2.
31. Carstensen, interview.
32. Kaufman, "The Fifth Army Mobile Radio Station."
33. Carstensen, interview.
34. General Mark W. Clark to First Lieutenant Vernon Carstensen, "Award of Bronze Star Medal," June 24, 1945, http://www.fiftharmymobileradio.com/.
35. First Lieutenant Vernon Carstensen, *Guide to Operation Practices Policies, Mobile American Expeditionary Radio Station*, 1945. Archived at http://www.fiftharmymobileradio.com/Operations_Guide/AERS_Guide.pdf.
36. Carstensen, 4.
37. Carstensen, 39.
38. Bryan Compton, interview by the author, January 13, 2011.

Chapter 20
It Was Surprising

1. Isaac Franklin Caudle to the author, February 3, 2011.
2. Warren L. Nicely to the author, January 12, 2011.
3. Dr. Russel Weiskircher to the author, January 11, 2011.
4. Derk Doombos to the author, January 15, 2011.
5. Howard R. Waugh to the author, February 7, 2011.
6. Don Welling, interview by the author, January 10, 2011.
7. Vere "Tarzan" Williams, "Autobiography of Vere Williams, 157th Infantry Regiment, Part 3," n.d., http://www.45thdivision.org/Veterans/VWilliams2.htm.
8. "Fifth Army Has Radios in Foxholes," *The Austin Statesman*, June 30, 1944.
9. Lucy Beebe, "Let's Rock," *Ocala Star-Banner*, May 18, 1991.
10. Harry Evans W2MIB, "Strays," *QST*, June 1945, 50.
11. *Photograph 111-SC-282167 "Tec 5 Hidenobu Hiyane of the 100th Infantry Listens to the U. S. Fifth Army Mobile Station over His Combination Mess Kit and Radio Set,"* 1944, 1944, Records of the Office of the Chief Signal Officer, Record Group 111, National Archives at College Park, College Park, Maryland.
12. *Photograph 111-SC-282168 U. S. Fifth Army Mobile Unit Programs Can Be Heard over Razor Blade Sets*, 1945, 1945, Records of the Office of the Chief Signal Officer, Record Group 111, National Archives at College Park, College Park, Maryland.
13. *Photograph 111-SC-282165 Tec 5 Hidenobu of the 100th Infantry Turns on a Program Coming over a Radio Set Made from a Mess Kit*, 1945, 1945, Records of the Office of the Chief Signal Officer, Record Group 111, National Archives at College Park, College Park, Maryland.
14. *Photograph 111-SC-282167*.
15. *Photograph 111-SC-282166 Sprawled out on a German Pup Tent, Private James Kubokawa of Hawaii Listens to Program from U. S. Fifth Army Mobile Station*, 1945, 1945, Records of the Office of the Chief Signal Officer, Record Group 111, National Archives at College Park, College Park, Maryland. Private First Class Kubokawa was killed in action in the Vosges Mountains on November 2, 1944.
16. "Manchester Eighth Army Veterans Association," May 9, 2006, https://web.archive.org/web/20060509005220/http://www.eavm.co.uk/Articles/Anzio.htm.
17. *Wireless Receiver Made by 5th Divisional Signals*, 1944, 1944, Catalogue Number COM 993, Imperial War Museum, London.
18. H. W. Clarke, "Can You Help?," *Eighth Army News*, March 3, 1945.
19. "Razor-Blade Radio," *Eighth Army News*, March 15, 1945.

20. William Ahrens to Frank Ahrens, May 13, 1944.
21. "Wilbur Wannenburg,",
     http://saafww2photographs.yolasite.com/wilbur-wannenburg.php.
22. "456th Bomb Group Association Bob Reichard Material: 745th Bomb
     Squadron," February 3, 2004,
     http://www.456thbombgroup.org/reichard/745th.html.
23. Vic Politi, "Foxhole Radios.... Again,"
     https://admin.qsl.net/pipermail/boatanchors/2002-October.txt.
24. Larry Wolters, "American Radio Follows Yanks Right to Dugout,"
     Chicago Daily Tribune, July 30, 1944.
25. Bill Bastian to the author, November 27, 2014.
26. Bastian to the author.
27. Victor V. Kubilius to the author, November 19, 2007.
28. "Strays," *QST*, July 1944, 62.
29. "Beachhead Gadget," *Time Magazine*, July 17, 1944, 88.
30. "Razor as Radio," *The Northern Miner*, July 12, 1944.
31. "Strays," *QST*, August 1944, 58.
32. "A Razor Blade and Cat Whisker," *Electronics*, September 1944, 332.
33. John W. Campbell Jr., "Radio Detectors and How They Work," *Popular
     Science*, October 1944, 206.
34. "Radio Made Out of a Razor Blade," *Popular Mechanics*, October 1944,
     11.
35. Justin Garton, "Foxhole Radio," *QST*, October 1944, 86.
36. "Amateur Activities," *QST*, January 1945, 70.
37. Hugo Gernsback, "Foxhole Emergency Radios," *Radio Craft*, September
     1944.

Chapter 21
A Cockeyed Invention

1. Sgt. Stanley Fink, "Radio in Every Foxhole," *Leatherneck: Magazine of the
   Marines*, July 1945. Raymond Gram Swing was a journalist who reported
   for the Mutual Broadcasting System during WWII.
2. "NATTCen Newsreel," *Jax Air News, U. S. Naval Air Station and Naval
   Air Technical Training Center, Jacksonville, Florida*, May 17, 1945.
3. Moving the needle did not actually select stations, rather it was done to
   find a sensitive spot on the razor blade "crystal".
4. "NATTCen Newsreel."
5. *Photograph 80-G-49100 Radio Made by Bourgault, Edward E. (8D3) out of
   Edged Razor Blade, Bent Safety Pin & Loop of Wire, Somewhere in the Pacific.*,
   1945, 1945, National Archives at College Park, College Park, Maryland.
6. "Yank Ingenuity," *Nebraska State Journal*, May 17, 1945.

7. "Seabees Come up with Another Impossible in War," *Greenfield (Indiana) Daily Reporter*, August 2, 1945; similarly "Razor Blades Make Good as Foxhole Radio," *Porthole: The Newspaper of the U. S. Naval Barracks, Tampa, Florida*, September 15, 1945.

8. "Fan Mail," *All Hands: The Bureau of Naval Personnel Information Bulletin*, October 1945.

9. Frank DeAngelo, "Sound Off," *Leatherneck: Magazine of the Marines*, October 1945, 7.

10. Fink, "Radio in Every Foxhole."

11. Alio J. Benedetti, September 14, 2011, Alio J. Benedetti Collection (AFC/2001/001/80396), Veterans History Project, American Folklife Center, Library of Congress, http://memory.loc.gov/diglib/vhp/story/loc.natlib.afc2001001.80396/

12. Paul M. Cornell, "Fox-Hole Radio," *QST*, September 1945, 53. Cornell's letter reads "Many reports have been circulated concerning the various types of fox-hole radio sets constructed by members of the armed forces throughout the world. Naturally, tubeless and batteryless radios must be used by most of the boys in the field. Few parts are required for a razor-blade set. The most difficult item to locate is a pair of 'phones. The wire may be hard to obtain, but the rest of the parts usually will be available. Fig. 5 shows both the schematic and pictorial diagrams of a typical razor-blade set using parts found in most localities. Armed Forces radio stations up to twenty-five miles away have been heard, using a fairly good antenna and ground. Greater distances have been reported on similar sets. - *Lt. Paul M. Cornell, SC, W8EFW*."

13. Paul Cornell W8EFW to Lance Borden WB5REX, March 5, 1999.

14. Lawrence E. Davies, "KGEI Tells Them," *New York Times*, July 19, 1942.

15. American Forces Radio and Television Service, *History of AFRTS: The First 50 Years* (American Forces Information Service and Armed Forces Radio and Television Service, 1993), 5.

16. Major Spencer M. Allen, "Mosquito Net Finds Home Methods Best," *Broadcasting*, April 30, 1945.

17. Allen.

18. S/Sgt. Garth P. James, "Rock Radio," *Radio News*, June 1944.

19. Cornell W8EFW to Borden WB5REX, March 5, 1999.

20. "Scrap Pile Radio," *San Antonio Express*, December 21, 1944.

21. William Lloyd Wiley, interview by the author, November 16, 2007.

22. Wiley.

23. Wiley.

24. "Seaman Makes It Simple," *Berkeley (California) Daily Gazette*, February 1, 1945.

25. "Razor Blade Aids Seaman Build Radio," *San Antonio Light*, December 17, 1944.

26. "Razor Blade Aids Seaman Build Radio."
27. Captain Ernest Shackleton, *Wireless Equipment, Receiver (POW-Constructed), British*, wood, metal, plastic, glass, cardboard, 315mm x 415mm x 130mm, Imperial War Museum, London, http://www.iwm.org.uk/collections/item/object/30005281.
28. "131st Battalion Survivor Knew Only Work," *The Paris (Texas) News*, October 21, 1945.
29. "Improvised Radio to Help Yank Prisoners," *Tucson Daily Citizen*, May 12, 1945.
30. "Scrap Radio Tells Prison War News," *The Miami Daily News*, February 1, 1945.
31. *Wireless Equipment, POW-Constructed Receiver in Broom Head, Australian*, 1944, 1944, Imperial War Museum, London, http://www.iwm.org.uk/collections/item/object/30005330.
32. *Wireless Equipment, POW-Constructed Receiver, British*, 1943, 1943, Imperial War Museum, London, http://www.iwm.org.uk/collections/item/object/30005461.
33. E. H. Marriner W6BLZ, "Amateur Ingenuity," *CQ*, October 1965, 64–65.
34. "Homemade Radio Gave PWs News," *Indiana Evening Gazette*, September 19, 1945.
35. Jack Stinnett, "Washington Daybook," *Daily Capital News*, October 12, 1945.
36. N. Norris, *Wireless Equipment, Receiver Type Crystal (in Water Bottle, POW-Constructed), British*, Imperial War Museum, London, accessed August 15, 2017, http://www.iwm.org.uk/collections/item/object/30005782.
37. G. C. Dobbs and Bernard Robinson, *Making a Transistor Radio* (Loughborough: Ladybird Books, 1972).
38. "Secret Camp Radios - John Chew PoW History," https://sites.google.com/site/johnchewpowhistory/home/stories/secret-camp-radios.
39. Charlie Plumb and Glen DeWerff, *I'm No Hero* (Mechanicsburg, PA: Executive Books, 1973), 199.
40. Charlie Plumb to the author, "POW Radio," July 29, 2016.
41. Paul C. Wilson, *The Sunset War: The 41st Infantry Division in the South Pacific* (Bloomington, IN: 1stBooks, 2003), 131.
42. Vic Politi, "Foxhole Radios.... Again," October 10, 2002, https://admin.qsl.net/pipermail/boatanchors/2002-October.txt.
43. "40th Division Offers Radio Course," *Stars and Stripes, Pacific Edition*, March 19, 1954.
44. Karl Kolbus, "Foxhole Radios," May 21, 2001, http://www.madsci.org/posts/archives/2001-05/990554457.Eg.r.html.

Chapter 22
Midnight Requisitioning

1. *Boy's Fun Book of Things to Make and Do* (New York: Grosset & Dunlap, 1945), 152.
2. John W. Campbell Jr., "Radio Detectors and How They Work," *Popular Science*, October 1944, 206.
3. "Foxhole Radios from Italy," *Auckland Weekly News*, April 24, 1945.
4. "Razor-Blade Radio," *Eighth Army News*, March 15, 1945.
5. "Razor as Radio," *The Northern Miner*, July 12, 1944.
6. "'Foxhole' Radio Receiver," *Sydney Morning Herald*, July 2, 1947.
7. "Superboy's Workshop," *Superboy #6*, February 1950.
8. Westinghouse Electric Corporation, *How Does It Work?* (Pittsburgh: Westinghouse Electric Company School Service, 1950).
9. Boy Scouts of America, *Official Handbook for Boys* (Garden City, NY: Doubleday, Page & Company, 1911), 210.
10. Boy Scouts of America, 32.
11. "The Hobby Shop," *Boys' Life* 1, no. 12 (February 1912): 36–37.
12. G. E. Clark, "A Bantam Radio," *Boys' Life*, February 1951.
13. William W. Conner, "Razor Blade Radio," *Boys' Life*, November 1959.
14. "Scrap Pile Radio," *San Antonio Express*, December 21, 1944.
15. Art Trauffer, "Improved Razor-Blade Detector," *Elementary Electronics*, no. 657 (1963): 142.
16. Jack Gould, *All About Radio and Television* (New York: Random House, 1953).
17. Jack Gould, "One Thing and Another Along Radio Row," *New York Times*, June 25, 1944.
18. Lewis L. Gould to the author, "Jack Gould," November 9, 2005.
19. For more on Jack Gould and his career see Jack Gould and Lewis L Gould, *Watching Television Come of Age: The New York Times Reviews* (Austin, Tex.; Chesham: University of Texas Press ; Combined Academic, 2003).
20. John Blaine, *The Blue Ghost Mystery* (New York: Grosset & Dunlap, 1960).
21. John Blaine, *Rick Brant's Science Projects* (New York: Grosset & Dunlap, 1960).
22. "Things for Children to Do," *New York Times*, February 28, 1947.
23. "Hayward Area School News," *The (Hayward) Daily Review*, December 21, 1950.
24. "2nd Annual Southern Colorado Regional Science Fair," September 18, 2004, from an archived copy of http://www.canoncityschools.org/scsciencefair.htm.

25. Shriver L. Coover, *Drawing, Sketching and Blueprint Reading* (New York: McGraw-Hill, 1954), 40.
26. Paul Franz Brandwein et al., *You and Science: Science for Better Living* (New York: Harcourt, Brace & World, 1960), 622.
27. Alan H. Humphreys, *Modern General Science* (Austin, Tex.: Steck Co., 1964), 254.
28. James Brown, *Casebook for Technical Writers* (San Francisco: Wadsworth Publishing Company, 1961), 17–18.
29. Ann Landers, "Advice from Ann Landers," *Reno Evening Gazette*, April 19, 1960.
30. Ann Landers, "Advice from Ann Landers," *Salisbury Times*, June 27, 1960.
31. Landers.
32. "The Dick Cavett Show," March 7, 1974.
33. Landers, "Advice from Ann Landers," June 27, 1960.
34. "Mythbusters," *Penny Drop* (The Discovery Channel, October 17, 2003).
35. "Mail Call," *Military Pilot Training* (The History Channel, October 12, 2003).
36. Erik Barnouw, *The Golden Web: A History of Broadcasting in the United States 1933-1953* (New York: Oxford University Press, 1968), 192.
37. Byron G. Wels, *Transistor Circuit Guidebook* (Blue Ridge Summit, PA: TAB Books, 1968).
38. Byron G. Wels, "Foxhole Radio," *Electronic Projects You Can Make*, 1958, 108–9.
39. Joe Tartas, "Razor-Blade Radio," *Popular Mechanics*, October 1962, 203.
40. John G. Borkman, "Ye Olde Razor Blade Radio," *S9 The Citizens Band Journal* 4, no. 7 (July 1964): 22–23.
41. Anson MacFarland, "Foxhole Radio Receiver," *Popular Communications*, March 1983, 23.
42. Penn Clower, "World War Wireless," *73 for Radio Amateurs*, August 1985, 32–34.
43. "Letters," *Radio-Electronics*, April 1987, 12.
44. Thomas P. Smith, "The 'Fox-Hole' Radio," *Radio-Electronics*, July 1987, 14.
45. T. J. Byers, "Build a Foxhole Radio," *Hands-On Electronics*, January 1988, 27–28.
46. "Foxhole Radio," *Minneapolis Star Tribune*, November 19, 1994.
47. Phil Anderson W0XI, "The Carbon and Steel Detector Set, AKA 'The Foxhole Radio,'" *The Xtal Set Society Newsletter* 7, no. 34 (1997); reprinted in *Crystal Set Building: The Xtal Set Society Newsletter Volume 6 and 7* (The XTAL Set Society, 1998).
48. Dave Ingram K4TWJ, "World of Ideas," *CQ*, July 2001, 56–61.
49. Shannon Huniwell, "Do-It-Yourself Radio," *Popular Communications* 23, no. 10 (June 2005): 74–79.

50. Reverend George Dobbs, "Carrying On the Practical Way," *Practical Wireless*, January 2008, 36–39.
51. "Remember This?," *Ex-POW Bulletin*, no. 5/6 (June 2011): 23.
52. Lance Borden, "Build A World War II Foxhole Radio," *Electronics Handbook*, no. XVII (1995): 47–55.
53. "Borden Radio Company - Radio Kits and Designs for Old and New Styles," http://www.xtalman.com/.
54. *Rocky Mountain Evening Telegram*, May 19, 1953.
55. *Popular Mechanics*, May 1945, 60.
56. *Popular Science*, July 1945, 61.
57. *Popular Science*, May 1947, 69.
58. *Popular Mechanics*, July 1970, 51.
59. "Crystal Set Society," http://midnightscience.net/home.html.
60. Greenleaf Whittier Pickard to Paul I. Murphy, July 11, 1948, Estate of Greenleaf Whittier Pickard, courtesy Ben Pickard.
61. "Antique Radio Forums - Foxhole Radio Coil Inductance?," http://www.antiqueradios.com/forums/viewtopic.php?p=942342.
62. "Foxhole Radio," EDN, http://www.edn.com/electronics-blogs/living-analog/4415140/Foxhole-radio- "I've long been amused at the name 'foxhole radio,' since I doubt many soldiers in war had the spare time, or parts, to build one..."

Chapter 23
Tops in Patience

1. Baldwin and Mermey, "Press Release Prepared for the Marlin Firearms Company," June 9, 1944.
2. "NATTCen Newsreel," *Jax Air News, U. S. Naval Air Station and Naval Air Technical Training Center, Jacksonville, Florida*, May 17, 1945.
3. *Boy's Fun Book of Things to Make and Do* (New York: Grosset & Dunlap, 1945).
4. John Blaine, *Rick Brant's Science Projects* (New York: Grosset & Dunlap, 1960), 103.
5. Jack Gould, *All About Radio and Television* (New York: Random House, 1953), 60.
6. Reverend George Dobbs, "Carrying On the Practical Way," *Practical Wireless*, January 2008, 36–39.
7. "Fifth Army Has Radios in Foxholes," *The Austin Statesman*, June 30, 1944.
8. Byron G. Wels, "Foxhole Radio," *Electronic Projects You Can Make*, 1958, 108–9; Art Trauffer, "Improved Razor-Blade Detector," *Elementary Electronics*, no. 657 (1963): 142; Anson MacFarland, "Foxhole Radio Receiver," *Popular Communications*, March 1983, 23; Penn Clower,

"World War Wireless," *73 for Radio Amateurs*, August 1985, 32–34; Dave Ingram K4TWJ, "World of Ideas," *CQ*, July 2001, 56–61, to name a few.

9. Anson MacFarland, "Foxhole Radio Receiver," *Popular Communications*, March 1983, 23.

10. Jack Gould, "One Thing and Another Along Radio Row," *New York Times*, June 25, 1944.

11. Byron G. Wels, *Transistor Circuit Guidebook* (Blue Ridge Summit, PA: TAB Books, 1968), 12.

12. Gillette Customer Service to the author, "Gillette Blue Blades," January 26, 2006.

13. Gerard B. Lambert, *All Out of Step: A Personal Chronicle* (New York: Doubleday, 1956), 189.

14. Albert R. Stargardter, Method of treating steel, US1948192, filed March 10, 1932, and issued February 20, 1934.

15. Stargardter.

16. Gillette Safety Razor Co. v. Triangle Mechanical Laboratories Corp., 13 Federal Supplement Reports (District Court, Eastern District of New York 1935).

17. Gillette Safety Razor Co. v. Triangle Mechanical Laboratories Corp., 4 Federal Supplement Reports (District Court, Eastern District of New York 1933).

18. United States Trademark 345,427, applied for on November 7, 1936, states that the Marlin logo was used on razorblades since November 1, 1935.

19. During WWII, when Marlin supplied about 10% of the blades sold to the Military, 90% of Blue Strike's production was sold by Marlin, according to William S. Brophy, *Marlin Firearms : A History of the Guns and the Company That Made Them* (Harrisburg, PA: Stackpole, 1989), 88.

20. "Letters," *Time Magazine*, August 7, 1944, 4, 7.

21. *Photograph 80-G-49100 Radio Made by Bourgault, Edward E. (8D3) out of Edged Razor Blade, Bent Safety Pin & Loop of Wire, Somewhere in the Pacific.*, 1945, 1945, National Archives at College Park, College Park, Maryland.

22. Clark Pettingill, "Novel Detector," *Modern Electrics*, January 1909, 352.

23. "Fifth Army Has Radios in Foxholes."

24. Dobbs, "Carrying On the Practical Way."

25. "Razor-Blade Radio," *Eighth Army News*, March 15, 1945.

26. *Photograph 111-SC-282168 U. S. Fifth Army Mobile Unit Programs Can Be Heard over Razor Blade Sets*, 1945, 1945, Records of the Office of the Chief Signal Officer, Record Group 111, National Archives at College Park, College Park, Maryland.

27. Gould, *All About Radio and Television*.

28. Dr. Ray McAllister, interview by the author, January 23, 2006.

29. Gould, "One Thing and Another Along Radio Row."

30. William Ahrens to Frank Ahrens, May 13, 1944.
31. "Razor-Blade Radio."
32. Justin Garton, "Foxhole Radio," *QST*, October 1944, 86.
33. Sgt. Stanley Fink, "Radio in Every Foxhole," *Leatherneck: Magazine of the Marines*, July 1945.
34. *Photograph 111-SC-282168*.
35. *Photograph 80-G-49100*.
36. Lt. William H. Rosee, "Music (?) For Your Dugout," *Field Artillery Journal*, July 1944.
37. Thomas Daniel Murphy, *Ambassadors in Arms: The Story of Hawaii's 100th Battalion* (Honolulu: University of Hawaii Press, 1955), 181.
38. Private Ralph E. Evans, "Radio in a Nutshell," *Stars and Stripes Mediterranean Naples Edition*, June 1, 1944.
39. Paul M. Cornell, "Fox-Hole Radio," *QST*, September 1945, 53.
40. G. E. Clark, "A Bantam Radio," *Boys' Life*, February 1951; Shriver L. Coover, *Drawing, Sketching and Blueprint Reading* (New York: McGraw-Hill, 1954); Joe Tartas, "Razor-Blade Radio," *Popular Mechanics*, October 1962, 203; John G. Borkman, "Ye Olde Razor Blade Radio," *S9 The Citizens Band Journal* 4, no. 7 (July 1964): 22–23; MacFarland, "Foxhole Radio Receiver"; Clower, "World War Wireless."
41. Raymond F Yates, *Fun with Electrons* (New York: Appleton-Century, 1954), 69.
42. William W. Conner, "Razor Blade Radio," *Boys' Life*, November 1959.
43. Art Trauffer, "Improved Razor-Blade Detector," *Elementary Electronics*, no. 657 (1963): 142.
44. "Scrap Pile Radio," *San Antonio Express*, December 21, 1944.
45. Dan Wissell N1BYT, "The HZX Headphone Adapter," *QST*, September 1998, 67, 97. Available online at https://www.arrl.org/files/file/Technology/tis/info/pdf/9809067.pdf.
46. Antique Electronic Supply https://www.tubesandmore.com/ is one of several sources for crystal radio earphones and diodes.
47. The Xtal Set Society is a good place to start https://www.midnightscience.net/home.html
48. There are a few radio clubs specializing in crystal radios, for example, the Birmingham, Alabama Crystal Radio Group http://www.crystalradio.us/ , and the Heart of England Crystal Radio Club http://crystalradioclub.co.uk/

A Mostly Chronological List of
Foxhole Radio Sources

The sources in this list describe or mention foxhole radios in
varying amounts of detail. Generally only one source is given for a
syndicated article, though they may have appeared in dozens of
newspapers across the country. Further sources are, no doubt,
awaiting discovery.

World War II Sources and Later Military Accounts

"Music Helps in a Foxhole." *The Salt Lake Tribune*, April 28, 1944.
   Typical of the many articles about Eldon Phelps and his
   radio that ran in papers across the country. Most of the
   articles about Phelps in civilian newspapers refer to his set as
   a "razor blade radio" but not a "foxhole radio".
"G. I. Uses Razor as Radio." *New York Times*, April 29, 1944. The
   Eldon Phelps story as it appeared in the *Times*.
"Flashes from the Italian Front Lines." *Stars and Stripes, Mediterranean
   Algiers Edition*, May 6, 1944. Eldon Phelps as reported by the
   Stars and Stripes. This is the earliest printed use of the term
   "foxhole radio".
Rupert, Maxie L. Letter to the Marlin Razor Blade Division, May 9,
   1944. Rupert's original letter to Marlin, written on Red Cross
   stationary, describing the foxhole radio. Includes a sketch
   that was reproduced in the *New York Times* and other papers.
   The original letter is lost but was reprinted in Marlin

advertising materials.

"Flashes from the Italian Front Lines." *Stars and Stripes, Tunis Edition*, May 12, 1944. A slightly later printing of the Phelps story that ran in the Stars and Stripes Algiers edition.

Ahrens, William. Letter to Frank Ahrens, May 13, 1944. Includes William Ahrens' sketch and description of a foxhole radio.

"Front Line Radio." *Daily Boston Globe*, May 24, 1944. A soldier describes building a razor blade radio at Anzio in a letter home. He calls it a "foxhole radio", making this likely the first appearance of the term in a civilian newspaper.

"Soldier Makes Radio of Odds and Ends." *Biloxi Daily Herald*, May 31, 1944. Corporal Fred B. Cassel builds a radio from a razor blade which is copied by several men in his unit. He does not refer to it as a "foxhole radio".

Evans, Private Ralph E. "Radio in a Nutshell." *Stars and Stripes Mediterranean Naples Edition*, June 1, 1944. A unique microphone style detector using two carbons from flashlight batteries straddled by a razor blade. With an illustration by the author.

Butterfield, C. E. "Radio Day by Day." *St. Petersburg Evening Independent*, June 12, 1944. Article describes Maxie Rupert's set, referred to as a "fox-hole" radio, and modifications made by N.B.C. engineer O. B. Hanson.

"The Radio." *The Zanesville (Ohio) Signal*, June 12, 1944. One of the 1,300 articles written about Maxie Rupert's radio in newspapers across the country.

"Foxhole Radio Made of Razor Blade and Pin." *Chicago Daily Tribune*, June 13, 1944. A longer version of the Maxie Rupert article.

"Radio Is Made for a Fox Hole." *The Chillicothe (Missouri) Constitution-Tribune*, June 13, 1944. Another article about Maxie Rupert and his radio, this time referring to the set as a "foxhole radio", as Rupert did in his letter to Marlin.

Peterson, Marvin. "With Uncle Sam." *Chicago Daily Herald*, June 16, 1944. A soldier's letter mentions a razor blade radio built by a buddy.

"Foxhole Razor Blade Radio Set." *Broadcasting*, June 19, 1944, 67. Rupert's radio and Hanson's modifications, along with the Hanson N.B.C. photo.

Gould, Jack. "One Thing and Another Along Radio Row." *New York Times*, June 25, 1944. The author describes Maxie Rupert's radio and improvements made at N.B.C. by O. B. Hanson. Includes much of Rupert's letter to Marlin and his sketch of the radio.

"Fifth Army Has Radios in Foxholes." *The Austin Statesman*, June 30, 1944. Building a foxhole radio, as described by Corp. John Savacool, and a shrapnel detector by Sgt. Charles Myrick.

Rosee, Lt. William H. "Music (?) For Your Dugout." *Field Artillery Journal*, July 1944. A wartime microphone detector style foxhole radio, with a diagram by the author.

"Strays." *QST*, July 1944, 62. Toivo Kujanpaa's brief description of a razor blade set at Anzio.

"Razor as Radio." *The Melbourne Argus*, July 1, 1944. Eldon Phelps' story makes it to Australia.

Pitman, James H. "It Even Works in Newark." *New York Times*, July 2, 1944. Letter in response to Jack Gould's *Times* article describing a reader's successfully built foxhole radio in Newark.

"Razor as Radio." *The Northern Miner.* July 12, 1944. Phelps as reported in Australia, again.

"Beachhead Gadget." *Time Magazine*, July 17, 1944, 88. Rupert's radio with a new illustration by staff illustrator James Cutter.

"Razor-Blade Radios." *Electronics*, August 1944, 294–96. A brief description of Rupert's radio, again with the Hanson N.B.C. photo.

"Strays." *QST*, August 1944, 58. A brief letter mentioning foxhole radio sets in Italy.

"Letters." *Time Magazine*, August 7, 1944, 4, 7. Letters reporting more or less successful foxhole radios, responding to the July 17 *Time* article.

"A Razor Blade and Cat Whisker." *Electronics*, September 1944, 332. A brief mention of the Phelps set.

Gernsback, Hugo. "Foxhole Emergency Radios." *Radio Craft*, September 1944. Hugo Gernsback traces foxhole radios back to razor blade "microphone" detectors of the early 20th century.

"Unbiased." *Wireless World*, September 1944, 302. A humorous assessment of Rupert's set, with Rupert's illustration.

Campbell, John W., Jr. "Radio Detectors and How They Work." *Popular Science*, October 1944, 206. Several detector types and their operation are described including Rupert's foxhole set.

A photo of the O. B. Hanson N.B.C. set is included.

Garton, Justin. "Foxhole Radio." *QST*, October 1944, 86. Describes a basic foxhole radio set built at Anzio, with an illustration by the author.

"Radio Made Out of a Razor Blade." *Popular Mechanics*, October 1944, 11. A single paragraph article about the foxhole radio, including the Hanson N.B.C. photo, but not mentioning Rupert.

"Razor Blade Aids Seaman Build Radio." *San Antonio Light*, December 17, 1944. The most detailed article about William Lloyd Wiley and his radio, despite his last name being misspelled (as "Miley") in the photo caption.

"Scrap Pile Radio." *San Antonio Express*, December 21, 1944. Photo of two airmen in San Antonio with their radio.

Josowitz, Edward L. *An Informal History of the 601st Tank Destroyer Battalion.* Salzburg, 1945. The foxhole radio is mentioned while describing life at Anzio.

"Amateur Activities." *QST*, January 1945, 70. Brief mention of a foxhole radio in news of the Tucson Shortwave Association.

"Seaman Makes It Simple." *Connellsville (PA) Daily Courier*, January 29, 1945. One of many articles about William Lloyd Wiley's razor blade radio printed in papers across the country. It is never referred to as a "foxhole radio".

"Makes It Simple." *Mason City (Iowa) Globe-Gazette*, January 30, 1945. One of many articles about William Lloyd Wiley's razor blade radio printed in papers across the country. It is never referred to as a "foxhole radio".

"Seaman Makes It Simple." *Dunkirk (NY) Evening Observer*, January 31, 1945. One of many articles about William Lloyd Wiley's razor blade radio printed in papers across the country. It is never referred to as a "foxhole radio".

Clarke, H. W. "Can You Help?" *Eighth Army News*, March 3, 1945. A British soldier letter requesting more information about foxhole radios.

"Razor-Blade Radio." *Eighth Army News*, March 15, 1945. Descriptions of several sets sent in to the *Eighth Army News* by servicemen, with illustrations.

"Foxhole Radios from Italy." *Auckland Weekly News*, April 24, 1945. A reprint of the March 15, 1945 *Eighth Army News* article.

Wireless Receiver Made by 5th Divisional Signals. 1944. Catalogue Number

COM 993. Imperial War Museum, London. A razor blade radio made from a bottle by British troops at Anzio, part of the Imperial War Museum collections.

"At Last - Use for Old Razor Blades." *Traverse City (Michigan) Eagle-Record.* May 11, 1945. Typical of the many articles about Ed Bourgault and his radio, which he referred to as a "foxhole companion".

"NATTCen Newsreel." *Jax Air News, U. S. Naval Air Station and Naval Air Technical Training Center, Jacksonville, Florida*, May 17, 1945. A longer version of Bourgault's story.

Evans W2MIB, Harry. "Strays." *QST*, June 1945, 50. A soldier's letter describing a microphone style detector as well as field-made galena crystals.

Fink, Sgt. Stanley. "Radio in Every Foxhole." *Leatherneck: Magazine of the Marines*, July 1945. A description of Ed Bourgault's radio and how his directions for building one were distributed.

"Seabees Come up with Another Impossible in War." *Marysville (Ohio) Evening Tribune*, August 18, 1945. Another, longer version of Bourgault's story.

Cornell, Paul M. "Fox-Hole Radio." *QST*, September 1945, 53. One of the first detailed plans of a foxhole radio printed. With a diagram and schematic by the author. Established the variable coil "Cornell" type radio.

"Razor Blades Make Good as Foxhole Radio." *Porthole: The Newspaper of the U. S. Naval Barracks, Tampa, Florida*. September 15, 1945. Bourgault's radio, this article is similar to the longer syndicated newspaper article.

DeAngelo, Frank. "Sound Off." *Leatherneck: Magazine of the Marines*, October 1945, 7. A letter responding to the July Leatherneck article on Ed Bourgault, giving original credit to a Fifth Army lieutenant at Anzio.

"Fan Mail." *All Hands: The Bureau of Naval Personnel Information Bulletin*, October 1945. Some of the many letters Ed Bourgault received after his story was printed.

Anzio Beachhead, 22 January - 25 May 1944. American Forces in Action Series. Historical Division, Department of the Army, 1948. The foxhole radio is mentioned in describing life on the beachhead.

Sheehan, Fred. Anzio, Epic of Bravery. Norman, Oklahoma: University of Oklahoma Press, 1964, 169-70. The author, who was at Anzio, briefly describes a foxhole radio.

Beebe, Lucy. "Let's Rock." *Ocala Star-Banner*, May 18, 1991. A crystal set built with galena at Anzio.

Benedetti, Alio J., September 14, 2011. Alio J. Benedetti Collection (AFC/2001/001/80396), Veterans History Project. American Folklife Center, Library of Congress. http://memory.loc.gov/diglib/vhp/story/loc.natlib.afc2001 001.80396/. The interviewee describes a razor blade radio built while he was on Guadalcanal.

Failmezger, Victor. *American Knights: The Untold Story of the Men of the Legendary 601st Tank Destroyer Battalion*. Osprey, 2015. Includes a soldier letter mentioning hearing Rome on a foxhole radio.

Bailey, Douglas M. "Diary Entry, May 11, 1944." The 463rd Parachute Field Artillery Official Website. http://www.ww2airborne.net/463pfa/trooper_bailey.html. The author mentions in his diary seeing a radio built using a razor blade.

McAllister, Dr. Ray. "Ray McAllister." 45th Infantry Division : Ray McAllister. http://www.45thdivision.org/Veterans/McAllister.htm. The author recalls making a razor blade radio at Anzio.

Nishime, Saburo. "Memories: From Anzio To Civitavecchia." http://www.100thbattalion.org/archives/puka-puka-parades/european-campaigns/italian-campaign/anzio/memories-from-anzio-to-civitavecchia/. The author describes building a foxhole radio after reading about hem in Stars and Stripes.

Williams, Vere "Tarzan." "Autobiography of Vere Williams, 157th Infantry Regiment, Part 3." http://www.45thdivision.org/Veterans/VWilliams2.htm. Listening to Axis Sally on the foxhole radio.

"40th Division Offers Radio Course." *Stars and Stripes, Pacific Edition*, March 19, 1954. An army radio course includes instruction for making a foxhole radio.

Plumb, Charlie, and Glen DeWerff. *I'm No Hero*. Mechanicsburg, PA: Executive Books, 1973. A razor blade radio built by a Vietnam War P.O.W. is described.

Postwar Sources

Boy's Fun Book of Things to Make and Do. New York: Grosset &
Dunlap, 1945. The first foxhole radio article to appear in a
book marketed to children, details are given for the
construction of a receiver based on Maxie Rupert's design.
Features a photo of the set built by O. B. Hanson of N.B.C.

Popular Mechanics, May 1945, 60. An early classified ad for foxhole
radio plans available by mail order.

Popular Science, July 1945, 61. Another classified ad for foxhole radio
plans.

"Things for Children to Do." *New York Times,* February 28, 1947.
Mentions an exhibition of projects built by the Brooklyn
Children's Museum Science Club including a razor blade
radio.

"'Foxhole' Radio Receiver." *Sydney Morning Herald,* July 2, 1947.
Construction of a basic foxhole radio is described. Includes
a schematic illustration.

Westinghouse Electric Corporation. *How Does It Work?* Pittsburgh:
Westinghouse Electric Company School Service, 1950. An
educational comic including a very brief description of a
foxhole radio, with illustration.

"Superboy's Workshop." *Superboy #6,* February 1950. Full page,
illustrated instructions for building a standard receiver.

Clark, G. E. "A Bantam Radio." *Boys' Life,* February 1951. Boys' Life
magazine's take on Paul Cornell's radio. Half page, with an
illustration of the radio and a schematic.

Gould, Jack. *All About Radio and Television.* New York: Random
House, 1953. Detailed and well-illustrated multi-page
instructions for building a Rupert style foxhole radio,
including much of the theory behind it.

Rocky Mountain Evening Telegram, May 19, 1953. A newspaper ad
offering plans for a razor blade radio.

Coover, Shriver L. *Drawing, Sketching and Blueprint Reading.* New York:
McGraw-Hill, 1954. A Cornell style foxhole radio used as an
example of orthographic projection.

"Local Boy Makes His Own Radios." *San Saba News.* October 7,
1954. Features J. L. Warren Linn, who built foxhole radios
during WWII and continued making them in Korea and
after.

Wels, Byron G. "Foxhole Radio." *Electronic Projects You Can Make*, 1958, 108–9. The author, who built foxhole radios during the war, recounts how to do it.

"Superboy's Workshop." *Superboy #68*, October 1958. A reprint of the article from Superboy #6.

Conner, William W. "Razor Blade Radio." *Boys' Life*, November 1959. A stripped-down radio with only a razor blade detector, pencil lead, antenna, ground and phones. With illustrations.

Blaine, John. *The Blue Ghost Mystery*. New York: Grosset & Dunlap, 1960. The title character builds a foxhole radio as part of the narrative.

Blaine, John. *Rick Brant's Science Projects*. New York: Grosset & Dunlap, 1960. A more detailed description of the radio built in *The Blue Ghost Mystery*.

Brandwein, Paul Franz, Leland G. Hollingsworth, Alfred D. Beck, Anna E. Burgess, and Violet Strahler. *You and Science: Science for Better Living*. New York: Harcourt, Brace & World, 1960. A science textbook recommends making the foxhole radio from All About Radio and Television for further study.

Landers, Ann. "Advice from Ann Landers." *Salisbury Times*. June 27, 1960. A reader describes a foxhole radio built during the war as response to Landers' article on receiving radio signals in one's dental work.

Brown, James. *Casebook for Technical Writers*. San Francisco: Wadsworth Publishing Company, 1961. A description of a foxhole radio is given as an example of technical writing.

Tartas, Joe. "Razor-Blade Radio." *Popular Mechanics*, October 1962, 203. Instructions for building a Cornell style radio. With photographs and illustrations.

Trauffer, Art. "Improved Razor-Blade Detector." *Elementary Electronics*, no. 657 (1963): 142. A radio similar to the November 1959 *Boys' Life* minimalist set.

Humphreys, Alan H. *Modern General Science*. Austin, Tex.: Steck Co., 1964. School textbook with plans for a crystal radio, suggesting a razor blade can be substituted for the diode.

Borkman, John G. "Ye Olde Razor Blade Radio." *S8 The Citizens Band Journal* 4, no. 7 (July 1964): 22–23. Article featuring a Cornell style set.

Barnouw, Erik. *The Golden Web: A History of Broadcasting in the United States 1933-1953*. New York: Oxford University Press, 1968.

The foxhole radio is mentioned briefly in a description of troop listening habits.

Wels, Byron G. *Transistor Circuit Guidebook*. Blue Ridge Summit, PA: TAB Books, 1968. The author mentions making foxhole radios during the war in the introduction.

Popular Mechanics, July 1970, 51. A later classified ad for foxhole radio plans.

Four Star Spectacular. New York: DC Comics, 1976. Another reprint of the article from Superboy #6.

MacFarland, Anson. "Foxhole Radio Receiver." *Popular Communications*, March 1983. Another Cornell style radio.

Clower, Penn. "World War Wireless." *73 for Radio Amateurs*, August 1985. An account of the Cornell radio, this time giving credit to Cornell. The author provides plenty of detail, and goes on to modify it by adding a detector bias and tuning capacitor.

"Letters." *Radio-Electronics*, December 1986, 33. Part of an ongoing discussion and letters about the foxhole radio that continued with the April and July 1987, the latter including a letter than mentions a copy of the Illustrated Evening News story of Maxie Rupert which was still hanging in the AFRTS office in California.

Byers, T. J. "Build a Foxhole Radio." *Hands-On Electronics*, January 1988, 27–28. A Rupert style set including an amplifier so that it could be used with newer headphones.

"Foxhole Radio." *Minneapolis Star Tribune*, November 19, 1994. Basic plans for a Rupert style radio with pin, pencil lead and razor blade detector.

Borden, Lance. "Build A World War II Foxhole Radio." *Electronics Handbook*, no. XVII (1995): 47–55. Nicely detailed instructions for building a Cornell style foxhole radio.

Anderson W0XI, Phil. "The Carbon and Steel Detector Set, AKA 'The Foxhole Radio.'" *The Xtal Set Society Newsletter* 7, no. 34 (1997). An overview of the foxhole radio including tips for building one.

Ingram K4TWJ, Dave. "World of Ideas." *CQ*, July 2001, 56–61. A survey of crystal radios including mention of the foxhole set. Includes a diagram similar to the "minimal" Boy's Life set.

"Mail Call." *Military Pilot Training*. The History Channel, October 12, 2003. The host demonstrates foxhole radios sent in by viewers.

"Mythbusters." *Penny Drop*. The Discovery Channel, October 17, 2003. A foxhole radio is constructed (successfully) to demonstrate the theory behind radio reception in dental work.

Huniwell, Shannon. "Do-It-Yourself Radio." *Popular Communications* 23, no. 10 (June 2005): 74–79. The story of a group of boys who are taught how to make a foxhole radio by a radio station owner.

Dobbs, Reverend George. "Carrying On the Practical Way." *Practical Wireless*, January 2008, 36–39. Reverend Dobbs discusses making radios from odds and ends, including a razor blade radio. He reports greatest success with an ordinary, rusty blade and pin.

"Remember This?" *Ex-POW Bulletin*, no. 5/6 (June 2011): 23. A description of a foxhole radio including an illustration from All About Radio and Television.

Photographs

Included here are WWII era photographs of foxhole radios built by military personnel. Photographs and drawings of civilian made models, like the set built by N.B.C. engineers based on Maxie Rupert's design, are listed with the articles or books they appear in.

Photograph 111-SC-282168 U. S. Fifth Army Mobile Unit Programs Can Be Heard over Razor Blade Sets. 1945. Records of the Office of the Chief Signal Officer, Record Group 111. National Archives at College Park, College Park, Maryland. Anonymous soldier listening to a foxhole radio at Anzio. This is one of two known photographs of a foxhole radio in use at Anzio or anywhere in Europe during WWII. Details of the receiver can be clearly seen.

Waldon H. Johnson, William "Bill" Dodd Jr. and Milton Fauch operating their receiver near their dugout. 1944. The only other known photograph of an Anzio foxhole radio. From the collection of Waldon H. Johnson.

Photo inscribed "Note our aerial for razor blade radio set" by Wilbur Wannenburg of the South African Air Force. April 1945. The foxhole radio is not visible but the aerial is, just barely, in the background of this photograph taken at the Celone Airfield near Foggia. Estate of Wilbur Wannenburg, online at http://saafww2photographs.yolasite.com/wilbur-wannenburg.php.

Photograph 80-G-49100 Radio Made by Bourgault, Edward E. (8D3) out of Edged Razor Blade, Bent Safety Pin & Loop of Wire, Somewhere in the Pacific. 1945. National Archives at College Park, College Park, Maryland.

William Lloyd Wiley and his set. 1945. Photograph Section, Landing Craft School, Amphibious Training Base, Coronado, California. Courtesy William Lloyd Wiley.

Pfc. Elias Vivero and Pfc. Huel Butler with their "scrap pile radio". San Antonio Express, December 21, 1944. The original photograph is likely lost.

Original Sets

Very few WWII era sets made by military personnel are known to survive. More may be waiting to be discovered, stored away in a footlocker, and not recognized for what they are. It is hoped that this book will help bring more of them to light.

Two receivers built by Paul Cornell while on Saipan, one complete with original razor blade, are owned by his family. These are, so far, the only known extant foxhole radios made by American military personnel.

Vic Politi brought his foxhole radio home with him, sent it to his brother in Germany during the occupation, and was still using it in the 1950s after replacing the razor blade with a diode. It is likely lost.

Wireless Receiver Made by 5th Divisional Signals. 1944. Catalogue Number COM 993. Imperial War Museum, London. The only British made set known to survive and the only WWII service built razor blade radio known to be in a museum collection.

Several museums display reproductions of foxhole radios, including one at the Museum at Mountain Home, East Tennessee State University; the radio room of the Ponce De Leon Inlet

Lighthouse & Museum in Florida; a set built by the Sydney Group of the Historical Radio Society of Australia for display at the Hellfire Pass Memorial Museum in Thailand; and, until it was stolen, a set built on a single board, its coil wrapped loosely at one end and secured by thumbtacks, razor, pin and pencil lead at the other end, at the American Airpower Museum in Farmingdale, New York.

Index

Printed in Great Britain
by Amazon